Mr. Stanley of Estes Park

Mr. Stanley of Estes Park

by James H. Pickering

Published by the Stanley Museum, Inc.
Kingfield, Maine and Estes Park, Colorado
Susan S. Davis, Editor

Mr. Stanley of Estes Park
by James H. Pickering

First edition: July 2000 (reissued September 2011)

For further information, contact:
The Stanley Museum
40 School Street
PO Box 77
Kingfield, Maine 04947
Telephone: (207) 265-2729
Facsimile: (207) 265-4700
Website: www.stanleymuseum.org
Email: maine@stanleymuseum.org

Library of Congress Cataloging-in-Publication Data

Pickering, James H.
    Mr. Stanley of Estes Park / by James H. Pickering.
        p. cm.
    Includes bibliographical references and index.
        1. Stanley, Freelan Oscar, 1849-1940 2. Stanley Steamer automobile.
        3. Estes Park (Colo.)--Biography. 4. Tourism--Colorado--Estes Park
        --History. I. Title

    F784.E85 .P52 2000
    978.8'69031'092--dc21
    [B]   00-040051

ISBN 1-886727-05-8 Paperback • ISBN 1-886727-06-6 Hardcover

Paper: Lynx Opaque
Typefaces are Palatino for body copy and Caslon Openface for heads

Designer, Michel Reynolds
Editor, Susan S. Davis

Cover: Original painting © 1998 by Seamus Berkeley—www.sbart.com

The Stanley Museum's Mission Statement

The Stanley Museum keeps and shares the traditions of Yankee ingenuity and creativity as exemplified by the Stanley family in order to inspire these values in children and adults.

Institutional Vision & Values

The Stanley Museum shall be for all an institution of learning dedicated to a celebration of Yankee ingenuity as exemplified by the Stanley twins, Freelan Oscar and Francis Edgar, their sister Chansonetta Stanley Emmons, and their American contemporaries.

The Stanley Museum shall strive to preserve the history of their achievements and the artifacts and technology relevant to them for the purpose of arousing in the public pride of heritage and promoting those values most cherished and valuable in the American experience – Family Excellence, Integrity, Creativity, a Love of Learning, Tenacity, and Good Citizenship.

Adopted Unanimously October 14, 2000

Table of Contents

List of Illustrations

This book has been published in part through the generous support of

The Kenneth Kendal King Foundation
Denver, Colorado

The Strake Foundation
Houston, Texas

Introduction

Rarely has such a big story taken so long to be told.

The Stanley Museum was founded in 1981 in Kingfield, Maine, to save a building—and the Stanley story. Few at the time realized how deeply that story was entwined in the history of Colorado. The 1903 Georgian-style Stanley School in Kingfield, a gift from the identical Stanley twins, F.E. and F.O., to the town where they were born, was going to be torn down and made into a parking lot. After saving the building, it become clear that the Stanley story itself needed preservation.

That preservation effort is finally bearing fruit. It begins, ironically, not with the Stanley Steamer or with photography, but with the Colorado part of the story and Freelan Oscar Stanley through the publication of *Mr. Stanley of Estes Park* by the Stanley Museum and its author, James H. Pickering. In the next several years, three more volumes are to be published by the Museum: the Stanley history of Newton, Massachusetts, the first history of the Stanley Steamer automobile, and a major book on the Stanleys' famous sister, Chansonetta Stanley Emmons.

In all of this, nowhere is the discrepancy between importance and the known greater than with F.O.'s story. Although Stanley Museum archives in Maine held more Estes Park Stanley history than was known in Estes Park, the Stanley Museum spent virtually no time on the story until it was invited to Colorado by the Stanley Hotel in 1997.

When the Museum arrived that year, it realized the immensity of its responsibility and work: virtually no attention was being given to the man behind the Stanley Hotel, Stanley Park, the Stanley Power Plant—and so much other Colorado history. Pickering himself indicated after a luncheon interview that it would not be a long story. But before long, it was 40 pages longer than his 1999 history of Estes Park, "*This Blue Hollow*."

F.O. Stanley himself may be partly responsible for such lack of attention. A self-effacing man of great self confidence and composure, he shunned attention and credit for himself. The clearest example of that was his intention to name his Colorado resort "The Hotel Dunraven" rather than "The Stanley." The citizens of Estes wouldn't allow it and petitioned him to name it "The Stanley Hotel."

Stanley wrote virtually nothing about himself, nor about the projects that bore his stamp. His talent was in making things happen, from recognizing need and choosing people, to the money that greased the wheels. He was very clear about not being the man who did the labor, trying at every opportunity to give credit to those who did, from bank teller Sidney Sherman for starting Estes Park Bank, to Enos Mills for making Rocky Mountain National Park a reality, to his superintendent-of-the-works, "By" Hall, who completed all of Stanley's projects from road building to the construction of the Stanley Hotel and of the Stanley Power Plant.

Seriously ill from tuberculosis when he arrived in 1903, F.O. Stanley came to Estes Park to regain his health. To him, everything else was a bonus—and to Estes Park, a boon, one that prepared a Rocky Mountain community for the 20th century. F.O. Stanley's greatest gift may be yet to come: a model for others of a creative but selfless man who cared for people, for their comfort and happiness— and for community that ensured a future for those who followed.

Susan S. Davis, Editor
For the Stanley Museum, Inc., Publisher
Kingfield, Maine

Preface

For a summer resort, nature has endowed Estes Park in a
wonderful manner. The grandeur of its scenery, its deep blue
skies, its clear, cool and invigorating air, its mountain streams of
sparkling soft water, its sunny days and delightfully cool nights,
are things the summer visitor never forgets, and having enjoyed
once, desires to enjoy again.

Estes Park is not a place to "go through." It has no geysers, no
hot springs, no cliff dwellers, and no grizzly bears. But as a place
in which to spend the summer in perfect comfort, either in a
hotel, or a private cottage, it is unsurpassed.

—F.O. Stanley (1928)[1]

This book had its origins during the summer of 1997 when my
wife, Pat, and I were invited to lunch at the Stanley Hotel in Estes
Park by Betty and Eldon Freudenburg. Alma and Frank Hix, Estes
Park residents, and Susan Davis, executive director of the Stanley
Museum in Kingfield, Maine, were the Freudenburg's other guests.
It was a memorable occasion. It coincided with the opening of a
branch of the Stanley Museum at the hotel and we were sharing a
table with individuals who were as passionate as I was about pre-
serving and celebrating Colorado, Estes Park, and Stanley history.
While I don't remember all of our conversation, I do remember the

concluding remark of our young waitress, who leaned in to say, "You know, you people are really interesting!"

At some point during the meal, Sue Davis turned to the subject of the day: Would I be interested in writing "the Stanley history of Estes Park?" Like most people familiar with Estes Park, I knew something about the Stanley legacy and its importance. Having just finished a history of early Estes Park, I was generally familiar with the facts of F.O. Stanley's life and his contributions to Estes Park. In giving my immediate assent, I thought we were talking about an 80-page book, 20 of which could be devoted to photographs.

I also knew that the timing was right. The new owners of the Stanley Hotel had recently invested significant sums in its refurbishing and had invited the Stanley Museum of Kingfield, Maine, to provide tours and establish an exhibit space at the hotel; a group of dedicated local citizens had embarked that summer on an ambitious campaign to restore Stanley Hall (originally the Casino) to use as a community venue for the arts; and the town of Estes Park was in the process of nominating the Fall River Hydroelectric Plant for inclusion on the National Register of Historic Places. The success of such projects would depend on external support and funding, and both, it seemed to me, would be more likely to succeed if people better understood the historic significance of what they were being asked to preserve.

What I didn't understand, or at least underestimated at the time, was how much of a story there actually was. A great deal more than 80 pages!

As anyone interested in the early history of Estes Park quickly learns, published sources of historical information are surprisingly limited. An additional handicap is the fact that for nearly half of its recorded history, until 1921, Estes Park had no permanent year-round newspaper to provide a day-to-day account of events.

In the case of F.O. Stanley, the problem is compounded by a comparative lack of personal correspondence and other documentary evidence to detail and illuminate his Estes Park years. Stanley was a modest, self-effacing man who spent little time talking about himself or writing about his experiences. Even late in life, at a time when many famous men give themselves over to sharing their stories, the record is sparse, except for what he had to say about his early involvement with dry plate photography and the Stanley automobile—achievements that predate his arrival in Estes Park.

Henry Lynch, manager of the Stanley Hotel in 1928–1929 and again in 1948–1952, understood this dilemma all too well. Writing in 1949 to University Press in Dallas, which had commissioned a book on Estes Park for its American Resort Series, he lamented the fact "that there should have to be a rush in the preparation of copy for the book you are publishing . . . for the value of the book will undoubtedly suffer as a result of misinformation or the lack of full information." "There is considerable historic background in connection with a number of the hotels in the region, including the Stanley," Lynch went on to explain,

> and though I think that I know quite a little of that history, I would not want to be a party to having supplied information which later, after publication in a book such as you are preparing, might prove to be incorrect, and be embarrassing.
>
> As an example of what I have in mind, quite a good case in point: When I returned to Estes Park last year to manage the Stanley—I had managed it in 1928 and 1929 for Mr. F. O. Stanley, the builder—I happened to get into a discussion with a number of old-timers regarding the date the hotel was opened for the first time, and at least three different individuals on whose accuracy I would normally rely on such matters, had three different opinions as to what the actual year was that Mr. Stanley built and opened the hotel. . . . I hope that the information which you say is being incorporated in the book about Mr. Stanley has been authenticated.[2]

Henry Lynch's cautionary note notwithstanding, the materials to write such a history do exist. As might be expected, the Stanley Museum itself has by far the greatest concentration of Stanley material, much of it dutifully saved by family members after F.O. Stanley's death in 1940. But materials are also to be found in the newspapers of Longmont, Loveland, Lyons, Fort Collins, Boulder, and Denver; in the public records of Larimer County and the State of Colorado; in the hands of private individuals; in the oral histories and published reminiscences of Stanley's contemporaries; and in a variety of other documents located in museums and libraries in

Colorado and across the country. Taken together these sources have provided more than enough information, much of it new, to create the history *Mr. Stanley of Estes Park*.

During our lunch at the Stanley we all agreed on the importance of getting the story told, however incomplete it might turn out to be. Sue Davis was very clear that its publication would provide the occasion for the discovery of still more information about F.O. Stanley and his Estes Park story. Though the "brief" history I once visualized has become a full-length book, there are still gaps in the historical record, for which additional materials may well exist. It is the Stanley Museum's hope and my own that this book will lead to the recovery of still more documentary evidence.

Historical research inevitably involves debts to people, and I have contracted many. At the risk of slighting any number of individuals who have so graciously responded to my letters and other requests, I do need to thank some by name. Sue Davis for her initial invitation and confidence, for sharing with me her knowledge of the Stanley story, and for her skills and abilities as an editor; Betty and Eldon Freudenburg and Alma and Frank Hix for support and encouragement; and my wife, Pat, for her general indulgence (once again), this time in a project that consumed far more of our life together than I had so rashly first promised. I owe a special debt to six individuals who were particularly helpful in moving the project forward: Pat Burdick of the Stanley Museum at Kingfield, who patiently sifted the Stanley archives for materials that might be of importance; Marjorie Trenholm who kept the physical material flowing and the lines of communication open; Frank Hix, who drew upon his extensive knowledge of Estes Park, Stanley automobiles, and hydroelectric power to add details and facts that I could have come upon no other way; Julie Franklin Jones of Estes Park, who volunteered her time to diligently scour the deed books of Larimer County to help establish the record of F.O. Stanley's property transactions; Sybil Barnes, the local history librarian at the Estes Park Public Library, who in addition to using her special abilities to track down pieces of information, agreed, perhaps all too willingly, to edit with blue pencil a final draft of the manuscript; and Frank Normali of Estes Park and Cleveland, Ohio, a former owner of the Stanley, who made available to me his important collections of F.O. Stanley and Enos Mills materials.

Others that I need to mention by name include Betty Kilsdonk, Lisl Goetze Record, and Lisa Hanson of the Estes Park Area Historical Museum; Judy Visty of the Park's interpretive staff; Walter Emery of Denver and Rowena Emery Rogers of Parker, Colorado; Karen Dacey of Newton, Massachusetts; and Bob Bemiss, Curt Buchholtz, the late Ted James, and Marty Yochum-Casey, all of Estes Park.

There were also those individuals who were kind enough to read and comment on an earlier version of my manuscript and to offer comments and suggestions. In spite of the redundancy I would like to thank them here. Proceeding alphabetically, they include Sybil Barnes, Bob Bemiss, Gary Brown, Kelley Brown, Curt Buchholtz, Pat Burdick, Norm Carver, Karen Dacey, Bernie Dannels, Sue Davis, Bob Dekker, Betty Freudenburg, Eldon Freudenburg, Lisa Hanson, Alma Hix, Frank Hix, George Hix, Pieter Hondius, Ted James, Julie Franklin Jones, Terry License, Enda Mills Kiley, Betty Kilsdonk, Jack Melton, Frank Normali, Eleanor James Owen, Mary Pratti, John Ramey, Lisl Goetze Record, Rowena Emery Rogers, Paula Steige, Marjorie Trenholm, Bill Van Horn, Judy Visty, and Marty Yochum-Casey. To state the obvious, this book has been made a good deal better because of their active involvement.

Finally, I owe a special debt to Bob Sweeney and the other trustees of the Kenneth Kendal King Foundation of Denver and to George Strake and the Strake Foundation of Houston, Texas, for the significant financial support they have provided to help underwrite the cost of research and publication. I can only hope that what I have written justifies the support and encouragement that I have received, and that readers will find the pages that follow as rewarding as our table conversation apparently was that day for the young lady at the Stanley.

James H. Pickering
Houston, Texas, and Estes Park, Colorado

CHAPTER

1

Beginnings

On the morning of June 30, 1903, Freelan Oscar Stanley left Welch's ranch hotel on the north fork of the St. Vrain River above Lyons. Following meager directions, he drove his small steam automobile up the rough winding wagon road toward the mountain resort of Estes Park. One hour and 50 minutes later he came to a stop in front of the general store owned by a tall, redheaded Irishman named Sam Service. For Enos Mills, the region's first historian, Stanley's arrival was

> The epoch-making event in the history of the Park. . . . The investment of a half million dollars in a modern hotel in the wilds twenty-five miles from a railroad startled the business world; this also gave the Park publicity far and wide and greatly hastened its development. This large and adventurous investment showed great confidence in the future of Estes Park, required nerve, good business sense, the capacity to see the recreation needs of the near future and also something more and greater than these.[1]

That "something more" had to do with vision. Immediately grasping the future prospects of Estes Park as a modern resort community and the role that automobile transportation was destined to play in developing tourism, F.O. Stanley set about using his Yankee ingenuity and considerable wealth to turn those convictions into reality. He designed and built the Stanley Hotel complex, 11 buildings in all. He improved access to and from the Park, a boon to the newly arrived automobile, by reconstructing the North St. Vrain road from Lyons and then incorporated a transportation company so that people could make the trip. He built Estes Park's first power plant and helped establish its water system and first bank.

With this infrastructure in place, Stanley turned to an even larger project, the creation of a national park in the Estes Park region. The direct influence of F.O. Stanley would continue to linger over town and region for another quarter of a century. The story of Mr. Stanley of Estes Park is not, however, just a textbook lesson in civic high-mindedness and entrepreneurial success. It is part of the larger story of the development of the resort industry in Colorado and the West.

What made all of this even more remarkable, even improbable, was the fact that when Stanley came to Estes Park in 1903, he was a very sick man for whom the outlook was grim. Four months earlier, on

Estes Park in 1903. Courtesy Estes Park Area Historical Museum.

February 27, when his family physician in Massachusetts found evidence of recurring tuberculosis, Stanley had been ordered to start at once for a different climate. Like so many before him, he chose Denver and the mountains.

This unexpected event marked a turning point in F.O. Stanley's life, and he quickly proved himself more than equal to the challenge. Shaped by inheritance, environment, and circumstance, Stanley had taken good advantage of all three. At age 54 he had accomplished much, was a competent judge of people and events, and had the experience and wealth to do pretty much as he pleased. Measured and thoughtful, with the ability to express with irony and humor his sense of the world around him, Stanley's very presence inspired the confidence and trust of others.

His physical appearance was deceiving. Though five feet, 10½ inches in height, the slender, erect Stanley gave the impression in person or photograph of being a distinctly taller man. His presence and effect on others also had much to do with manner and deportment. Speaking slowly and deliberately, in a voice that never lost its accent or composure, he seemed very much at ease with himself and with the world. Strangers and friends alike were instinctively attracted by his cordiality and openness, qualities that spoke of natural kindness, good nature, and genuine interest rather than simply politeness and courtesy. Small wonder that when F.O. Stanley began to talk about new possibilities in the West, other people should listen and respond. Stanley had the advantage of arriving in Colorado at a time when business frontiers remained unconquered. Bringing with him a lifetime of accomplishment, as well as the inclination and determination to confront new challenges, F.O. Stanley was fully prepared to take advantage of the opportunities that came his way.

New England Origins

"You can't throw a stone without hitting a Stanley."
—Kingfield, Maine, saying, c. 1860

By the time F.O. Stanley arrived in Denver, he was a man of reputation as well as means. Together with his talented twin brother, Francis

F.O. Stanley. From the collection of the Stanley Museum.

Edgar Stanley (1849–1918), he had already made major contributions to the dramatic industrial and technological expansion that characterized post–Civil War America. Though best known for their "Stanley Steamer" automobile, the two brothers, who came to be known as F.O. and F.E., had also done pioneering work in the field of dry plate photography, from which had come their wealth.

The Stanleys owed much of this success to traits long associated with their New England roots. Shrewd, practical, and hardworking—quintessential Yankees through and through—the Stanleys could trace their American origins back to three brothers who had arrived at the port of Boston from England in the 1660s and then, as so often happened in the New World, went their separate ways—to Connecticut, New Hampshire, and Massachusetts.[2]

F.O. and F.E. Stanley belonged to the branch that remained, at least initially, in Massachusetts. Their paternal grandfather, Liberty Stanley (1775–1863), was born in Attleborough, Massachusetts, south of Boston, in February 1775. His name reflected local anti-British sentiment and the revolutionary ferment that would erupt just two months later at Lexington Green and Concord Bridge. On the day of the battle, his father, Solomon Stanley, with a party of 60 other minutemen, had marched as far north as Roxbury "to make as much show of numbers as possible in view of the British" and to harass their return to the safety of Boston.[3]

Liberty Stanley's stay in Attleborough, however, was relatively brief. Located in the corridor that included Newport and Providence as well as Boston, the town remained open and vulnerable. By the spring of 1779, when Liberty was four, his parents, Solomon and Patience Stanley, sought the safety and opportunities of Winthrop, Maine, 200 miles to the north, transporting themselves and their precious household goods over roads and cartways that were in places scarcely more than four-and-a-half feet wide.

By purchasing sizable tracts of land, Solomon Stanley gave notice of being a man of consequence. Winthrop's other residents almost immediately elected him town moderator and thrust him into the center of local affairs. His son, Liberty, attended the local schools, and then, continuing a family tradition of business ownership, was apprenticed in a fulling (wool processing) mill near Lake Annabessacook. When Solomon Stanley purchased the mill and its equipment in 1797 and put him in charge, Liberty, now 22, immediately became someone with prospects. It did not take him long to demonstrate the fact.

In November of the following year Liberty Stanley married 17-year-old Hannah Fairbanks, the daughter of Revolutionary War veteran Colonel Nathaniel Fairbanks, one of Winthrop's most prominent citizens. Hannah brought to the marriage a story of her own. Her father had the distinction of having lived in Dedham, Massachusetts's famous Fairbanks House, built by a lineal ancestor in 1636 and said to be one of the oldest homes in America. It was a fact that his descendants, including the children of Liberty and Hannah Stanley, would later point to with considerable pride.

Though known locally as "an excellent mechanic, and a superior workman,"[4] Liberty Stanley was not a successful businessman. He was never able to run the mill at a profit and by 1800 had sold his interest and turned to other pursuits. The first was an attempt to support his family as an inventor, a hope based on the fact that he had already developed a very successful cloth-shearing machine. He also gave expression to a love of music by designing and constructing bass viols, selling them as he could. Tragedy, however, followed.

In July 1813, 27 days after giving birth to Solomon, named for Liberty's brother in Kingfield, Hannah Stanley died at the age of 32, leaving Liberty with seven children. The oldest, Isaac Newton Stanley, was just 13. Unable to cope with the situation, Liberty allowed the family to be broken up. The two youngest children were sent to live with others, while Liberty and the rest struggled on as best they could with the help of relatives and friends. Liberty finally left Winthrop for Dixfield, 45 miles distant, where he made his home with Isaac Newton, until his death in 1863.

Solomon Stanley (1813–1889), the future father of the Stanley twins, was fortunate. Only 27 days old at the time of his mother's death, Solomon lived with a neighboring family until he was nearly three. Then, in 1816, his uncle, Solomon Stanley (1780–1875), the man after whom he had been named, returned to Winthrop, adopted the boy, and brought him 60 miles north to Kingfield, the village that he had helped to pioneer and settle.

Solomon Stanley, Esquire—the family called him "Solomon One," his nephew "Solomon Two"—had first visited the future site of

Kingfield in the fall of 1807 while acting as a surveyor for William King, a wealthy merchant capitalist from Bath. Earlier that year King and several others had obtained title to a vast tract of land known as the Bingham purchase, which included what is now Kingfield, Concord, and Lexington Townships in the mountainous region of northwestern Maine. Though his efforts to promote settlement were only partially successful, the enterprising William King left his mark in two important ways. He gave the town of Kingfield his name, and 13 years later, in March 1820, he became the state's first governor, in large measure because of his efforts in securing statehood. King and others had struggled successfully to have Maine separated from Massachusetts and then enter the Union as part of the Missouri Compromise.[5]

Though little more than a wilderness when Solomon Stanley first saw it, Kingfield offered promise. Returning in 1808 with his wife, Susanna, Esquire Stanley, now serving as William King's first agent, built a small log house and helped to establish a village. Securing a choice tract of land on both sides of the Carrabassett River, he erected a mill dam, a mill for grinding corn, and a dye house for coloring cloth. He also built and operated a store and, in 1818, constructed what was said to be Kingfield's first framed house on a 150-acre tract that he had acquired on the east side of the river. This house, the Stanley homestead, still remains. Prominent in town affairs from an early date, Esquire Stanley became Kingfield's first town clerk and, later, town treasurer, pound keeper, and justice of the peace.

During this period, Kingfield prospered. By 1850 the population of the town had reached 662. According to the census of that year, while the largest group of men—150—listed their occupations as "farmer," the village of Kingfield could boast five blacksmiths, seven merchants, three carpenters, three shoemakers, a miller, two schoolteachers, a mason, a sawyer, and nine who listed themselves simply as "laborer."[6] Solomon Stanley prospered with the town, living into ripe old age and dying on April 12, 1875, the 68th anniversary of his marriage, well into his 96th year.

Solomon Two attended the local schools and then began a highly successful career, first as a teacher and later as a farmer and shopkeeper. While operating a general goods store, he survived a partner who drank and gambled the enterprise into debt. Though it took years to pay off the creditors, the younger Solomon persevered. In so doing he provided his children with a powerful, and lasting, lesson about the evils of drink.

Solomon Stanley, like the Stanleys before and after him, deeply valued education. He served for many years as a member of Kingfield's school committee and, later, as the town's supervisor of schools. Having become the leading advocate for the building of a controversial graded schoolhouse for the village, he skillfully outmaneuvered his opponents to obtain the needed votes. When the new school opened in 1875, his fourth son, Solomon Liberty Stanley, sometimes known as Solomon Three, taught the lower grades.

Solomon Two also served Kingfield as a selectman, assessor, surveyor, and overseer of the poor; was elected for two different terms to the Maine legislature as a Republican (despite the fact that the town always carried a Democratic majority); and in 1876 became a member of the Governor's council. In his role as a county commissioner, he helped bring the Franklin and Megantic Railroad to Kingfield in 1884, the single most important event in the economic history of the town and northern Franklin County. Named for Franklin County, Maine, and Lake Megantic, Quebec, the F & M was a branch of the better-known Sandy River and Rangeley Lakes Railroad; with over 120 miles of track and 13 locomotives, it was one of the most extensive networks of narrow-gauge railroads in the country, and one of the few to operate consistently at a profit.

In an age that demanded progress, Solomon Stanley championed its most potent symbol. "Amid the doubts of timid men as to the policy of building any railroad, the best route and the means with which to build," one of Solomon Two's contemporaries later wrote, "he saw clearly, was independent and firm and was always ready to raise his voice for the construction of the railroad that he knew he could not long enjoy, but which he knew that all who came after would be sure to use and highly appreciate."[7]

On December 16, 1840, Solomon Stanley married Apphia Kezar French (1819–1874), the daughter of one of Kingfield's first settlers. Over the next 21 years she became the mother of six boys and a girl, including the twins, Freelan Oscar and Francis Edgar, born on June 1, 1849. The others were Isaac Newton (1841–1910), John Calvin French (1852–1883), Solomon Liberty (1854–1881), Chansonetta (1858–1937), and Bayard Taylor (1861–1915), each of whom was given a name with

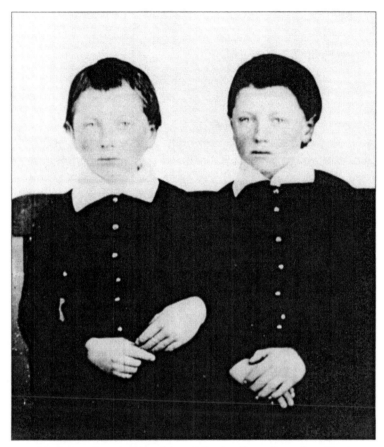

The Twins, Francis Edgar left, and Freelan Oscar. From the collection of the Stanley Museum.

scientific, religious, cultural, or family significance, reflecting their parents' education, interests, and values. The names of the twins were said to have come from the writings of Sir Walter Scott.

Kingfield, with its village green, small white houses, church steeples, and surrounding mountains—Abraham, Sugarloaf, Bigelow, Vose, and Black Nuble—was picturebook New England. Here were forests, ponds, and streams—cool green summers, golden autumns, crisp winters—a delightful place in which to be young. According to family tradition, the twins' childhood was full, happy, and comparatively uneventful.

It was, nonetheless, a time of preparation. In a rough, unfinished autobiographical essay found in his desk after his death, Freelan Stanley described the origins of their interest in technology:

> The Stanley twins inherited from both father and mother quite unusual mechanical ability. While Solomon Stanley was by occupation chiefly a farmer, yet he always kept his farming tools in the best possible condition. His carts, sleds, harrows, and stone drags he made himself and they were models of their kind. His post and rail fences were the best in town, and in making ox-yokes he was unexcelled. The mother of the twins was equally gifted and came from a family of mechanics. Her brother Josiah French was by far the most skillful carpenter in town and her brother Ira was the leading millwright. So it was not surprising that the twins very early in life showed a mechanical bent.
>
> At the age of four they showed a passion for whittling, and before they were five their father had bought each of them a jackknife, and for a number of years the jackknife and gimlet constituted their principal mechanical equipment. With these simple tools they made from pine and cedar, of which the farm furnished an abundance, their own toys, which consisted of wooden oxen and horses, bows and arrows, kites.[8]

In another incomplete essay, written about 1930, Freelan recalled the twins' first entrepreneurial efforts at age nine, when they used the lathe at their father's mill to manufacture wooden tops that they sold to playmates. Quickly saturating that market, the enterprising twins then turned to making replacements for a critical piece of a loom that frequently broke, which they offered to the women of the town.

The following year the Stanley twins entered the maple sugar business. Carefully making 60 sap buckets from staves of well-dried birch, held together with steamed strips of white ash, they traded a mink that Freelan shot for the needed sugaring-off pan. The $34 they earned from their efforts was enough to purchase their first store-bought woolen cloth for suits then made by their mother and a much-prized, and thoroughly-mastered, copy of Benjamin Greenleaf's famous *National Arithmetic*.[9]

Efforts at enterprise were punctuated by long-remembered episodes of boyish playfulness. "Dear Sewall," F.O. Stanley wrote from Newton, Massachusetts, on Stanley Dry Plate Company letterhead in December 1894,

> You will find inclosed our check for $20.00. Now will you please cash the same and take the cash to Wm Lane as a present from the two boys that have stolen more apples from his back orchard than any other two boys in existence.[10]

If identity and self-confidence begin with a developed sense of place and belonging, then Freelan and Francis Stanley began life with a decided advantage. In Kingfield the name "Stanley" was everywhere about them. There was Stanley Hill, the gently sloping pasture southeast of the old Solomon Stanley homestead on Maple Street, with its sweeping view of Kingfield and the Carrabassett River valley; and Stanley Brook, the small stream that ran behind the house itself. There was also Stanley Mill Pond, by whose reflecting waters the twins'

The Stanley Homestead, Kingfield. From the collection of the Stanley Museum.

grandfather had once ground corn for the new town. In Kingfield it was said that "you could not throw a stone without hitting a Stanley."[11] By 1903 there would also be Stanley School, which the twins designed and helped to build at a cost of $12,000 as a way of remembering and celebrating their own beginnings.

Surveying the jobs available to them in a community such as Kingfield, Freelan and Francis decided to follow an old and honorable New England tradition. They became teachers—a choice that clearly reflected the emphasis that their parents placed on education. Graduating from Kingfield's school, the twins (known as Freel and Frank to their relatives and closest friends[12]) left home in the fall of 1869 to travel 20 miles to the new Western State Normal School (now the University of Maine at Farmington), a type of institution that pioneered in linking higher education to the preparation of teachers. Though it was apparently about this time that F.O. had his first bout with tuberculosis, he managed to graduate with the class of 1871.

F.E.'s career at Farmington, on the other hand, ended almost as soon as it began. Within months of his arrival, his ability to draw a map of the United States from memory led to an accusation of cheating.[13] His honor challenged, he quit and almost at once became a teaching principal at North New Portland, eight miles southeast of Kingfield. There F.E. met, and on January 1, 1870, married, an elementary schoolteacher named Augusta May Walker (1848–1927), affectionately referred to as "Gusti."

Continuing to teach, F.E. took a position at Strong, 15 miles southwest of Kingfield, where he again assumed the combined role of principal and teacher. While at Strong, the headmaster of the Maine Youth Center at Portland was fired after an incident involving a youth who had been allowed to die from exposure. F.E. Stanley agreed to assume the position on an interim basis, performing so well that he was asked by the trustees to stay on the following year. Slowly, however, F.E. Stanley began to gravitate toward a new career—one that within a decade would make him one of the leading portrait artists in New England.

F.O. Stanley's formal education lasted somewhat longer than F.E.'s. After graduating from Farmington Normal, F.O. taught in district schools at Andover, Farmington, and Lisbon and then in the summer of 1872 began to prepare (or "fit" as it was called) for college by entering Hebron Academy, the school founded in 1804 among the rolling hills of Oxford County northwest of Lewiston.

Coming initially as an assistant in writing under newly appointed principal John F. Moody, Stanley matriculated as a student with the class of 1873 but apparently never received a diploma.[14] Though his stay was brief, the educational experiences at Hebron Academy were the happiest of F.O. Stanley's life, a debt he would later repay with three decades of service and considerable financial support.

In the fall of 1873, F.O. Stanley entered Bowdoin College at Brunswick, Maine, to pursue the same course of classical study that had produced, within a single class, Nathaniel Hawthorne, Henry Wadsworth Longfellow, and President Franklin Pierce. Unlike these three members of Bowdoin's famous "Class of '25," Stanley stayed but a single year. As was the case with F.E. at Farmington, he was soon called upon to choose between authority and principle.

The defining event of F.O. Stanley's collegiate career was the cause célèbre known as the "Drill Rebellion." Its origins could be traced to a decision made the previous fall by Bowdoin's illustrious president, Joshua Lawrence Chamberlain, who drew upon his Civil War fame to institute a system of military drill.

Chamberlain had impeccable credentials. An 1852 graduate of the college, to which he returned in 1857 to teach rhetoric and modern foreign languages, Chamberlain had gone off to fight for the North as lieutenant-colonel with the 20th Maine, rising to the rank of brigadier-general. Glory came in July 1863 at Gettysburg. Commanding the left flank on Little Round Top, Chamberlain so distinguished himself that he was awarded the Congressional Medal of Honor "for daring heroism and great tenacity." Two years later, at Appomattox Courthouse, Joshua Chamberlain was chosen to receive the formal surrender of the arms and colors of Lee's Confederate Army.

Returning to Bowdoin as president in 1871, after four terms as Maine's governor, Chamberlain was alarmed to find a lack of military fitness among the student body. His remedy was a new three-year program in military science, beginning in the freshman year with a course titled "Infantry Tactics: School of the Soldier." Implementation was placed in the hands of a diminutive and somewhat austere army officer, Major Joseph P. Sanger, handpicked by Chamberlain and assigned to the college by the War Department, together with 12 pieces of artillery.

By the fall of 1873 the purchase of a uniform had been made compulsory, and, as Stanley quickly learned, a majority of the "cadets" were unhappy with Chamberlain's program. As the student biweekly paper, the *Bowdoin Orient*, described the situation that July, "Many heartily like the 'drill'; many are carelessly indifferent; many, very many, are quietly but thoroughly restless and dissatisfied, many are openly and bitterly rebellious."[15] A petition asking that the drill be abolished, signed by 126 of the 133 persons to whom it was submitted, was presented to the college governing board in November. When it went unconsidered, grumbling gave way to sedition. One of the cannons was dismounted; breechblocks were stolen. The climax occurred late one night. As one student wrote home to his father in a letter,

> A crowd of students unknown . . . painted some inscriptions in black paint on the front of the chapel and on the chapel door coming down profanely on the military department of this institution and the military officers placed here. They show a low sentiment enough but a true one on the part of the students. Such notices must gall Chamberlain as the military is his pet scheme.[16]

Joshua Chamberlain was unmoved. By May 1874, however, covert opposition had become open defiance. One Friday "the greater part of the Freshmen, Sophomore and Junior classes refused to report and let it be known that they "had bound themselves by written agreement to resist the drill at all hazards."

The faculty quickly saw its "duty." It denounced the "concerted rebellion against lawful authority" and voted to send home "every man who persisted in his refusal to comply with all the requirements of the College." This action was followed on May 28, 1874, by a form letter, signed by the president and sent to the fathers of some three-quarters of the student body. Each rebellious student was given until 7 P.M. on June 8, 1874, to return to campus and sign a pledge renewing "obedience to the Laws and Regulations of the College" or face expulsion.[17] To add to the discomfort of Chamberlain, Sanger, and the Bowdoin faculty, the goings-on at Brunswick were picked up and reported by the press, not only in Maine but in Boston and New York as well.

Only three students failed to return to campus. One of these was Freelan O. Stanley.

F.O. Stanley's college stay beneath the fabled pines of Bowdoin College was over. Though he took away with him a solid respect for education and the Greek, Latin, history, mathematics, and "Exercises in Elocution" that comprised Bowdoin's freshman course of study, in later years he came to regret the lack of a Bowdoin degree. "Your kind letter is at hand," Stanley wrote in November 1918 to an agent of the college, who had carefully tracked his career in hope of financial support, "and in reply I think I should much prefer being placed back in the class of '77 with a degree of A. B."[18] Bowdoin remedied the deficiency the very next year by awarding him an honorary one.[19]

For the next eight years, F.O. Stanley returned to teaching, briefly at Strong, Maine, with F. E, and then by himself at Mechanic Falls, Maine, 1875–1877; Columbia, Pennsylvania, in Lancaster County west of Philadelphia, 1877–1880; and at Farmington, Maine, 1880–1882. Unfortunately, neither of the Stanleys left reminiscences of their days as teachers in the small towns of rural Maine. Nor, apparently, did any of their students, many of whom as adults surely must have pointed with pride to the fact that they had been schooled by one of the amazing Stanleys.

Like his twin brother, F.O. married a fellow teacher. While at Mechanic Falls, a small, thriving village on the banks of the Little Androscoggin, he met Flora Jane Record Tileston (1847–1939), the daughter of Peter and Phoebe Tileston. They were married on April 15, 1876.

Despite a fondness for teaching and the young, predilections that F.O. Stanley would demonstrate in countless ways in future years, his restless, innovative nature eventually turned him to other ventures. In 1882 he returned to Mechanic Falls, purchased an abandoned factory, and began the manufacture and sale of school supplies.

Taking advantage of the increasing school market for mechanical drawing, F.O. Stanley soon developed "Stanley's Practical Drawing Set," consisting of a pair of compasses with a pen and pencil attachment, a ruler, triangle, and protractor, all packed in a neat case that sold for the very reasonable price of one dollar. Since the cost of production was only 25 cents, the potential for profit was clear. Orders flowed in. "It certainly seemed," he wrote years later, "that opportunity had not

Flora Jane Record Tileston Stanley, c. 1890. From the collection of the Stanley Museum.

only knocked on my door, but had flung the door wide open, and that I was on the road to prosperity."[20]

This prosperity was brief. It lasted only until a fire destroyed his factory. While the building was insured, its contents were not, and F.O. was left with "the loss of the savings of a lifetime."[21] Borrowing from F.E.—as much, apparently, as $5,000[22]—F.O. Stanley moved the business to Boston, opened a production facility at No. 17 Main Street in Cambridgeport (today's Cambridge), and tried, without success, to start over.[23]

town's commercial thoroughfare. In Lewiston, as in Auburn, his portraits were well received and before long most of the leading families had paid at least one visit to his large 40-foot-square display room and become clients. With success, all thoughts of studying law were put aside.

The Stanley Dry Plate Company (with its motto of the Scottish clans, "On, Stanley, On!") was a direct result of F.E. Stanley's experiments with airbrush portraiture. But this form of artistic rendering was also labor-intensive and far too slow for the volume of business he was now attracting. Old-fashioned portrait making required the subject to pose quietly, sometimes for hours, while the artist sought to capture just the "right" look or expression. F.E. discovered that by working from photographs rather than real life, he could greatly reduce the time it took to complete a work.

At first he employed a local photographer. Unfortunately, the man F.E. chose did not meet his artistic standards. Subcontracting the photographic work also added to the cost of doing business. It did not take F.E. Stanley long to realize that he could significantly improve quality and lower costs by doing the photography himself. Borrowing $300 from Isaiah Woodman, a distant relative of his wife, F.E. purchased a camera in New York City and began taking his own pictures.

The Stanley Dry Plate

Though he no longer had to rely on the photographic work of others, Stanley was soon experiencing all the irritations that went with the so-called collodion (or "wet plate") photography of the day. It required that exposure and development be accomplished with a glass plate that had been freshly coated with a highly unstable, toxic emulsion, and then photosensitized, just prior to exposure, by bathing it in a solution of silver nitrate. Reducing and fixing agents then had to be applied to achieve a glass plate with a printable negative image. All of this was messy, time-consuming, and frustrating in its complexity.

Like a number of his contemporaries, F.E. Stanley was soon experimenting with emulsions that would dry on the plate and still retain their photosensitivity. He read what he could on the subject, books and magazines of the day that introduced him to the recipes of

Englishmen and Europeans. Then he went to work in his basement laboratory formulating his own. Over a two-month period in 1880, through trial and error, F.E. developed and tested a highly satisfactory gelatin plate.[5]

The Stanley Dry Plate was one among many that helped to revolutionize the American photographic industry by making it possible for the competent amateur photographer to take quality pictures. No longer did photographers have to go through the cumbersome process of producing wet plates in their studios or in the field. Nonperishable plates could now be produced in large batches, with far better control of quality, and were ready in advance as needed.[6]

The market for the dry plate had long been in existence. What was needed was a technology that reduced the complexity of picture taking itself.[7] The Stanley dry plate, among others, did precisely that, and beginning in 1881, F.E. and his small production facility started to become a player in this new and expanding industry.

Three years later, F.E. took his wife's suggestion and asked his brother to join the growing business. Augusta conceived the arrangement as a way of allowing F.O. to discharge the debt he had incurred after the fire at Mechanic Falls while getting her husband help he could rely upon and trust.[8]

On Friday, May 30, 1884, F.O. left his job at G. L. Damon's safe factory in Boston, where he had been working as an assistant cashier, to investigate the possibilities of his brother's expanding photography business at Lewiston. Five months later, on October 27, 1884, having carefully weighed Frank's proposal and his own prospects, F.O. accepted. Within weeks they were full partners.

It was at this time—perhaps as a way of underscoring the equality of their new business relationship—that F.O. allowed his beard to grow in length to match his brother's and both began their lifelong habit of dressing alike in public.[9] Though there were differences between the two in appearance and mannerisms, these were so slight that even family members were hard-pressed to tell the twins apart. Augusta Stanley Tapley, F.E. Stanley's granddaughter, recalled with pride that as a young girl she knew at once—because the toes of F.O.'s shoes were wider than those of her grandfather's.[10]

By May 1885, after some initial difficulties, the Stanley Dry Plate Company had been firmly launched. The company's success, and its impact upon F.O.'s own future prospects, can be measured by the series of increasingly enthusiastic letters written that spring to Flora, who remained in Boston while their new house on Pine Street in Lewiston was being readied for them.

"We are surely on the road to wealth," he wrote her on May 7th. "Our monthly statement shows a profit of $2400 apiece for April. I am going to have all my debts paid the first of June, and shall have a good sum left, for my dear wife and me."[11]

"We are turning out lots of plates, and no losses," F.O. told Flora a week later. "We have enough to pay all our debts and leave us more than before the fire. We can count ourselves lucky to get over the fire so soon."[12] His estimates were very much on target. "I find by our monthly statement," he wrote on June 1, "that we can pay our last debt and have over three thousand left. Don't you feel good about it[?]"[13]

During these years of increasing financial success, the Stanley brothers went into the horse breeding business and built a large stable on Canal Street. F.O. was particularly interested in horses, and owned what were said to be some of the best trotting stock in Maine, including very fast horses with such names as "Black Amber," "La Mont," "Redwood Boone," and "Grover," which he both exhibited and raced.[14]

F.E. continued to make and sell portraits "of every description" finished "in Crayon, Pastel, Water Colors and India Ink . . . in the most artistic manner."[15] But with the success of the Stanley Dry Plate Company such efforts gradually became less important and far too time-consuming. By 1890 they were a thing of the past.

Though the Stanleys immediately established a comfortable working relationship in the dry plate business on Bates Street, it was F.E. Stanley who got most of the credit. When Lewiston produced a new history of its "leading business men" in 1889, F.E. was roundly praised as "one of the best-known photographers in the United States" and "one of the first to manufacture and use the now universally used [dry-plate] process." F.O. Stanley, perhaps because he was a relative newcomer to Lewiston and involved with the manufacturing and sale of dry plates rather than with the more visible photography studio, was not mentioned at all.[16]

For a time at the turn of the century, the names of the Stanley brothers and their accomplishments were usually linked together. But this lasted only until 1903 when F.O.'s tuberculosis took him off to Colorado and out of the public eye during those critical years that saw the sale of the Stanley Dry Plate Company to George Eastman and a number of the most dramatic accomplishments of the Stanley Steamer. Small wonder that when it came to publicity and reputation in the East, F.O. Stanley lived and labored in his brother's shadow. In time F.O. would have a reputation all his own, but only after he transported his Yankee skills and ingenuity some 2,000 miles to the west.

The dry plate business proved demanding. "I doubt if an enterprise of any considerable size ever started in a more primitive manner than we started the manufacture of photographic dry plates," F.O. Stanley would write in May 1936.

> We had, practically, no capital, no factory, and no customers. Cramer, Seed, and Eastman [the leading dry plate manufacturers of the day] were amply able to supply the demand, and the dealers did not want to be bothered with any more dry plates. But there was left the "forgotten man," the consumer. He, no matter who he was, or what he was, is always anxious to buy something just as good cheaper, or to buy something better at the same old price. We decided to do both, to give him a cheaper, and a better plate. This was the problem that confronted us, and its solution meant success.[17]

The story of that success is far more complex than F.O. makes it sound in the retelling. Much of the Stanleys' accomplishment had, in fact, to do with F.O.'s knowledge of papermaking, an expertise he had gained through careful observation at the paper mills at Mechanic Falls. By 1885 that knowledge allowed him to conceptualize, design, and build a dry plate coating machine that reduced the time needed to coat an 8 x 10–inch plate by hand from 60 plates an hour to 60 plates a minute by machine, astounding industry competitors. This increase in productivity and competitiveness allowed the Stanleys to reduce the price of their plates, further increasing profit margin and market share.

Adding to the Stanleys' success was their marketing strategy. By selling directly to a number of New England's leading photographers, cutting out the middleman or jobber, they were able to make well-

The Stanley Dry Plate. From the collection of the Stanley Museum.

established dealers like the large New York firm of E. & H. T. Anthony and Company willing, and even anxious, to carry plates so much in local demand.

In 1893, at the invitation of William Notman, the Stanleys further increased their penetration of the market by opening a highly profitable production facility and wholesale outlet in Montreal. Notman Photography Studios operated galleries in Montreal, Ottawa, and Halifax as well as in Boston, New York, and Albany. As Notman's son, Charles, recalled in 1955:

> My father started to make [dry plates] in the studio but soon found out it would require a special factory to keep up the quantity required and corresponded with English manufactur-

ers asking them to open a factory in Montreal. They turned the proposition down, so he arranged with the Stanley Bros. of Lewiston, Maine to open a factory here.[18]

Well before the Notman invitation, the influx of orders had overburdened existing facilities. On May 1, 1888, the Stanleys broke ground for a new factory in Lewiston, which they occupied for two years. In 1890 the entire dry plate business was transferred to Watertown, Massachusetts, a vibrant manufacturing center on the Charles River near Boston.

Looking back from half a century, F.O. Stanley also tended to underestimate the extent to which the twins' success was the result of good old-fashioned, face-to-face salesmanship, in particular F.O.'s own ability in a highly competitive market to convince dealers that they should stock the Stanley product. While F.E. remained in Lewiston and later in Watertown, tending the factory and making sure that the quality of their glass dry plates remained high, F.O. took to the road calling on dealers.

The record of one of his trips, made during the late winter and early spring of 1889, is contained in a lengthy series of some 80 letters written to Flora. "I want to visit St. Paul, Milwaukee and Minneapolis north of here, and St. Louis, Kansas City & Denver west," he wrote her from Chicago on February 10, 1889,

and return home by the way of Washington[,] Baltimore and Philadelphia.

I am doing finely and shall increase the sale of the Stanley Plate.

How do you like being a "widder"[?] I find a steam radiator to help a feller keep warm nights cant [sic] hold a candle to a sweet wife.[19]

Subsequent letters suggest that F.O. pretty much followed the itinerary described, beginning in Chicago, which, he told Flora, "beats any town I was ever in for business."[20] "Chicago is the hardest town to drum in the world. Most dry plate drummers are pointed towards the door quite lively. But I have succeeded a fair trial in every place."[21] Despite some initial qualms, F.O. Stanley discovered that he liked playing the salesman role and, moreover, that he was good at it. His letters radiate increasing confidence and success, as well as a growing optimism about the future of the Stanley Dry Plate Company.

Stanley's letter of April 13, 1889, written on the road from Buffalo, is typical:

> I am going to do the Stanley D P Co a grand job in this town. If I could be on the road all the time for six months more I think we could not fill our orders. It is hardly possible to estimate the value this trip has been to me. It required much nerve to stick to it so long and I did not intend to let go till we were in fine working shape.[22]

He was particularly proud of his results in Chicago, given its reputation as a tough place to make a sale. "I have succeeded in getting the best concerns in Chicago to using our plate," he wrote Flora on February 24, "a thing which all pronounced impossible when I landed here. The work is not so disagreeable as I anticipated. All accord me with being in my methods the most original drummer they ever saw."[23] Those "methods" apparently worked everywhere, including Denver, where he reported "a clean sweep."[24] They worked so well, in fact, that he could report to Flora on April 15, on his way home to Lewiston, that "on my return we shall have connections with every dealer in the U. S. east of the Rocky Mts, except a few in the south."[25] F.O. returned to Boston on April 24, 1889, after an absence of more than 12 weeks. The success of that trip, and the new business that followed, made the removal to suburban Boston not only inevitable but necessary. Stanley would later put these same sales and marketing skills to use in Colorado—and with similar results.

The Stanley Dry Plate Company in Watertown

The move to Watertown and nearby Newton, where the twins and their wives took up residence, was a matter of economics. The Stanleys used glass shipped through the port of Boston. By establishing themselves at the edge of Watertown near Boston rail lines, they were able to save on transportation costs and be closer to their major markets. By March 25, 1890, they had received a permit from the local selectmen to build a new three-story building "north of Maple St., near a proposed new Street, in the vicinity of Elliott Machine Shop on South side of the Charles River."[26] "Six years today," Flora Stanley wrote in her diary on May 31, 1890, "Freelan left Boston for L. [Lewiston] to establish D. P. business. Today he goes to Boston to arrange for its establishment there."[27] He almost did not make it. "In removing the machinery," the Lewiston paper reported, "Mr. F.O. Stanley fell from a ladder about twelve feet . . . , getting quite a shaking up, but pluckily kept at work, taking the train for Boston later in the day to expedite matters at their new quarters."[28]

Two days later, on June 2, 18 tons of machinery were shipped from Lewiston, and the rest of the move was accomplished without incident. There was now, however, a backlog of orders to fill. When the production of plates began again that summer, the Stanleys almost immediately encountered difficulties. As Flora confided in her diary on June 26, "We are having terrible luck."[29] Shipments of defective plates began to come back, one lot alone amounting to $40,000. For photographic producers this was more than simply "terrible luck": a crisis was at hand. The problem, it turned out, had to do with the chemicals in the local water supply, which spoiled the gelatin plates within days of production.

According to John Allen, who had worked for the Stanleys in Lewiston since December 1885 and then accompanied them to Boston, these unexpected expenses, coming as they had on top of the cost of building and equipping the new factory, almost brought the Stanley Dry Plate Company to its knees. Borrowing money that Augusta Stanley had saved and invested, the brothers had to drill an artesian well to the unprecedented depth of 303 feet, all but 29 of which was through solid rock, before locating a fine supply of fresh water that remedied the problem.[30] Success returned. By November 8 Flora could report, "Great days in the dry plate business."[31]

Though the panic of 1893 posed yet another significant threat, the Stanleys survived, and even prospered, by once again doing the unconventional. Refusing to remain part of the association formed by fellow manufacturers to raise and fix prices, the twins overcame a subsequent boycott by continuing their practice of selling directly to photographers and amateurs at a substantial discount. Following the lessons learned from F.O.'s experiences in 1889, they kept three salesmen more or less continuously on the road, and identified cut-price dealers in all the major cities north of Washington. The brothers also briefly established a distribution center in Chicago. Inventiveness, stubbornness, and the willingness to take calculated risks, together with a strong Puritan work ethic, underlay the Stanleys' success. By 1900 the Stanley Dry Plate Company was selling nearly $100,000 worth of plates a month.

Life in Newton

Newton, the "Garden City of the Commonwealth," was a fine place to live. Originally one of 11 New England villages clustered about Boston, by the late nineteenth century, Newton had become a distinctive suburb of rolling hills, wooded slopes, and winding roads, whose wide and shaded streets, neat hedges and lawns, and setback houses exuded an air of affluence and well-being.

Though the banks of the nearby Charles River had become at an early day the site of cotton, paper, and leather mills and ironworks, Newton's residential areas remained quiet and picturesque, not unlike the place that Ralph Waldo Emerson had bragged about in 1834 during his brief residency. "Why do you not come out here, and see the pines and the hermit?" Emerson wrote a friend. "It is calm as eternity and will give you lively ideas of the same. 'Tis Sunday in this woodcock's nest of ours from one end of the week to the other."[32] The Stanleys and their wives evidently thought so too, for by the mid-1890s they had firmly established themselves as contributing members of a community they found both accepting and congenial.

During their first years in Newton, F.O. and Flora lived next door to the Stanley Dry Plate Company with Sterling Elliott and his family, from whom the Stanleys had purchased the property for their new plant. Elliott, the so-called Bicycle Man, was owner of the Elliott Machine Shop, the unused bicycle manufacturing facility adjacent to the dry plate building that later, in 1898–1899, would become the first home of the "Stanley Bros." steam car factory.

In 1894, as a sign of their intention to stay, F.O. and Flora built a small but impressive, three-story Georgian Colonial Revival–style house at 165 Hunnewell Street, within easy walking distance of the factory, which would remain their home until 1913. The task was not without its difficulties, for when it came to designing and building houses, Stanley could be a difficult man for whom to work. A surviving letter from J. C. Rochford, a Newton carpenter and builder, openly scolds his client for the "various changes . . . ordered . . . in the house" and for insisting that he work from an "entirely different set of plans . . . from what we had agreed upon."[33] Presumably someone other than Rochford later installed the small, foot-operated turntable in the rear carriage house so that F.O. could exit his steam car by driving forward rather than backing it out.[34]

F.E. and Augusta were not to be outdone. The following year, 1895, they gave up the small three-story, hip-roof Victorian house with a two-sided stone veranda they had built four years earlier on Franklin Street in favor of a much grander Georgian mansion with rounded portico and half-circle drive. A grand home by any standard, it occupied the whole corner of Hyde Avenue and Centre Street on a city block, all but one piece of which was owned by F.E. and Augusta, in an area then still surrounded by woods. The house had a large playroom with pool table and bowling alley in the basement. But its most distinguishing feature, reflecting the owner's deep interest in music, was the large central Music Room with its Steinway grand piano. Located on the midway landing of the grand staircase, this theatrelike room, for which the second-story landing served as a balcony, occupied the middle of the house, beginning below the second floor and rising to meet the ceiling of the third. The entrance was off a broad landing, 13 steps up from the wide front hall. The room itself was striking: light ivory woodwork, sky-blue walls, and a ceiling decorated by a painting depicting "cherubs playing different instruments [while] floating about on fleecy clouds."[35]

Both Stanley families invested in their neighborhoods beyond their current needs, purchasing a number of choice lots, on several of which they would later build homes.[36] They invested civically as well, beginning in 1895, when F.O. Stanley and several others formed the Hunnewell Club for the exclusive use of 40 local residents living within a two-mile-square area. Two years later, in 1897, with the demand for membership expanding, the brothers together financed the building of a much larger clubhouse at the corner of Eldredge and Church Streets, adapting for the purpose the same distinctive Georgian Colonial style of architecture, with majestic ornate columns and balustrades, that by now had become something of a trademark. It embodied engineering originality as well. Set on a foundation of granite, the new clubhouse was one of the first private buildings in Boston to use steel-frame construction.

In external appearance and internal appointments, the new building of the Hunnewell Club of Newton, Massachusetts, as the organization was rechartered in November 1898, would have done credit to any late nineteenth-century genteel community. Nothing that might facilitate the leisure-time activities of the 250 members or their wives was overlooked.

The first floor, with its combination billiard and pool room containing four tables, and its library, reading room, office, and men's coatroom and lavatory, belonged exclusively to the male members. The second floor contained a serving kitchen; a large room used for both dining and card playing; a second, smaller card room; and a lady's combination parlor, coat, powder room, and toilet. On the third floor was a good-sized ballroom and assembly hall complete with stage, capable of accommodating several hundred persons. Located in the basement were the men's lockers and shower room, four bowling alleys (later expanded to six), and a full kitchen, where meals were prepared and sent by dumbwaiter to the serving kitchen on the second floor.

From the time it first opened its doors in April 1898, the Hunnewell Club was a great and continuing success. Unsurpassed in the greater Boston area, it quickly became the recognized center of community life in Newton. To be a member of the Hunnewell Club, particularly during the heyday of its early existence, was considered a "position of considerable prestige."[37]

F.O. Stanley, though seldom a club officer, continued to play a leadership role at Hunnewell. It was through his interest and efforts during the early years that a series of popular Sunday afternoon concerts, with teatime intermission, were begun, which continued into the 1930s.[38] The membership was appreciative. The contribution of both brothers was formally recognized on the evening of February

22, 1909, when on George Washington's birthday an "old folks ball" was held in the third-floor ballroom. As Augusta Stanley explained that night in her diary,

> I was one of the matrons. I wore my white lace dress over yellow. Freel & Flora & Frank & I led the grand march. It was a part of christening of the new Hall named "Stanley Hall" in honor of the boys. The boys looked very fine in strict evening dress and Flora in white lace over yellow also.[39]

The clubhouse building remained the legal property of the Stanley families until 1929, when F.O., serving at the time as president, offered to sell it to the membership for $25,000, the original cost of construction. By then, as Flora's and Augusta's diaries had testified, it had served the Stanleys as an important social outlet for better than three decades. F.O., on his part, kept up an active presence at the club even into his 80s, when, it was said, his opponents at pool and billiards still had a difficult time in winning.[40]

From Photography to Steam Cars

In his 1936 essay, F.O. Stanley dismisses the final years of the Stanley Dry Plate Company with characteristic succinctness. "In the meantime," he wrote, "we had become much interested in the `horseless carriage.' There was more fun in riding in a machine of our own make than there was in making dry plates, so . . . we sold the dry plate business to the Eastman Kodak Company."[41]

The fact of the matter was that despite the quality of the Stanleys' product, the American photographic industry of the 1890s had become ferociously competitive, forcing smaller producers out of business, fostering regional concentration, and increasing the need for improved products and trained, in-house technical personnel. It had also become fertile ground for the sort of monopolistic behavior employed so well by America's captains of industry who created large holding companies to reduce costs and control prices.

Of the new combinations in the photography industry, George Eastman's was by far the most successful. Having acquired two other major competitors by 1902, Eastman took his time in finally coming to terms with the Stanleys, even though their dry plate continued to maintain strong market share. After having made an offer in the spring of that year, conditional on an inspection of the company's books by "experts" during the summer, Eastman then changed his mind. Negotiations, conducted by F.E. Stanley as president of the Stanley Dry Plate Company—F.O. was then convalescing in Colorado—did not resume until November 1903. Though the selling price did not change, the Stanleys now lowered the cash portion by $85,000 in exchange for excluding "the Newton real estate and all Machinery and fixtures therein excepting those which are used exclusively for the dry plate business."[42] The reason for the change of terms had to do with the needs of their emerging steam car business.

A final agreement with George Eastman came on January 5, 1904, when F.E.'s newfound interest in steam automobiles and F.O.'s ongoing battle with tuberculosis in the West made selling out far more attractive than hanging on. The price they negotiated (based on the company's profits for the previous three years) was some $430,000 for the company and its goodwill, and another $110,000 for its equipment and supplies.[43] Once out of the Stanleys' hands, the business remained in Newton about a year and was then transferred to Rochester where Eastman continued for some time to produce and sell the Stanley plate under the Stanley Dry Plate name.

The sale to Eastman and its timing were fortuitous. Photographic historian Reese Jenkins takes nothing away from the enterprising Stanleys when he writes that for all their early success "the Stanley brothers were not deeply committed to long-term goals of growth, technical innovation, and imaginative business practice in the photographic industry."[44] F.O. Stanley suggests as much in the tribute to George Eastman with which he closed his 1936 essay on the Stanley Dry Plate Company:

He alone had the vision. While the rest of us were striving to improve our products in order to secure the patronage of the leading photographers, he saw that the way to make a great industry was to make everybody a photographer, and with the film and the Kodak he did this and developed one of the big industries in the country and could count his profits in millions, while we counted ours in thousands.[45]

The transaction had an interesting footnote. According to F.E.'s son, Raymond, George Eastman wanted to pay for his purchase, at least in part, with Eastman stock, an offer that the cash-conscious brothers refused. That was, Frank later told his son, the most "awful mistake" he had ever made in his life.[46]

3

The Stanley Steamer

If the electric [automobile] is a "peach," the Stanley is a "peacherina."

—George Eastman,
Letter of January 8, 1902

Three years before they moved the Stanley Dry Plate Company to Boston in 1890, the Stanley twins reportedly had seen a crude steam car built and operated in Lewiston. Their own entrance into steam locomotion did not begin, however, until April 1897, when F.E. Stanley began to construct an automobile largely of his own design at the house of his employee and friend, John Allen, while Augusta was touring Europe with their daughter Blanche.[1] Allen, a native of Kingfield, was brought by the Stanleys to Lewiston in 1885 and moved with them to Watertown-Newton in 1890.

The First Steam Car

If F.E. Stanley knew little about automobiles, he knew less about internal combustion gasoline engines, then still considered something of a novel technology. Steam, on the other hand, was a logical choice of locomotion. It had been harnessed successfully for more than a century as a source of power for steamboats and locomotives. Steam also powered the stationary steam engines that drove the industrial revolution, including, presumably, the production machinery at the Stanley Dry Plate factories. In short, steam was a subject that F.E. Stanley knew something about.

In adopting steam for his automobile, F.E. may also have been influenced by the example of fellow Bostonian George Eli Whitney who, a year earlier, in June 1896, had produced a steam carriage that was featured in *Horseless Age* and widely publicized by the local press. There was also Sylvester Roper of nearby Roxbury, who as early as 1863 had produced a small lightweight, steam-powered carriage. He also invented a much celebrated steam bike on which Roper himself set a world speed record three decades later, in June 1896. While circling the Charles River bicycle track in Cambridge, the 73-year-old Roper suffered a heart attack and died. As the *Boston Globe* put it in its headline, Roper had quite literally "Died in the Saddle."[2]

F.E. Stanley started to build his own car pretty much from scratch. As a result, he had plenty of questions. "There is one thing I want you to keep your eyes open to see," he wrote the touring Augusta on June 14, 1897,

and that is the motor carriages . . . you will see them in Paris, and I want you to ascertain the price at which they sell. . . . And also the kind of motor in most common use, whether the steam engine, the gasoline engine or the electric motor with storage battery. . . . I am still out of horses and I shall not own a horse again until I have seen the outcome of the motor carriage movement if it is not for 10 years.[3]

Though Augusta apparently did not respond to her husband's request, by July 1897 F.E. was far enough along to bring his wife up-to-date. "I wrote you some time ago about motor carriages," he reminded her on the 11th.

Well, I am building one. I am making all the plans and it will weigh only 350 pounds and will be four inches wider and five inches longer than our best buggy was. It will cost me about $500, and will be finished the first of September or soon after you

get home. It will not be afraid of a steam roller and will have no
bad habits. It will stand without hitching, and perhaps that is all
it will do.[4]

Parts were difficult to come by. Practically everything that went
into the first car, as well as those that followed, were borrowed from
other vehicles of the day or manufactured by the Stanleys themselves.
F.E. bought a light buggy from the Piper Tinker Bicycle Frame Shop in
Waltham, adding to it his own steering gear and drive chain. That was
the easy part.

For the power plant, F.E. had ordered a small two-cylinder, double-
acting steam engine from the Mason Regulator Works of Milton and
a boiler from the Roberts Iron Works Company. The problem, as
Stanley quickly discovered during assembly, was that engine and
boiler—built for stationary application—together weighed 600
pounds, some 250 pounds heavier than the anticipated weight of the
entire vehicle.

F.O. Stanley's later comments notwithstanding,[5] the primary impetus for that first steam car came from F.E. Stanley. But it is also clear that
F.O. was more involved in the early stages of the car—from the development of its engine to the November 1897 purchase of the Elliott bicycle and machine shop—than some members of F.E.'s family were later
willing to allow. It is equally clear, however, that after the completion of
the first vehicle, F.O.'s own enthusiasm and inventiveness were thoroughly engaged and he willingly became part of the doing.

Working together, the twins were able to produce a much lighter
vehicle. They did so by turning to F.O.'s old friend, machinist A. R.
Penney, of J. W. Penney and Sons in Mechanic Falls, who had built the
machinery that Stanley needed to manufacture his mechanical drawing tools. Penney was able to build the twins an engine weighing only
35 pounds.[6] This they combined with a new Roberts boiler weighing
90 pounds, whose sheet-copper outside shell they wrapped with high-
grade steel piano wire to give it the strength to carry 250 pounds of
pressure.[7] Thanks to Penney's ingenuity and their own, the Stanleys'
new automobile was almost 500 pounds lighter than its unfinished
predecessor.

By September 1897 this steam car, a two-seater complete with
leather dash, whipsocket, 28 x 2–inch bicycle wheels, and steering

lever handle, was ready for testing. The genealogy of the first car was not difficult to trace. As *Steam Car* magazine explained in 1917:

> It was a hybrid that carried earmarks not only of the buggy it was destined to replace, but of the bicycle, which was then reaching the zenith of its popularity. The steel tubing of the underframe, the light wire wheels, the pneumatic tires, the single chain and sprocket drive—in fact, the entire running gear of the car, was an adaptation of bicycle design. And the body, with its straight leather dash, single high seat, steps, backrest and open sides, was unmistakably made in the wood working shop of some unimaginative carriage builder.[8]

That hybrid nonetheless worked, and worked well. Its entrance into the world was celebrated by one of the most famous photographs of the new age of automobiling. It captured the black-bearded twins, ramrod straight, sitting side by side, impeccably dressed in long dark overcoats and black derby hats, knees covered by a blanket, in their wonderful horseless carriage. "Firing up" the gasoline burner, they set out on a trial run to Newtonville and back. "I shall never forget our first ride," F.O. Stanley wrote in 1930.

> We went out our alley way on to Maple Street, and turned towards Galen Street. A horse hitched to a produce wagon was standing headed toward Galen Street. He heard the car coming, turned his head around, took a look, gave a snort, and jumped so quickly that he broke the whiffletree, but did not move the wagon, ran out to Galen Street, through Newton Square and did not stop running till he reached Newtonville Square. That occurred in the forenoon. That afternoon the owner called at our office and told us we owed him $25.00. We claimed we owed nothing; at the same time if he would take his harness and wagon up to Murray's and have them repaired, we would pay the bill. The bill amounted to $2.00.[9]

A second trip, this time to Cambridge, followed the next day. According to F.O. Stanley's memoir, three more steam automobiles were made during the next year—two of them two-passenger cars

The Stanleys and their first Steam Car, September 1897, Watertown, Massachusetts. From the collection of the Stanley Museum.

and the other a four-passenger surrey. The twins sold one of the passenger cars to a Bostonian named Methot for $600;[10] the surrey was dismantled because they were not satisfied with it. For all the excitement of the new venture, however, the Stanley Dry Plate business still came first. "Up to this time," F.O. recalled, "we had not the slightest idea of ever engaging in the manufacturing of automobiles as a business. It was an interesting hobby, and not a trade."[11]

Things at first did not always go smoothly. F.E.'s attempt to take his new car from Newton to Poland Spring in Maine in a single day, for example, turned out to be something of a disaster. "I have something to tell that will amuse you," F.O. Stanley wrote Flora from Newton on July 9, 1898—she was then at the Stevens House at Lake Placid, New York:

Frank started for Poland Spring yesterday morning at 4 o'clock. He got as far as Mystic Park and punctured a tire. But he had taken the precaution to take a new one, so he stopped and in about 20 minutes he had the new one [put] on. Everything went finely till he reached Hamilton where he punctured another tire that hung him up. So he went to a long distance telephone and called me up and I sent a boy on a wheel with a new tire. He then returned to the shop, a distance of 39 miles in coming back, or 78 miles, and he got here at 12:30. Before starting he was told to give his carriage a more thorough test as he had put on a new body, a new engine, and two new tires of a different make.

Well he worked on his carriage all yesterday afternoon and got it in fine shape and started at 4 a.m. today to do the trick. Everything went to perfection till he got to Kennebunk Port. There his steering bar broke when he was going at high speed and the carriage ran plum into a ledge breaking both front wheels and damaging the body badly. Frank jumped landing in a brush pile and escaped uninjured. Had he met with no accident he could easily have reached Portland by noon and Poland Spring by 5 p.m. His handle bar has broken once before and was entirely unsafe.

F.O., on his part, was clearly undisturbed by his brother's trials, for he concluded his letter to Flora, "By the time you get home my carriage will be ready and we will have some fun."[12]

Charles River Park

Then came November 1898 and what was arguably the first automobile show ever held in New England at Boston's Mechanics Hall, an event, the *Boston Herald* told its readers, that "brought Boston up to date with London and Paris."[13] Though most of the exhibit space was given over to bicycles, four cars were on display: two gas cars (one a De Dion racer from France, the other a Haynes-Apperson), a Riker electric car, and a steam car built by the well-publicized George Whitney. The small number of automobiles were to be expected, for that year only 800 were registered in the entire United States.

The twins attended, where they were caught paying more than ordinary attention to the Whitney automobile. They became so absorbed in Whitney's machine, in fact, that when Whitney himself entered the basement of Mechanics Hall, he found one of the Stanleys taking photographs of his car, the other lying on his back under the vehicle closely inspecting its chassis. One observer recorded the event:

> I saw the Stanley steamer brothers at the bicycle show in Boston where Mr. Whitney's car was on display. It stole the show much to the displeasure of the bicycle people. It was in the basement where it had all the room to run around. The Stanley brothers, big, tall, bearded fellows like the Smith Cough Drop Brothers, were all over that car and under it, too, measuring.[14]

What made the auto show memorable, however, was not the Stanleys' rather outrageous behavior, or Whitney's indignant, if fruitless, protest to the show's manager. Rather it was the events that took place on the velodrome track at nearby Charles River Park during an open-air meet held on November 8, 1899, immediately after the close of the exhibition at Mechanics Hall.

Because the Stanleys' machine had not been part of the exhibition, it was not originally scheduled to be part of the trials for speed and hill climbing. The twins were persuaded at the last minute by the sports editor of the *Boston Herald* and the show's manager to enter their small two-seater. For the promoters it was a way to increase interest in what otherwise would have been only a field of four.

Following a parade of motor carriages from the Mechanics Hall building on Huntington Avenue to the park, the day's events began. With F.E. at the wheel, the Stanleys' "light and trim" steam carriage established a new world record in the speed trials, circling the one-third-mile oval track before 1,500 spectators three times in two minutes and 11 seconds, defeating Henri Fournier's low-slung De Dion. F.E. then added to the day's triumphs by beating Whitney's steam car in the hill climbing event. "Never, before or since," F.O. recalled,

> have I seen such enthusiasm as was created by these two performances of this little car. This [the hill climb] was the last event of the day, but we were kept there over an hour answering questions and explaining the construction of the car. And in less than two weeks from this event we had received orders

for over 200 cars similar to the one shown there. It was then, for the first time, we decided to engage in the manufacture of automobiles.[15]

F.O. Stanley's story is one that has been repeated many times. It is wrong, however, in several respects. According to the August 1898 issue of *Horseless Age*, the decision to enter the car business had been made several months before, and no later than July:

F.E. Stanley of the Stanley Dry Plate Co. is about to embark in the motor carriage business, having constructed a steam carriage which gave good service and which he sold at a round price. He is now building a number of carriages embodying several improvements over the first model.[16]

It should also be noted that the number of orders received was over 100, not 200. Most of F.O.'s reminiscences about dry plates and steam cars come from the 1930s, when Stanley was in his 80s, and many years removed from the events he was trying to retell. Age combined with F.O.'s well-known storytelling abilities, rather than any conscious "disremembering," doubtless accounts for his factual discrepancies.

The events at Charles River were clearly important for the Stanleys and the future of their automobile enterprise. The *Boston Herald* prophetically placed the day in an even larger context:

The fair has done much already to familiarize people with automobilism, but this contest must give a tremendous impetus to interest in this invention. A good many of us can recall the day when the bicycle began its career in pretty much the same way. But the bicycle is an old story, and the auto carriage is the new one. It is doubted if any of the spectators at the racing meet yesterday said they did not care to have such a vehicle. The impression gathered from many bystanders was to the effect that the horse would soon be deprived of his occupation, and that he might as well take off his shoes and retire to newer pastures for the next century or so. . . . One of these days in the near future they [auto carriages] will be in every family precisely as the bicycle is there now. We shall all own our auto-

The Stanleys at Charles River Park, November 1898. F.O. Stanley with stopwatch in hand. From the collection of the Stanley Museum.

mobiles, and then we can snap our fingers at subways and elevated roads, and not care a button about "trackless wastes," or anything else.[17]

To meet the demand generated by their success at Charles River, the Stanleys made use of the shop once occupied by the Sterling Elliott Machine Company, which stood empty adjacent to their dry plate plant. Utilizing some of Elliott's equipment, which F.O. had purchased in November 1897, and ordering whatever else they needed, the Stanleys began to assemble the components of their first steam cars, relying heavily on available and proven technology and using standardized, interchangeable parts. "I think we can truthfully say," F.E. Stanley wrote in 1917, "that that hundred cars were the first lot of automobiles of that number that were constructed of standardized parts, and really represented a manufacturing business as distinct from making things by hand."[18]

John Brisben Walker

During the winter and spring of 1898–1899 the Stanleys were visited on two occasions by John Brisben Walker, editor of *Cosmopolitan Magazine* and an early automobile enthusiast. Walker wanted to own an automobile company, and the Stanleys were a suitable target.

John Brisben Walker (1847–1931), whose monuments and success F.O. would later encounter in Colorado, was a fascinating character, and a determined one. Born in Pittsburgh and educated in Washington, D.C., Walker had accepted an appointment to West Point in 1865, only to abandon it three years later in favor of a trip to China with the new American minister. In return for helping to reorganize the Chinese army, Walker, not yet 30, was given the title of general. After returning to America, Walker made millions manufacturing iron in West Virginia, only to lose heavily in the panic of the 1870s. In 1889, having recouped his fortune by investing in Denver real estate and alfalfa farming, Walker bought and revived *Cosmopolitan Magazine*, in five years increasing its circulation from 16,000 to 400,000 by creating a popular, inexpensive, but well-illustrated magazine in touch with current affairs. And automobiles were very current.

Walker made his first visit to the Stanleys in early February 1899. Identifying himself, Walker announced that he had come to buy a half-interest in their new business. "We told him we didn't know as we had what might be called an automobile business," F.O. Stanley later wrote with his customary good humor,

> and we certainly did not want a partner; that we had difficulty enough in getting along with each other, and we did not want to increase our trouble by taking in a third party. He cited the great advantage offered by the *Cosmopolitan* as an advertising agent. We told him what we seemed to need was not advertising, but cars to fill our orders, and we could not see how the *Cosmopolitan* could help us in that. He was very persistent . . . but we were stubborn. . . .[19]

So was Walker. Two months later, in April, he was back. Though the Stanleys had by then produced only three cars, Walker now offered to buy the entire business. Since "this was an entirely different proposition, . . . we told him if he would call in the morning we would give him our price." Though the brothers decided that evening not to sell, they had agreed to offer Walker a price, a promise they were unwilling to break. The figure named the next morning was $250,000, more than 12 times their entire investment, and deliberately calculated to "drive him away . . . disappointed."[20] Walker astonished the twins by immediately accepting.

Walker soon located a partner, Amzi Lorenzo Barber, president of the Barber Asphalt Company of Bridgeport, Connecticut, the so-called king of asphalt. Barber agreed to give Walker part of the cash he needed to settle with the Stanleys in exchange for a half-interest in their company. Under the agreement reached with the Stanleys, the purchasers received the factory and equipment, the cars under manufacture, their automobile patents, and an agreement not to compete in the steam car business for a year beginning May 1, 1899. During that year, as a way of publicizing the new Barber-Walker venture, the Stanleys were required stay on in the role of "General Managers" and consultants.

The Walker-Barber partnership, incorporated on June 17, 1899, as the Automobile Company of America (a name changed within a month to the Locomobile Company of America), soon found itself in trouble. Within weeks the principals had quarreled over policy and choice of manager, and agreed to go their separate ways. In the "partition of interests" that followed, Barber kept the name Locomobile and the factory at Watertown, while Walker received $75,000 and started a new company, the short-lived Mobile Company of America, headquartered at Tarrytown, New York, where he had a large home. Under its new name, Barber's Locomobile Company produced some 100 of the original Stanley automobiles that had not yet been assembled at the time of the purchase, offering them for sale at a price of $600 F.O.B. Newton.[21] By 1901 the Locomobile would become America's largest selling automobile, turning out some 1,600 units in that year alone, an impressive accomplishment by the production standards of the day.[22]

On November 8, 1898, F.E. had been the star performer at the velodrome on Charles River. The next year, on August 31, 1899, it was F. O

Stanley's turn to make automobile history. As part of his agreement with Barber, he and Flora, at the tiller of a Locomobile, made the first automobile trip up New England's highest mountain, New Hampshire's 6,288-foot Mt. Washington. They completed the 7.6-mile trip up an average grade of 12 percent in the time of two hours and 10 minutes. "The thing we had undertaken to do was done," Flora later wrote of their adventure, "and the triumph of the Locomobile was published to the world! Our running expenses up and down the mountain were 26 cents and everything about the carriage and machine was as perfect as when we left Newton."[23]

F.O. Stanley followed this achievement with yet another. Taking his steam car to Washington, D.C., he chauffeured a less-than-enthusiastic President William McKinley on an automobile tour of the capital, the first sitting President to ride in an automobile. McKinley is reported to have confided to a friend that throughout the ride, he expected the car either to blow itself to bits or to run away, out of control, with him and its inventor.[24]

F.O. and Flora Stanley on Mt. Washington, August 31, 1899. From the collection of the Stanley Museum.

The Stanleys Reenter the Automobile Business

The Stanleys, their appetites clearly whetted by the possibilities of the steam car, were soon back in the car business. Within a short time of the expiration of their noncompetition agreement with Barber and Walker on May 1, 1900, they were ready with an almost totally redesigned car. A year later, in May 1901, when Barber moved the Locomobile Company to Bridgeport, Connecticut, the Stanleys bought back their Watertown factory, together with all the patents they had sold, and started into production. The cost of the repurchase was a mere $20,000. As in 1898, the Stanleys were once again swamped with orders—even without advertising. On August 24, 1901, the brothers produced the first of their new Stanley automobiles, a two-seater weighing a mere 650 pounds.

It was during this period that their old rival George Eli Whitney, now with Locomobile Company as its chief engineer, reentered the picture. Whitney claimed that part of the chain drive tensioning device on the Stanleys' new car constituted a patent infringement. A suit was threatened, incited, it has been intimated, by Amzi Barber, as a way of slowing down the Stanleys' return to the automobile business. A lawsuit was forthcoming. Instituted by Whitney in the federal District Court of Boston in February 1902, it led the Stanleys to redesign the engine so that it connected directly to the rear axle—an improvement in efficiency that Whitney himself later praised.

George Eastman was among the earliest Stanley enthusiasts. The Stanleys' car had attracted Eastman's attention in 1899, when he was becoming increasingly interested in acquiring their dry plate business. But what may at first have been merely a strategy to encourage the twins to focus on new pursuits by August 1901 had ripened into genuine enthusiasm. Since "I have seen a new machine that Stanley is getting out at Newton," Eastman wrote his friend, Frank Seaman, on August 6, 1901, in a letter worthy of the kind of advertisement that the Stanleys disdained,

> I have altogether changed my ideas about steam machines. They appear to have simply eliminated trouble instead of putting on devices to overcome it. I rode in the Stanley machine and ordered one. He superheats his steam to such an extent that there is little

or no vapor. This, of course, is unimportant but he claims the superheating allows him to run twice as far on the same amount of water and to save about one third of his gasoline. He can carry gasoline for 140 miles of good roads. It is not under pressure except about one pint of it at a time. Cylinder lubrication will lubricate the engine absolutely for exactly 50 miles run. No steam air pump is required and the burner is a wonder. . . . It has an extra long wheel base and will run 30 miles an hour and keep steam up. The price is only $600 and the machine is so simple that it almost looks unfinished. . . . you had better see his machine.[25]

By January 1902, with the arrival of his new car, Eastman was even more lavish in his praise. "If the electric [automobile] is a 'peach,'" he wrote on the 8th, "the Stanley is a 'peacherina.'"[26]

In 1902 an even newer Stanley made its appearance, and before the year was out the twins had sold some 170 machines at a price of $600 each, matching the price of Barber's Locomobile. The following year, as a result of Whitney's threatened suit, the Stanleys (as noted above) improved their automobile by gearing the engine directly to the rear axle. At this time they also covered the engine and gears in a metal

AN EARLY STANLEY RACE WINNER!

George Herring at Denver's Overland Park, 1905. From the collection of the Stanley Museum.

case to protect them from dust. The number of Stanleys produced and sold in 1903 almost doubled. They nearly doubled again in 1904, the year George Eastman completed his purchase of the Stanley Dry Plate Company.[27]

Tuberculosis

At the very moment when the prospects of the Stanley brothers seemed brightest came Dr. Baker's announcement that F.O.'s tuberculosis had recurred. Though clearly a blow, his diagnosis cannot have been totally unexpected. Stanley had experienced several occurrences of lung problems, including tuberculosis, as far back as his school days. Flora had been so distraught over his health in 1899, in fact, that she noted in her diary entry for January 1900: "This year I kept no diary. It has been a year of much sickness and anxiety for us. Freel had pleurisy in May and was confined to his bed 5 weeks."[28]

A predisposition to pulmonary problems, moreover, ran in the Stanley family. The twins' mother, Apphia Stanley, died of tuberculosis in 1874, at the age of 55. Within a decade, two of their brothers, John Calvin French Stanley and Solomon Liberty Stanley, died of the disease as well. Dr. Baker's news and the advice that accompanied it, were therefore to be taken very seriously. Within days F.O. and Flora had wound up their affairs in Newton, boarded a train, and started west to Denver.

Their choice of destination was eminently logical. Since the 1870s there had been endless talk about the amazing effect of the Colorado climate upon the victims of tuberculosis and other diseases. In fact, so many came west that those in the East were often left with the impression that the state was, as the celebrated English traveler Isabella Bird put it, "the most remarkable sanatorium in the world." "The climate of Colorado is considered the finest in North America," she wrote of her visit of 1873, "and consumptives, asthmatics, dyspeptics, and sufferers of nervous diseases, are here in hundreds and thousands, either trying the 'camp cure' for three or four months, or settling here permanently."[29]

Even P. T. Barnum, the great American showman (who admittedly had property for sale in suburban Denver), professed to be astounded by Colorado's wonderful restorative powers. "Two-thirds of them come here to die," he is said to have remarked, "and they can't do it!"[30] Barnum's hyperbole aside, consumption brought more people to Denver than did gold. Tuberculosis became such a stimulus to the Colorado economy, in fact, that one journalist quipped, not without cause, that its bacillus "might justly be commemorated in stone."[31] Sadly, not all who sought a cure in Colorado recovered their health or even survived. F.O. Stanley would be among the fortunate.

CHAPTER

4

First Years in Colorado

Out where the handclasp's a little stronger,
Out where a smile dwells a little longer,
That's where the West begins.

—Arthur Chapman
"Out Where the West Begins"

"The Queen City of the West": Denver, 1903

The city of Denver was very different from the cosmopolitan, sophisticated world of Newton and Boston that F.O. and Flora had left behind. Though Denver, once the so-called braggart city, was rapidly sloughing off what one contemporary resident called "its old 'wild West' provincialism" and taking on the "air of a real metropolis,"[1] evidence of the city's raw frontier past was still in evidence. Visitors had only to look, for example, at the piles of gravel along the banks of Cherry Creek to be reminded of the glory days of 1859 when throngs of miners lined the stream panning for gold.

Their train arrived in Denver on March 4, 1903, at 8:45 A.M., after a nightlong ride "over the great level prairies." The Stanleys went directly to the nine-story Brown Palace Hotel at 17th and Broadway, since 1892 one of Denver's architectural triumphs. There, early the

N

Denver 1900. From the collection of James H. Pickering.

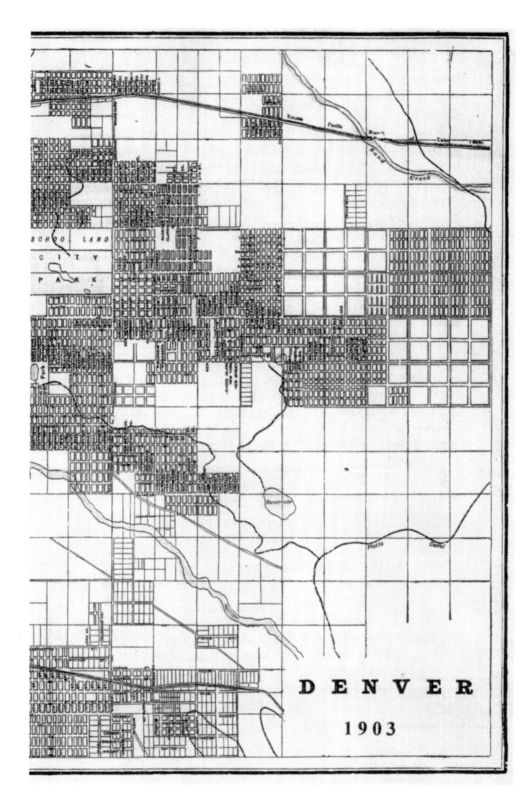

DENVER

1903

next day, they were visited by Dr. Sherman D. Bonney, who would serve as F.O. Stanley's personal physician throughout their stay in Colorado.

Bonney, a native of Maine, had been notified in advance of the Stanleys' coming, and their meeting was something in the nature of a reunion. The Stanleys had known Bonney and his wife, Nancy, at least casually, as far back as their days in Lewiston. The Harvard-trained physician had attended Lewiston's Bates College as an undergraduate and briefly practiced there before moving to Denver in 1890 because of his wife's health.[2] Flora, in fact, had seen both the Bonneys as recently as the previous April, when during her four-day visit in Denver as a delegate to the General Federation of Women's Clubs, she had been invited to dinner at their home.[3] Sherman Bonney's career had flourished in Colorado, where he enjoyed a substantial reputation as an expert diagnostician of diseases of the chest. That reputation would be further enhanced after 1908 with the publication of his widely used text, *Pulmonary Tuberculosis and Its Complications*.[4]

The Bonneys were fully prepared to take their Lewiston friends in hand. Sherman Bonney's first act was to relocate patient and wife to the new Adams Hotel at the corner of 8th and Welton. The next day, March 6, he examined Stanley at his office in the Steadman Building. While the precise nature of Dr. Bonney's prognosis is unknown, he clearly forecast a prolonged stay in Colorado. The very next day F.O. told a reporter for the *Denver Republican*, during the course of an expansive interview on the prospects of the Stanley steam car, that he would probably be a resident of Denver for at least a year and "was so delighted with the climate and the surroundings that he [had] started out to look for an investment in the way of a home."

When the *Republican*'s reporter suggested to Stanley that the fog that accompanied his arrival "was not a propitious introduction to the famous Colorado climate," F.O. had responded: "Oh, I called that a good day, but they told me it was the worst you had experienced in 20 years. If that's bad weather, what is your fine weather like?"[5] Though Bonney's report cannot have been overly encouraging, F.O. Stanley was obviously determined not to surrender to his illness and just as determined to like his new home. He also knew from his days on the road as a drummer for the Stanley Dry Plate Company that it never hurt to make friends in new places.

The fact that Stanley was suffering from consumption either was little known or, as seems more likely, simply didn't matter. In 1903, consumptives were still welcome in the state. It is a good thing, however, that Stanley arrived when he did. Within five years there would be a decided shift in attitude. Fear replaced compassion. "Because of the presence of consumption," one sufferer-turned-author wrote in 1908, "the heart of the average Denverite has become hardened toward the tuberculosis patient [and] . . . human sympathy is conspicuously lacking."[6] That same year the Colorado legislature even debated the proposition that consumptives be required to wear a warning bell. Had such a proposal become law, Thomas Galbreath wrote, clearly in anger, "the clatter [in Denver] would have been so great, the street gangs and automobile horns could not be heard above the din."[7]

According to Flora's diary, the search for a permanent residence began the following day, when Nancy and Sherman Bonney took the Stanleys out "driving to see houses with a view to hiring or buying one." Flora herself wasted little time becoming acclimated, and was soon following in Denver much the same kind of active social schedule she had pursued in Newton and Boston. Before the month of March was out she had visited Boutwell's art goods store on 16th Street, which was exhibiting the oil and watercolor paintings of Charles Partridge Adams,[8] and had purchased an old English plate and a statue of St. Peter at M. J. Kohlberg's Curio Store on 17th Street.

Flora Stanley was a knowledgeable if eclectic gatherer of art and antiques. She did not allow the fact that she was in Denver to dampen her enthusiasm. She also rode by carriage regularly to City Park, with its 320 acres of lakes and trees, and around the city; went to see Duncan Thompson in *Our Very Majesty* at the Tabor Grand Opera House, one of Denver's grand buildings; and attended an exhibition at the Denver Art Club and a meeting of the Social Union—a branch of the Denver Woman's Club.

As March came to an end, Flora Stanley's presence in Denver was acknowledged at a luncheon of the Colorado Society of the Daughters of the American Revolution, the third largest in the country, which invited her to sit at the central table and make a few remarks.[9] She also managed to find time to engage the services of a Swedish maid named Minnie Lundburg, a young woman of 22, just recently arrived from Iowa where she had been born and raised.[10]

By March 17, the Stanleys had settled on a rental at 1401 Gilpin Street.[11] F.O. was clearly feeling better, so much so that Flora optimistically recorded in her diary that he was gaining a pound a day. By April 3, F.O.'s steam car finally arrived by train from Boston, giving them additional independence. Daily drives about the city now became extended, often taking them in the direction of Overland Park along the Platte, the site of horse racing and, increasingly, various kinds of automobile events.

Dr. Bonney had advised F.O. that he should summer in the mountains beginning in July. But that was still several months away. Flora, who, according to Raymond Stanley, suffered headaches and nosebleeds because of the elevation, used the interval to return to Newton for a monthlong visit. She was glad to be back in Massachusetts. "The month of May was beautiful here in the East," she confided in her diary. "I spent the entire month at home and had a delightful time." Flora was in Denver again by June 2, to find Colorado enjoying high spring.

F.O. Stanley in his Model B Runabout, fall 1902 or January 1903. This is the exact model and car that Stanley drove into Estes Park on June 30, 1903. From the collection of the Stanley Museum.

One of those who long remembered that Denver spring and summer and the "stately-looking" Mr. Stanley was a boy of five named Channing Sweet. His father, William Ellery Sweet, Colorado's future governor, was then trying to establish himself in the investment securities business. The Sweets lived in a gray, three-story brick house at 1370 Gilpin Street, kitty-corner from the Stanleys. Years later, Channing Sweet recalled with obvious pleasure:

> I was full of importance when he [F.O. Stanley] allowed me to ride with him in his amazing car. My place was on a small seat just in front of the steering rod. . . . Mr. Stanley and I kept up our friendship for years. . . . Later I met his niece [Dorothy Stanley Emmons] in Boston, who allowed me to drive her Steamer. I almost wrecked it because the lever below the steering wheel worked just the opposite to that of a Ford.[12]

Much of the friendship of which the younger Sweet speaks was kept up in Estes Park, where the Sweets vacationed and where in 1912, Governor Sweet would build the summer cottage above Fish Creek Road that he named "Tyrolerne."

Mr. Stanley Comes to Estes Park

On Monday June 29, 1903, Flora Stanley and Minnie Lundburg started for Estes Park, the mountain resort community some 65 northwest of Denver, where Dr. Bonney had prescribed, and then made arrangements for, a summer of rest. Taking the 9:30 A.M. Burlington train to Lyons, the two ladies continued on by horse-drawn stage wagon, reaching Welch's North Fork Hotel a short way up the canyon in time for midday dinner. At 2:20 P.M. they were again on their way, arriving about 7:00 P.M. at their destination after a long and full, but mercifully uneventful, journey.

Flora and Minnie had come on alone, because F.O., to the surprise of everyone except his wife and himself, was determined to make the trip by steam car. If he was to come to Estes Park, he wanted to do so, quite literally, under his own power. In addition, having his automobile at hand seemed a particularly good way of getting out and about, meeting people and taking in the scenery.

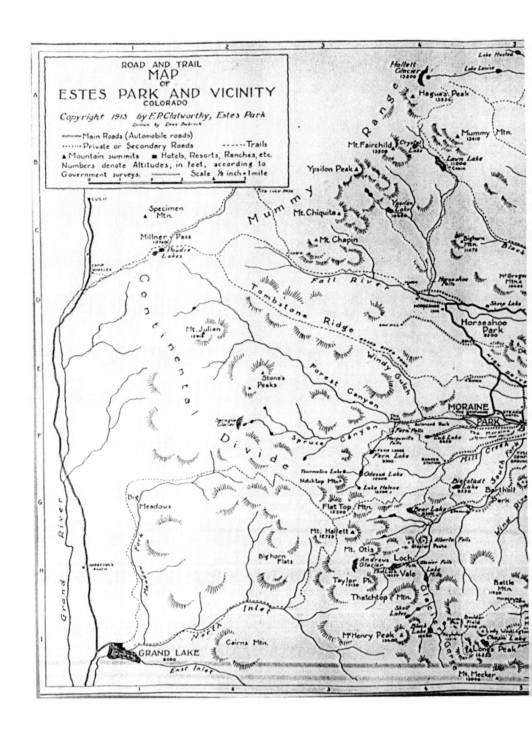

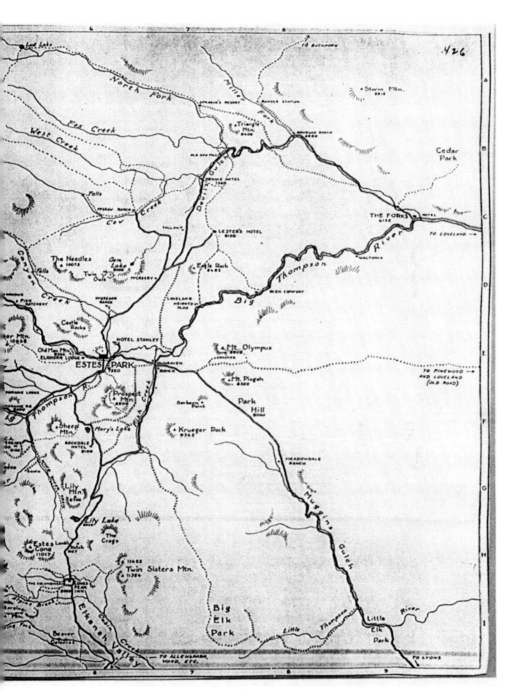

Estes Park, 1913, by Fred Payne Clatworthy. Courtesy Bill Van Horn.

Though the details of Stanley's remarkable journey have long since become clouded by legend, its outlines are clear enough. After seeing Flora and Minnie to the station, F.O. waited patiently at the Brown Palace for the arrival of a young man who had agreed to accompany him and do the heavy work of carrying water to replenish the steamer's boiler water supply. When by 3 P.M. this helper had not arrived, F.O. Stanley decided to set out on his own. Without a companion and, apparently, even a map, he missed the road to Longmont, only to find himself at sundown lost north of Boulder. Somehow—by asking directions, luck, or both—Stanley managed to make Welch's by nightfall.

William "Billy" Welch (1853–1938) was one of those original, interesting men who turn their back on the expected, embrace the independence of mountain life, and become known as "colorful characters." Born and raised in affluence in Philadelphia, he was the son of Aristides Welch, the owner of the famous Iroquois said to be the only American horse ever to win an English derby at Ascot. After receiving a first-rate eastern education, the younger Welch studied law at Oxford, was admitted to the Pennsylvania bar, but then declined to enter practice. Instead, in the early 1880s he came west to Colorado with his wife, Sarah, a Bostonian. By 1893 they had begun to develop their soon-to-be-popular resort on North St. Vrain Creek (located on the site now occupied by Shelly's Cottages), later adding considerable land to their holdings farther up in Big Elk Park where they ran cattle. Welch, who was well-read and had a considerable library, would later astound fellow resort owners by allowing "pulmonary invalids [to] use the grounds during the summer months so that they might have a new chance at life."[13]

Welch's, "four miles above Lyons on the North Fork," enthused a writer for the *Longmont Call* in July 1903, is

the prettiest place one can imagine. This is indeed a grand place to spend a few days or a month. One may have a cottage for himself with all the conveniences of a home at the hotel. Lights, water, and everything else enjoyed in the city. Welch's and the North Fork go well together, and neither would be at all satisfactory without the other.[14]

The worldly Welch was not greatly impressed by Stanley and his machine. When asked the next day to supply a companion for the 16-

mile ride to Estes Park, Welch reportedly replied that he declined to "sacrifice" a man to such a trip. (Adding to the rebuff, it was later said, no doubt apocryphally, were the derisive comments of four local farmers who then offered to pull Stanley's automobile.[15])

Welch had every right to be skeptical. Only a month before, on May 7, 1903, he had witnessed a similar attempt by a huge touring car, determined "to ascertain if it was possible and practicable to establish an automobile route to carry passengers between this place and Estes Park." Unlike Stanley's small two-seater, this earlier "machine was a monster. It was capable of carrying with comfort twelve people" and weighed, without passengers and baggage, a full two tons. The driver, T. A. Brady of the Chicago Motor Vehicle Company, was accompanied by R. W. Boone of Denver's Colorado Automobile Company, William F. Cantwell, a local stage owner, and H. C. Knight, editor of the *Lyons Recorder*. Brady and party found the going difficult and slow, for their car kept "going into mud up to the axle in numerous places."

Though they safely reached their destination, Elkhorn Lodge, future prospects did not seem particularly promising. The trip took a full four hours—"more time," the *Recorder* acknowledged, "than the present four-horse stage makes it in."[16]

Probably unaware of his predecessor, and certainly undeterred by Welch, F.O. Stanley drove on to Estes Park. He clearly had faith in his small machine, which was high-slung enough to ride above the deeply rutted, boulder-strewn road, and powerful enough to climb the steepest grade with comparative ease. Though details of what was nonetheless a remarkable journey are missing, we know from Flora's diary that he arrived in record time, phoning back the news from Sam Service's store to an astounded Billy Welch below. Welch asked to speak to Service, a former mayor of Lyons and an old acquaintance, who verified Stanley's report.[17] Though F.O. Stanley's automobile was not the first in Estes Park, as has sometimes been suggested, his entrance was by far the most dramatic and longest remembered.[18]

Estes Park, the "Gem of the Rockies"

F.O. Stanley apparently never described in writing his first glimpse of Estes Park as he came up the long treeless valley of Muggins Gulch to the top of Park Hill. But Flora Stanley did, in the article she wrote for publication during the summer of 1903 titled "A Tenderfoot's First Summer in the Rockies." To pause on the brow of the hill, she told her readers, is to be

> spellbound by the beauty of the scene. The mighty range, "Rockribbed and ancient as the sun" towers in a semicircle against the "turquoise sky of Colorado." Next are grouped the foothills, gray with granite, or dark with evergreens, and at their feet, like gay rugs, are spread the glades of the Park, bright with myriads of summer flowers, while through the midst of this coloring a mountain stream is woven like a silver thread, the shrubbery along its sides forming narrow lines of green.[19]

Though Flora then had little knowledge of the park's history, her initial response echoed those who had come before. "No words can describe our surprise, wonder and joy at beholding such an unexpected sight," Milton Estes had written about his own experience of mid-October 1859, when together with his father, Joel Estes, he first looked down upon the mountain valley (or "park") that would soon bear their name. That day they had forged their way back into the mountains on a hunting and exploring expedition. "We stood on the mountain looking down . . . where the Park spread out before us," the younger Estes continued.

> It looked like a low valley with a silver streak or thread winding its way through the tall grass, down through the valley and disappearing around a hill among the pine trees. This silver thread was Big Thompson Creek. It was a grand sight and a great surprise.
> We did not know what we had found. . . . We were monarchs of all we surveyed, mountains, valleys and streams. There was absolutely nothing to dispute our sway.[20]

Though others, including native Americans, had been there before, that moment on the crest of Park Hill marked the beginning of the recorded history of Estes Park.

Moving down into the valley, the Esteses erected several crude log buildings not far from the meandering Big Thompson, brought in cattle, and for seven years attempted to make a living ranching, while taking in occasional hunters, tourists, and other visitors. One of those who took advantage of their hospitality was William Byers, founding editor of the *Rocky Mountain News*, who arrived with three others during the summer of 1864 to make an attempt to climb Longs Peak. Byers failed (convinced, he told his readers, that "not a living creature, unless it had wings to fly, was ever upon its summit, and we believe we run no risk in predicting that no man will ever be"). In the process he gave Estes Park its name.[21]

The Esteses did not stay. Harsh winters and the desire to expand their cattle operation led to their departure on April 15, 1866. Joel Estes held nothing more than squatter's rights to his land and buildings, for the park was unsurveyed and legal entry was therefore impossible. He sold out for what he could get (according to Enos Mills, "Fifty dollars, a yearling steer, or a yoke of oxen. It is impossible to say which"[22]), and then made his way out of the valley, leaving little more than his name to confirm that he had once lived there.

By the fall of 1867, Estes Park had its second permanent resident. This was the genial Welshman Griffith J. Evans who, together with his wife, Jane, and their children, moved up from Lyons in a big two-wheeled cart and took over the Esteses' low log cabins. Like so many of those who followed, Griff Evans soon found himself in the tourist business. As the intrepid English traveler Isabella Bird, who visited in October 1873, remarked about her welcoming host, "He had the wit and taste to find out Estes Park, where people have found him out, and have induced him to give food and lodging, and add cabin to cabin to take them in."[23]

Griff and Jane soon discovered that sheltering and feeding guests, renting out horses, giving fishing and hunting directions, and guiding an occasional party to the top of Longs Peak were close to being a full-time occupation. Their guests were, however, appreciative. "It would be difficult to find jollier parties than at Evans's," another English visitor wrote home in 1873. "All summer there are lots of saddle ponies at the door—somebody going fishing, or someone going for a mountain sheep with a fine old dog, who understands the business and 'trees' his sheep every time."[24]

The first man to leave his physical mark on Estes Park, however, was not American but Irish. In late December 1872, Windham Thomas

Wyndham-Quin, the fourth Earl of Dunraven, came up from Denver to do some hunting, became enchanted with the sequestered valley, and decided to use his considerable wealth—which came, in part, from coal mines in southwestern Wales—to make as much of it as possible his own.

In the years that followed, it would be repeated again and again that Dunraven wanted to make Estes Park into an exclusive hunting preserve for himself and his aristocratic friends. Such a motive seems very unlikely. By 1872, Estes Park and what it had to offer were well known (as far away as London), and keeping out unwanted visitors— let alone good American citizens from Colorado—would have been impossible.

It is far more likely that what motivated the Earl of Dunraven is what motivated so many wealthy foreigners in the New World: the desire to make money. In Dunraven's case, he needed to secure an estate for his three daughters, for given the absence of a male heir, his property in England and Ireland would at his death under the laws of entailment and primogeniture pass out of his immediate family altogether. Estes Park offered a chance to put investment capital to work, and the Earl moved quickly to take advantage of the opportunity.[25]

Dunraven was able to arrange for the park to be surveyed in early 1874 so that it could be opened for legal entry. But prohibited as he was by American law from directly purchasing public land, subterfuge became necessary. Acting through his agent, a young Irish-Canadian mining engineer named Theodore Whyte, the Earl obtained the services of some 21 individuals, each of whom proceeded to file claim on 160 acres under the terms of the Homestead Act of 1862.

Once secured, these claims were turned over to Whyte for cash, for amounts that ranged from $700 to $2,000, or about $4.50 to $12.50 an acre. Two years later, in 1876, Whyte completed the transaction by transferring these deeds and others to the Estes Park Company Limited, an English holding company controlled by the Earl of Dunraven. Though challenged in court, these titles were never overturned, and for more than 30 years the Earl of Dunraven retained ownership of something more than 5,000 acres, for which he paid $38,100.

Whyte and Dunraven knew precisely what they were doing. In the West, controlling land meant controlling water: rivers, streams, and springs. By the summer of 1874, the Earl of Dunraven effectively controlled close to 10,000 of the best acres in Estes Park. In checkerboard fashion the Earl's claims ran for two miles on both sides of Fish Creek south of the Griff Evans ranch, in a strip as much as a mile wide along five miles of the Big Thompson, and for something less than a mile up Fall River from where the two joined. He also owned a mile-long strip up the Black Canyon, and four miles of spring-fed grazing land in the north end of the Park. In short he had all the land he needed, not for a private game preserve, but for a substantial cattle and tourist operation.

There was, as it turned out, plenty of land left over for others, and those others came. By the end of 1875 the Fergusons, Hupps, Spragues, Jameses, MacGregors, and Lambs had each taken up claims of their own. After a brief period of friction with Theodore Whyte and his cowboys, who tried to get them to leave through various forms of intimidation, these pioneers were living relatively peacefully alongside the Dunraven interests.

These new arrivals came to ranch and farm. But they soon discovered, in some cases somewhat reluctantly, that making a living in Estes Park meant finding ways to take advantage of the increasing influx of summer visitors, most of them from the valley towns along the Front Range, who came to relax or recreate amidst the breathtaking scenery. "The hotel business was forced on us," pioneer Abner Sprague would later write. "We came here for small ranch operations, but guests and visitors became so numerous, at first wanting eggs, milk, and other provisions, then wanting lodging, and finally demanding accommodations, that we had to go into the hotel business or go bankrupt from free company!"[26] Sprague's was a story often repeated.

In retrospect the coming of the Earl of Dunraven and his land acquisitions proved fortuitous. They both retarded and directed growth, and to that extent served Estes Park well. As Abner Sprague succinctly put it,

> We all began to see that the holding of so much of the Park by one company, even if it had been secured unlawfully, was the best thing for the place, particularly after it was proven that the place was only valuable on account of its location and its attraction for lovers of the out-of-doors.[27]

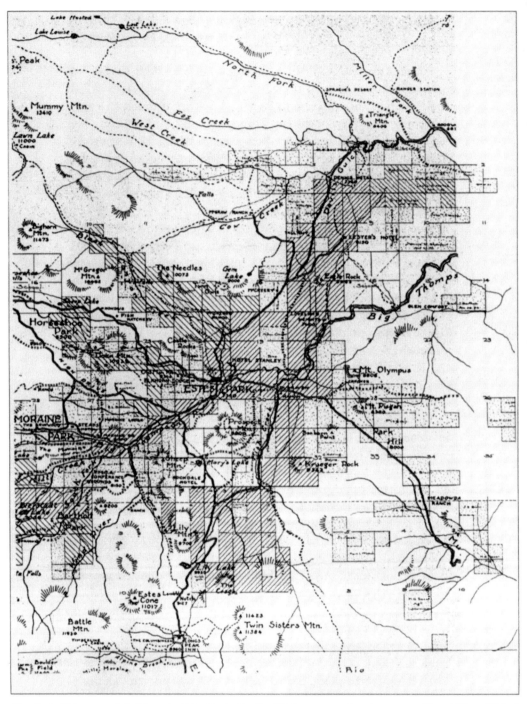

The Earl of Dunraven's holdings in Estes Park. On the 1913 map reproduced on pages 56 and 57, published and sold by local photographer Fred Clatworthy, has been superimposed an earlier map, presumably one drawn for Guy LaCoste and his partners in 1903, at the time they determined to acquire the whole of the Estes valley. It shows / / / / the lands then held by Dunraven's Estes Park Company and those that LaCoste and his associates also hoped to acquire \ \ \ \ . In addition it identifies, in the lightly shaded areas, the lands occupied by "various small ranches." Courtesy Frank Hix, Bill Van Horn, and Ricki Ingersoll.

About Dunraven's contributions Sprague might have added one thing more. When the Earl opened up his 40 x 100–foot three-story Estes Park (or "English") Hotel on July 9, 1877, on a site selected by German landscape painter Albert Bierstadt, he validated what Sprague and his neighbors had already discovered: running cattle in Estes Park was well and good as long as you were also prepared to take care of the needs of tourists.

The Stanleys' First Summer, 1903

Estes, Evans and Dunraven were pioneers all. Though the Stanleys could not possibly have known it at the time, they too would soon help shape the history of Estes Park. During that summer of 1903, like most first-time visitors, Flora and F.O. simply got to know the place. On the day of their arrival, Flora and Minnie's horse-drawn stage descended Park Hill to the old Dunraven ranch house with its log barns, pole corrals, and surrounding cabins. There was then no Lake Estes. Instead they followed the meandering Big Thompson River across the valley. On the left (the future site of the lake), they passed fields of ripening hay bordered by barbed-wire fences that within a decade would be known as Stanley Meadows.

Their immediate destination, however, lay farther on, across a rustic bridge spanning the Big Thompson. Here, near the upper end of what would later become Elkhorn Avenue, lay a small group of undistinguished buildings known as the "Corners," which in the summer of 1903 made up what there was of the hamlet of Estes Park. In addition to Sam Service's general merchandise store and John Cleave's frame house and 8 x 12–foot post office, these included a stage barn; a community building (the largest structure in town, which served as church, school, and meeting hall); a blacksmith shop run by Service's brother-in-law, Jim Boyd; William T. "Billy" Parke's photo shop; and the small general store operated during the summer months by two enterprising young women, Elizabeth Foot and Jenny Chapin. Nearby was a small shack that functioned as H. C. Roger's photographic studio.

"During the 'season'," Flora wrote later that summer, recording her impressions of life in the West, the "Corners" is a scene of life and gayety, when at nightfall, the stage comes in with the mail and passengers. The whole Park pours forth to meet it—ranchmen on their broncos, rigs from the scattered hotels, young men and maidens, usually on horse-back—all chattering and laughing, for in "no time" everybody knows everybody else, and the pleasant expectancy of "getting the mail" puts each one in good humor.[28]

The Corners. Courtesy Estes Park Area Historical Museum.

As Flora suggests, it was here at the Corners, the terminus of the stage lines, that arriving visitors were transferred to the smaller coaches and wagons sent to fetch them by the various hotels and guest ranches. These early resorts—offering rooms, cabins, and tents—lay "scattered" throughout the valley. The closest, just west at the foot of Oldman Mountain, was the Elkhorn Lodge, run by Ella James, a widow, and her sons, Howard and Homer. Farther away to the east-southeast, on lower Fish Creek back toward Denver, was the Earl of Dunraven's Estes Park Hotel, once the showplace of the park and still its most fashionable and expensive hostelry. But there was also Shep Husted's Rustic Hotel near the rim of Devils Gulch to the north, Horace Ferguson's Highlands to the southwest at Marys Lake above Beaver Point, Abner Sprague and James Stead's ranch resort back in Moraine Park, and Enos Mills's Longs Peak House (later renamed Longs Peak Inn) up in the Tahosa Valley nine miles to the south.

The Stanleys had rented two log cottages above the Corners. Obtaining keys at the Elkhorn Lodge, the two women settled in for the night.[29] Their quarters were comfortable if a bit primitive. Whatever they lacked in the way of amenities, however, was more than made up for by the splendid view spread out before them of the Front Range (or Snowy Range, as it was then often called). "Some of the cottages," Flora later wrote, "are built of logs, some are 'boarded.' Ours was for summer housekeeping only, and its unplastered walls were covered with canvas or paper, paneled with strips of wood, and our heating apparatus consisted of a fireplace in the living room, and a stove in the isolated region of the kitchen."[30]

With F.O.' s arrival the next day, the Stanleys began what would become more or less their routine for the next three months—despite

Elkhorn Lodge, c. 1880. Courtesy National Park Service.

the fact that their stay began with 10 days of cold and squally weather that left F.O. feeling poorly and Flora a bit depressed. Dr. Bonney came up from Denver on Sunday afternoons to examine his patient, and between visits Flora and her husband amused themselves at home with the local ground squirrels and a family of grouse, took photographs, and worried over their water supply. Rides in F.O.'s steam car became a favorite way to spend an afternoon.

On one trip they drove out to the English Hotel along Fish Creek, where they met Henry "Lord" Cornwallis Rogers, a 38-year-old architect who had come to Estes Park from London in 1895 because of his health. Since 1900 he had made most of his living selling his own photographs to visitors from his small studio near the Corners. During their conversation, Rogers told the Stanleys that he had designed their cottage. On another occasion they attended a "Broncho-busting exhibition" near the Dunraven stables, where they met a Mr. and Mrs. Woods, up from Denver in their Winton automobile.

The Stanleys also received visitors, among them Frank Crocker and his family. Crocker, founder of the Crocker Cracker Bakery of Denver, owned a large and impressive ranch at the foot of Mount Olympus, and the two families soon became friends. His secluded ranch, originally homesteaded by hunter Israel Rowe, and later acquired by John R. Stuyvesant, a relative of the famous first governor of New Amsterdam, now New York, remains today one of the private showplaces of Estes Park. Its plainly marked entrance is on the right as one descends Park Hill on Route 36 coming into the valley of Estes Park.

Another early visitor was the family of Charles Partridge Adams, the artist whose paintings Flora had seen at Boutwell's in Denver. Adams was renting a "cozy log house" that summer near the Dunraven ranch house, in front of which he had placed a small rustic sign saying "Adams Studio." When the Stanleys returned the visit, they took with them some of F.O.'s photographs of squirrels. Oddly enough, though Adams would leave a sprightly memoir covering his Estes Park years, in which he included a list of the "prominent people" who came as callers, he did not mention F.O. and Flora Stanley. Perhaps this was because, unlike "Mr. & Mrs. Wm. H. B., millionaires from Chicago" who "stayed an hour and carried away several of my pictures in exchange for $150.00," the Stanleys made no purchases.[31]

Dunraven's Estes Park (English) Hotel. Courtesy National Park Service.

Their favorite drive that summer—one they repeated at least once a week—took them out through Dry Gulch to the north end of the park toward the ranch hotel built and operated by Shep Husted and his wife, Clara. Husted would later become famous as the "prince of mountain guides," a man whom novelist Edna Ferber pronounced "too perfect" to be worked into one of her novels because "he left the imagination nothing to work on."[32]

The scene of the Front Range from the front porch of the Rustic was "magnificent," so much so that Stanley would later declare it his favorite in all the Park.[33] At the Rustic, F.O. also could visit with his new friend, Henry Rogers. Rogers had boarded with the Husteds upon his first arrival in the park, and had later agreed to draw up the plans for their new hotel provided he was allowed to build a cottage of his own nearby. Flora pronounced Rogers's cottage "a very pretty one."

Life was mostly uneventful. F.O.'s small steamer was obviously a novelty that attracted attention, for the most part without incident. The one apparent exception occurred on July 31. The day was "pleasant" and the Stanleys used the morning hours to call on "the artist Adams" and his family. They stayed long enough to allow a shower to pass,

F.O. Stanley and his Steam Car, summer 1903. Returning from Shep Husted's Rustic Hotel. From the collection of the Stanley Museum.

and then started for the Corners and home. The excitement of what happened next, and what might well have happened, is hardly conveyed by the three terse sentences that Flora recorded in her diary: "We started for home. Met a team—horse took fright—overturned carriage and occupants. No harm done except to wagon."[34] The Stanleys and the driver and passengers in the wagon were fortunate. In a similar episode five years later, in August 1908, a Mrs. Stover of Greeley was run over and killed near a bridge. Out driving with her husband and baby, she was thrown from her two-seat buggy when an auto came up from behind and frightened the horse.[35]

The Stanleys fell in love with Estes Park, even though summer and early fall were punctuated by poor weather, including an early, all-day snowstorm that arrived on September 15. They also endured a sudden earthquake, a most unusual occurrence in Estes Park, that in the early hours of September 6 rattled windows, shook houses, drained Marys Lake, and generally excited the entire community.

Weather notwithstanding, the only thing that seems to have bothered the socially active Flora was the solitude of the place. In her essay of that summer, Flora remarked on the apparent influence of the "solemn brooding of the mountains" on "the character of those who have lived continuously amid these impressive surroundings." She seemed particularly bothered by the children—"serious and thoughtful beyond their years"—whose "communications were of scriptural brevity."[36] For much the same reason, she further observed, "Estes Park is a bachelor's paradise. The isolation, and the dreariness of the cold season render it undesirable for women the year round, and their number is less than the male population."[37]

Flora was fully conscious of the positive impact of that mountain climate upon health seekers like her husband. F.O. improved dramatically, and in less than three months his weight had increased from 118 to 147 pounds. Following Henry Rogers's example, by mid-August they were looking at property with an eye to building a summer home of their own. Though Donald MacGregor showed them land, presumably in the vicinity of his ranch in the Black Canyon, the Stanleys ultimately chose 8.4 acres immediately adjacent to their rental cottages, which they purchased for $550.

Model CX Stanley Steamer, c. 1903–1905, in front of the Chapman house in Moraine Park. James H. Pickering collection.

The seller was Frank Gove, a prominent attorney who made his living in Denver and who owned considerable property just east of the Jameses on both sides of Fall River. This was on September 23.[38] The very next day, Gove and one of the James brothers from the Elkhorn Lodge called "to say the water supply for the new house would be all right."[39]

The Stanleys delayed their returned to Denver until October 2 in order to take advantage of the splendid weather ("days full of autumnal splendor, and of nights [when] the harvest moon lay ripening in the September skies"[40]). Back in the city, they rented a house at 2609 East 14th Avenue for $90 a month and prepared for their first full Colorado winter. By the end of that month F.O. had also established a business, the Automobile and Repair Company, at 1640 Broadway.[41] By 1910 this would become the Denver office of the Stanley Motor Carriage Company, and be relocated to 1523–1525 Cheyenne Place.

On October 13, 1903, F.O. and Flora Stanley made a surprise return to Newton. The occasion was the marriage of their oldest niece, Blanche Stanley, to Edward Merrihew Hallett. "Much to our amazement," Blanche later wrote in her memoirs, "Uncle Freel and Aunt Flora arrived the day before the wedding. Coming from Denver at that time of year, Uncle Freel was really taking his life in his hands."[42] In addition to a check for $1,350 for a new grand piano, Flora gave the bride a rare ruby-and-pearl East Indian mascot in the form of a spider to bring her luck. Wear it "invisibly if you wish," Flora told her. "It is my handful of rice."[43] Wedding and reception over, the F.O. Stanleys headed back immediately to their new home in the West.

The only other item of note concerning the Stanleys that year—a most dramatic one—was reported in the pages of the *Denver Post* on November 17. F.O. had been out and about as usual, that morning driving Sherman Bonney's Stanley steam car, which he was returning to the "barn" after leaving Dr. Bonney at his office at 17th and Broadway. He was proceeding at a leisurely pace, for the posted speed limit in downtown Denver was then eight miles an hour. On a nearly deserted 14th Street near Cleveland Place, Stanley was suddenly overtaken by a "maddened horse, wild-eyed, and with flaming nostrils . . . tearing to the northward at breakneck speed." Clutching the driver's seat of the attached open freight wagon was a badly frightened boy of 10, the son of the horse's owner. "The reins had fallen from his hands and nothing less than certain death seemed ahead of him."

Stanley responded at once. He turned his car around, hailed a passer-by, and with the words "Jump in here quickly and we'll save that lad," began to give chase. "You watch out that I don't kill anybody and that nobody runs into us . . . ," he told his startled passenger, "and I'll soon overtake that horse." The scene, as the *Post* reported it, was one of chaos and high drama:

> By this time the automobile had crowded the runaway horse up almost to the curbing on the right and this left the right of way clear for vehicles going in the opposite direction. Drivers ahead had also heard the clatter behind and pulling to the left they gave the racers a clear straightaway course.

At California Street an innocent pedestrian slipped and fell, only to scramble to his feet at the last moment, saving "his bones by a hair's breadth." At the corner of Stout Street a second accident was narrowly averted:

> An old woman in a phaeton, driving a shambling nag, turned the corner just ahead of the furious flyers. Apparently she heard nothing, and this time a crash seemed unavoidable.
>
> But a flying piece of paper scared the old horse and he balked. The driver plied the whip, but the horse refused to move, and the next instant the racers whizzed by.

Entering Curtis Street, both vehicles narrowly missed a trolley. Now, however, the runaway horse had begun to tire. By the time they reached Lawrence Street, the horse had settled down to an easy lope, and Stanley was able to reach out from his automobile, grab the bridle, and bring horse and wagon to a halt. "The suspense was ended; the race was won." In the aftermath the *Denver Post* reporter, largely unaware of the identity of the hero, commented that "Mr. Stanley is a veteran horseman, and he says he built the first automobile used in America."[44]

Even allowing for a good measure of sensationalism in the *Post*'s reporting, F.O. Stanley's driving prowess had saved the day. He was not nearly so fortunate eight years later, in February 1911, when he hit and killed a seven-year-old girl while driving through Malden on his way to Boston. Charged with manslaughter and forced to post a $1,000 bond, Stanley pleaded not guilty and was ultimately acquitted when it was proven that the girl ran directly in front of his car after he had stopped for her and that he was not going more than 10 miles per hour.[45]

By the time this story reached Denver, the *Post* had a far better sense of just who F.O. Stanley was. He was now identified as "the Denver millionaire and president of the Stanley Motor Carriage company of that city." The *Post* seemed, in fact, more interested in reporting his ownership of "the Hotel Stanley, a magnificent summer resort, and Stanley Manor, winter hotel," than detailing the events of the tragedy.[46]

The Stanleys' "Summer Cottage"

Much of the fall and winter of 1903–1904 were given over to planning and constructing the Stanleys' new summer home. "F.O. Stanley, a wealthy automobile manufacturer of Boston, Mass., has purchased land here," the Estes Park correspondent of the Fort Collins *Weekly Courier* reported on January 13, 1904, "and has carpenters at work building a fine residence for his use during the summer months. It will cost about $7,000."[47] Located immediately to the north and west of what would soon become the center of the village of Estes Park and nestled against the lichen-covered rocks of a sloping hillside above a beautiful meadow, the new house commanded the same fine panoramic view of Longs Peak and the snowcapped Front Range that the Stanleys had enjoyed the previous summer.

Making future prospects that much better was the letter Sherman Bonney sent back to Augusta Stanley in Newton on January 30, 1904. "I am very glad to state," Bonney wrote,

that Mr. F.O. Stanley is now doing exceedingly well. . . . He is not coughing or expectorating and says he feels as well as he ever did in his life. I am pleased to be able to report that the examination of the chest shows a continued diminution in the activity of the tubercular process. . . . I very much hope that you and Mr. Stanley will enjoy the best of health. I cannot tell you what a great blessing the automobile is and how we appreciate it.[48]

The house the Stanleys settled upon was clearly designed by F.O. himself. Its high foundation, imposing front entrance, Greek Doric columns, and classic ornamentation are an unmistakable part of the Georgian Colonial Revival style that graced almost every structure that F.O. Stanley and his twin brother ever built.

Although, as in the case of the Stanley Hotel, the original architectural and construction drawings have disappeared, the quality of work and design gives evidence of professional attention. The 14-inch beams, used throughout, and the unsupported archway in the divided staircase above the front entry hall—unusual in 1904—openly hint at the help of others. It is possible that F.O.'s friend of the preceding summer, Henry Rogers, played a role. At the very least the Englishman kept the Stanleys, wintering down in Denver, apprised of progress on their new home.

The Stanleys' roomy "cottage," with its 5,240 square feet on three levels, was at once elegant but simple. The second, or main, floor was the largest of the three. It opened off a long, 40-foot front veranda and into a large, illuminated front hall. Facing the front door was an impressive and airy central staircase leading to a landing and then continuing up on each side of the rotunda to the third floor above. This arrangement was typical of houses built by both Stanley brothers.

To the left of this entrance hall was the 15 x 28–foot drawing room, with bay window and built-in bench seat, to the right the 15 x 19–foot dining room (built to hold a Chippendale table capable of seating 22 to 24 people). Behind all three, across the rear of the house, were the functional areas: the butler's pantry, the guest bathroom and the kitchen with a great wood-burning stove. There was also an open porch on the back. The third floor, though a bit smaller than the second, was spacious enough to contain four bedrooms, each of identical size, as well as a library opening onto a deck over the front porch. The raised ground floor (or basement level) consisted of a single undivided room.

F.O. had his private space as well. To the left and slightly below the house, Stanley built a two-story carriage house and workshop. The

The Cottage at "Rockside." From the collection of the Stanley Museum.

lower level contained his billiard table, the upper the garage and his workshop. Here in future summers he would spend time playing at his favorite game, making his famous violins and crossbows, or just plain puttering about. The magnificent view of the Front Range from the workshop window was one that impressed everyone, including his not easily impressed sister-in-law, Augusta Stanley.

To the north of the house, connected by a path from the rear porch, there would in time be a well-used picnic area, which shared much the same view as the house itself. Beyond and above this area were gigantic boulders. There Stanley built himself a wooden bench, bolted directly to the rocks, where he could sit and play his violin or quietly watch the scenery and ever-changing hues of the range spread out before him.

Attention to detail was meticulous—from the printed wallpaper in the living and dining rooms, made to give the appearance of fabric, to the built-in custom dining-room buffet with leaded glass; from the imported green tiles in the drawing-room fireplace to the wood spindles of four different designs on the banisters lining the richly carpeted stairs. Many of these internal features and amenities, particularly the use of wood and tile, were borrowed directly from the

Stanleys' house on Hunnewell Street in Newton. As with the exterior Georgian design, when the Stanleys liked something, they tended to repeat it and, whenever possible, to improve upon it as well.

As might be expected, F.O. Stanley's practical, technological bent was also in evidence. There was a set of rudimentary wooden stairs leading from the kitchen area to the maid's bedroom above; an elaborate system of bells and call buttons, some foot-activated; and in the adjacent garage one of the turntables that were to become a Stanley legend.[49] The lack of central heating was compensated for by the use of what is commonly referred to today as passive solar design. The house's long front porch captured available light from the low winter sun to provide natural heat, while at the same time reflecting the intense rays of summer.[50]

No attempt was made to fence or wall the property. What was sometimes a necessity for Americans of wealth in places like Newport or even in Manitou, Colorado's most exclusive resort and spa, was unnecessary in the open, pastoral, largely unpretentious world of Estes Park.

The house's water system reflected F.O.'s agreement of the previous summer with Frank Gove and the Jameses that he make water available to summer cottages to the west and south as well as to the Elkhorn Lodge below. To do so, Stanley laid down an inch-and-a-half-diameter iron pipe from Black Canyon Creek above the MacGregor Ranch, burying it in a shallow ditch about six inches deep. The line then ran to an elevated wooden storage tank some 19 feet high and 15 feet in diameter located 200 feet west of the house. From there the water was distributed by pipe to the neighboring buildings.[51]

Clearly the grandest house in Estes Park, the Stanleys' new home, in the area the Goves called "Rockside," was waiting for them when they returned for their second summer. That August they purchased an adjacent parcel of seven acres for $700, assuring themselves of additional privacy in what was about to become an even more popular summer resort community.[52]

Platting and Laying out the Village, 1905

The Stanleys' decision to become permanent summer residents could not have been more timely. By the time they arrived for the summer season of 1904, change was decidedly in the air. Their return from Denver coincided with the opening of the new and much anticipated road up the Big Thompson Canyon. This road provided the long-complaining residents of Loveland, Fort Collins, and Greeley to the east with a direct, serviceable, and scenic access to the park. Though it would remain a dusty, narrow, and single-tracked affair for more than a decade, the new road was an immediate success.

This was but the beginning. Within little more than a decade, three major events set the stage for the years that followed: the laying out of the village of Estes Park in the spring and summer of 1905, the final decision by the Earl of Dunraven to relinquish his Estes Park holdings in 1908, and the establishment of Rocky Mountain National Park in 1915. These events quite literally changed the face of Estes Park forever, for they determined how, where, and on just what terms future development would take place. The decade also saw the beginnings of F.O. Stanley's active engagement in the life of both town and region.

Once a permanent summer resident of Estes Park, F.O. Stanley was quickly brought face-to-face with the realities of the tourist business, as well as with those factors that inhibited its expansion and limited its success. For all his subsequent involvement, however, it is unlikely that Stanley ever developed, let alone brought with him from the East, anything resembling "a grand design" or master plan. Rather, F.O. Stanley succeeded in Colorado for much the same reasons that he and his brother had succeeded in Massachusetts: simply put, they were constitutionally incapable of resisting opportunity. Though they were, first and last, shrewd, hard-headed, pragmatic realists, the Stanleys had the foresight and courage to seize the moment. They also had money. When it came to implementing their ideas, they had little need to rely on others. Quite the opposite: others needed them.

The catalyst for F.O. Stanley's own contributions was unquestionably the creation of the village of Estes Park and the rapid expansion of the local tourist industry that immediately followed. This was the work of four longtime friends and Loveland residents, Cornelius H. Bond, Joseph R. Anderson, William L. Beckfield, and John Y. Munson, who early in 1905 came together as partners for the purpose of buying property and laying out a town.

The land they selected was the 185-acre tract embracing the "Corners" owned by postmaster John Cleave and lying at the confluence of the Big Thompson and Fall Rivers. The site was as obvious as it was ideal, for with its intersecting network of roads and streams, post office, schoolhouse, and other buildings, Cleave's property, as Flora Stanley herself had discovered, was already the established center of community life. Happily, they found John Cleave, a resident of the park for more than 30 years, and tiring of it all, willing to sell. The $8,000 offered by Bond and his associates was quickly accepted.

The partners took possession in late April 1905, and within a month had the land surveyed and platted by Abner Sprague. Well before the tourist season arrived, they were doing a brisk business selling lots along what would be known as Elkhorn Avenue. Some would-be purchasers were so afraid they would be left out that they actually camped nearby in tents while the platting was completed. That August, Bond and the others organized the Estes Park Town Company to facilitate future development. Its first major project, completed the following spring, was to lay down a 14,500-foot, two-inch water pipeline between the new town and a small dam on Black Canyon Creek. That pipeline paralleled Stanley's own.

Buildings were thrown up hastily, seemingly overnight. As is so often the case with new towns, it was accomplished with little if any attention to style or taste. Some were little more than tent platforms given sides and a roof. New businesses included a shoe repair shop, bakery, barber shop, butcher shop, and livery stable, as well as Ye Little Shop, a studio/gift store built by Fred Clatworthy, whose photographs of such exotic places as Hawaii, Tahiti, and New Zealand would later grace the pages of *National Geographic*.

A year later, in 1906, at the corner of Elkhorn Avenue and Moraine Drive, Josephine ("Josie") Hupp opened her 23-room, steam-heated Hupp Hotel, providing the village with an even greater look of permanency. Such changes were not lost on returning visitors. "There is lots of new buildings here in Estes Park since you were here," a young woman named Audra wrote her cousin in May 1907.

They have moved the Post Office back towards Cantwell's barn, and have built a big Hotel on the corner where the P.O. was. They have also built a residence, a drug store, and a barber shop between the barn and where the Post Office used to stand. There are 8 or 10 new houses going up now and one steam laundry and one Livery Barn, right here on Main St. or rather Elk Horn Ave., as the people out here call it.[53]

Though Estes Park would not become formally incorporated as a town until 1917, the beginnings and character of "the village" were now already very much in evidence. With the completion of their new summer home on Wonderview, Flora and F.O. Stanley were about ready to play a role of their own.

Estes Park, c. 1908, looking west along Elkhorn Avenue. Courtesy Estes Park Area Historical Museum.

5

Mr. Sanborn, Mr Stanley, and the Earl of Dunraven

By the turn of the century the Earl of Dunraven, an absentee land-lord for almost 20 years, had all but lost interest in his holdings in Estes Park. As extensive as those properties were, the livestock busi-ness had never been much of a success, even during the heyday of western cattle ranching in the years before 1885. The Estes Park Hotel, the centerpiece of the Earl's Estes Park estate, had its admirers and its share of returning guests. But as the lack of continuity in its management suggests, it too was at best a marginal enterprise. Like the ranching operation, the hotel yielded little if any profit, particu-larly after the able and hardworking Theodore Whyte, Dunraven's resident overseer, returned to England in about 1890.

The idea of buying Dunraven out occurred to many. The problem, it seemed, was the difficulty in getting the Earl's attention. A number of individuals tried. From the turn of the century on, hardly a year passed without one or more stories appearing in the Colorado press about impending deals involving the Earl of Dunraven and his lands in Estes Park. When yet another such story began to circulate during the sum-mer of 1903 about the sale of Estes Park, the *Loveland Reporter* deliber-ately reminded its readers that this was "the third or fourth time this year" that such "paper deals" had been floated. "The plan looks very nice to those who are interested," the paper observed, "but it is a question of moment whether or not the plans can be completed."[1]

One man did finally succeed. Before the turn of the century, a young Denver newspaperman named Guy Robert LaCoste had homesteaded land above Wind River (on the future site of the YMCA of the Rockies). Though he soon controlled almost 1,000 acres of land, LaCoste was a man with even larger goals: he dreamed of one day owning hotels and inns "and other places of public entertainment" throughout the valley, including the properties of the Earl of Dunraven.

LaCoste had partners, at least some seed capital, and, most importantly, the gumption to try. Confident and determined, LaCoste made two trips to England. In December 1904 he announced matter-of-factly to Anna Wolfrom, who was then studying at Oxford, that he had come "to buy Estes Park." What LaCoste finally brought back from England was not, however, a bill of sale, but a seven-year lease beginning January 1, 1905. More significantly, that lease contained an option to purchase the properties of the Estes Park Company for $50,000.[2]

By the spring of 1905, for all intents and purposes LaCoste had achieved his goal. He had only to exercise the option that the Earl had given him. Then something went wrong. In all probability that something had to do with the inability of LaCoste and his associates to put together the necessary financing. Whatever the reason, on October 5, 1905, Lacoste and the others signed a quitclaim relinquishing their lease.

The dissolution was well planned and carefully negotiated. On the very same day, and under substantially the same terms, Frank Prestidge, Dunraven's Denver lawyer, executed a new agreement with Miller B. Porter, one of the principals of a Denver investment company. Porter too had both plans and partners. In February 1906 they organized the Estes Park Development Company in order to pursue them.

There were no further developments with respect to the Dunraven lands, however, until January 1907. Then, without warning, it was announced by the press that Burton D. Sanborn of Greeley (1859–1914) had agreed to purchase the Dunraven holdings for a price of $80,000.[3] When that sale was finally consummated, on June 16, 1908, Burton Sanborn had taken on a partner, Freelan Oscar Stanley.[4]

Estes Park in 1905. Courtesy Estes Park Area Historical Museum.

Prior to 1907, Sanborn was chiefly known in northern Colorado for his work as an irrigationist. A native of Vermont, he had come to Colorado from Ohio in May 1870 as one of the original members of the Union Colony, Horace Greeley's celebrated new agricultural cooperative. Sanborn remained in Greeley to become senior partner in a real estate, loan, and investment firm that had a stake in water projects. As president of the North Poudre Irrigation Company, Sanborn constructed the system of reservoirs known as the North Fork Ditch. Later he organized the Seven Lakes Reservoir Company to finance and build Boyd Lake Reservoir, the largest in Larimer County.

Burton Sanborn also had a long-standing interest in Estes Park. As early as August 1879, he had climbed Longs Peak with old-time guide Carlyle Lamb. Soon afterwards, summer visits to Estes Park became an annual ritual. On subsequent trips he not only met his future wife, but also experienced what he later described as "mental glimpses of the future." What those glimpses told him, the *Greeley Tribune* reported, was "that he would some day have to own all this, though how and why he had not the slightest idea."[5]

Burton D. Sanborn. Courtesy City of Greeley Museums, Permanent Collection.

Sanborn soon began to invest in the area. By the time he turned his attention to the possibility of acquiring the Dunraven property, he already owned Bear and Bierstadt Lakes, had helped to build the Eureka Ditch diverting water from the western drainage of Flattop Mountain into the Big Thompson,[6] and was in possession of the water rights on Fall River, which, it was said, he planned to use to generate hydroelectric power.

Much about the relationship between Burton Davis Sanborn and F.O. Stanley and the partnership they formed remains unclear. Part of the reason was that their partnership was dissolved in 1917. Until that date Stanley and Sanborn operated through the closely controlled Estes Park Development Company, which Miller Porter and his two partners had organized in 1906 at the time they assumed the lease-purchase agreement that Guy LaCoste had negotiated with the Earl of Dunraven. While it is likely that Stanley financed most of the original transaction with Porter and the others, with cash, and that some sort of agreement of understanding was signed between them, that document with its terms and conditions is now apparently lost. The Estes Park Development Company remained a distinctly private entity and as such, little or no public disclosure was ever required. Such an arrangement perfectly suited Stanley, who seldom talked to anyone about the details of his financial life.[7]

What is clear, however, is that by the late fall or early winter of 1906–1907, F.O. Stanley had developed plans to construct a major resort hotel in Estes Park and that those plans required property that belonged to the Earl of Dunraven. Those plans were far enough advanced to be made public at the time that Sanborn's purchase of the Dunraven lands was first publicly announced in late January 1907. More significantly in terms of the future, the two men were talking, even then, about some sort of future collaboration. As the *Longmont Ledger* reported on January 25.

> Mr. Sanborn is undecided as to what he will do with the property, but that it will be continued as a summer resort is a settled fact. He is at present negotiating with Stanley, of Denver, manufacturer of the Stanley steam automobile, the greatest hill-climber of the world. Mr. Stanley owns a cottage in the park and puts in all his spare time there, whenever the weather permits. He wants to erect an up-to-date hotel and put on a line of thirty steam autos to connect it with the outer world. If this be done, it will place the park to the fore as a summer resort and make it one of the best paying properties in the state, not excepting Manitou.[8]

These discussions went forward, and progress was made. Several weeks later, in a letter to the *Loveland Reporter* dated February 6, 1907, Sanborn himself reported, "I had the pleasure of an interview with Mr. Stanley yesterday and have hopes of cooperating with him in such a way that the best results can be reached."[9] Whatever the terms of their ultimate arrangement, when the final agreement with the Earl of Dunraven was announced in June 1908, Sanborn and Stanley were the joint recipients.

As with most such partnerships, theirs undoubtedly had to do with money. Part of Sanborn's initial payment to Dunraven had taken the form of a section of land near Fort Collins and stock in the North Poudre Irrigation Company. Stanley, on the other hand, brought to the table a ready supply of cash.

Burton Sanborn's Reservoir

The initial reaction of Estes Park residents to the news of Sanborn's purchase was one of apprehension, for it was accompanied by talk that the new owner intended to build "a large storage reservoir in the park and destroy it as a resort."[10] So pervasive was the rumor that Sanborn sent a lengthy letter of disavowal to the Loveland Chamber of Commerce, which saw to its publication in the *Loveland Reporter*. "I must say," Sanborn wrote, allowing irony to convey a clear sense of annoyance,

> that I am complimented by the confidence that the Estes Park people have in my ability to carry out such a stupendous project. They must think I have "money to burn," as it is a certainty that an irrigation reservoir of this character would cost enormously and there is no unappropriated water to fill it. . . . The matter is an absolute impossibility unless the United States government or someone should spend millions of dollars in tunneling the range and bringing in additional supplies of water. I wish the Estes park people to give me credit for having common sense and I wish to advise them that I know of no one, unless it is Mr. Stanley, who is more interested in developing the Park and making possible the glorious future of this vicinity, than myself.[11]

Sanborn did allow that "a large lake on which launches and rowboats might be placed would prove a valuable feature for the park."[12] His letter to the *Reporter* is interesting, however, for another reason as well: it demonstrated that Burton Sanborn, like his future partner, F.O. Stanley, was something of a visionary. Sanborn's suggestions about "tunneling the range" with federal dollars and building "a large lake" for recreation purposes anticipate with amazing accuracy the construction of the Alva Adams Tunnel and the damming of the Big Thompson to create Lake Estes four decades later.

Burton Sanborn clearly found reservoir-building intriguing. Within months of having assured residents of the park that no such scheme existed, his name was once again linked to an almost identical project. According to the September 19, 1907, edition of the *Loveland Reporter*, "B. D. Sanborn and other capitalists" proposed to build a three-mile-long, 125-foot-high dam for the generation of electricity, extending from the Dunraven ranch down into the Big Thompson Canyon to within about a mile of the summer enclave now known as Loveland Heights.[13]

Though there was no apparent public outcry, this time the rumor had substance. Surviving correspondence between Sanborn and one of his "capitalists," a 40-year-old lawyer from Colorado Springs named Orlando B. Willcox, indicates that Sanborn had taken the project directly to F.O. Stanley and asked for his help in dealing with Frank Crocker, "who owns perhaps 150 acres of the proposed project." Unfortunately, Crocker was in the East and unavailable. "I regret very much the delay," Sanborn wrote Willcox from Greeley on September 30.

> Mr. Stanley and Mr. Crocker are both jealous of the beauties of the Park, and as near as I could learn think that Mr. Stanley had promised Mr. Crocker that he would consult with him about any proposed reservoir site. If a division of the land could be made in such a way as to insure owners that the reservoir was only to be drawn off for power purposes and not during the summer months or tourist season to any extent and proper protection be given to the trout which would enter the lake in large quantities, he would favor a sale. . . .
>
> In a general way it looks probable that this site can be purchased and improvements settled for, not to exceed $90,000, but in settling with the County of Larimer, it would certainly be necessary to do some road work in the Canyon and building roads around the reservoir, involving in some places difficult and expensive work. It seems that the reservoir expenses outside of the dam will probably exceed slightly $100,000.

Mr. Stanley is not willing to have the reservoir built quite as high as we have planned. A reduction of two or three feet will suit him. His objection is that in building the $100,000 hotel he must have a garage and livery stable just below the town and the survey that was made is slightly too high for this site. In any event I do not think there will be any reduction in the size of the reservoir which will make the capacity less than 1,000,000,000 cubic feet.

I will write you just as soon as I hear from Mr. Stanley and have asked him if I should meet him in Estes Park or Denver for further negotiations after he hears from Mr. Crocker.[14]

Willcox responded two days later, on the 30th, with an eye to pushing the scheme forward just as rapidly as possible:

I hope you will be able to follow the matter up with Mr. Stanley and advise us soon as to his views.

I trust that you will be able to secure a satisfactory option from him so that we can determine the cost of the Reservoir by connection with the cost of the other projects on the Big Thompson.

Of course Mr. Stanley will realize that if his conditions or price are arbitrary the Company can condemn such land as it may require for the Reservoir site.[15]

We can only guess what F.O. Stanley thought of Mr. Willcox's veiled threats, had Sanborn even been willing to pass them along. Whatever the response, if there was one, nothing more is heard about the proposed reservoir and power plant until March 1908, when Sanborn quietly announced that it had been put off "on account of the recent money stringency."[16] There would be a hydroelectric plant in Estes Park. But it would be built up Fall River and with F.O. Stanley's money.

6

Racing Cars and Mountain Roads

The Stanley Racers

The spectators joined in three cheers and a chorus of "S-t-a-n-l-e-y! S-t-a-n-l-e-y!" as the flying car crossed the line . . . establishing a new record. . . . And the cry is, still, "On. Stanley, On!"[1]

The years from 1903 to 1910 were busy ones for the Stanley Motor Carriage Company of Newton, Massachusetts. Aided by the expansion of its factory and office facilities along the banks of the Charles River, output and sales climbed steadily. Production exceeded 500 units in 1904, 600 in 1905, and 700 in 1907. This growth was attributable to constantly improving product and performance and the resulting good publicity, for all of which F.E. Stanley was alone responsible.

Left in charge of the Watertown factory while F.O. was convalescing in Colorado, F.E. not only designed and built cars but raced them as well.[2] Though such activities may seem frivolous, racing then, as now, was the testing ground for much new and developing automo-

Francis Edgar Stanley with his driver, Fred Marriott, at Ormond Beach, Florida, January 1906. From the collection of the Stanley Museum.

bile technology. This was particularly true of the early days of automobiling. As Stanley driver, collector, and historian Brent Campbell puts it, during that era, "road races, hill climbs, endurance contests and speed records were the arenas in which manufacturers tested their ideas, refined their products, and relied on winning to bring both prestige and sales."[3] They were also fun. And for a time the Stanley Motor Carriage Company and its owners were willing and highly competitive participants.

Many of these events initially took place close to home. In April 1903, F.E. Stanley duplicated his earlier success at Charles River Park by winning a climbing test on a hill on the north end of Commonwealth Avenue, Boston's main thoroughfare. Driven by Frank Durbin, Stanley's two-seater runabout, with its 5½-h.p. engine, won the "Steam Vehicle" competition; then Durbin beat bigger, gas-driven competitors by a full 10 seconds going up the 15 percent grade in the "Grand Final." "The meteoric ascent of that remarkable steam carriage," one contemporary paper reported, "was the star performance of the afternoon. Up around the top a big crowd had gathered and as there was but one lonely policeman in sight they filled the road to their heart's content."[4]

The next month, the first aerodynamic and streamlined Stanley Steamer made its debut at the Readville Race Track near Boston, an event witnessed by Flora Stanley during her monthlong visit from Denver. With F.E. driving, the red, stunted, cigar-shaped vehicle set a new American record by finishing the mile in one minute, 2.8 seconds. "I predict that track racing is destined to be a great sport in this country in the future," he wrote in the aftermath, "as it combines the three essential elements which must underly [sic] any sport to make it interesting, viz., science, skill, and chance."[5]

In 1904 and 1905, F.E. entered cars in the eight-mile, 4,600-foot, vertical "Climb to the Clouds" up New Hampshire's Mt. Washington, by then a sanctioned racing event, repeating F.O.'s historic climb of 1899. "Steam upheld its reputation for mastering grades," *Automobile Weekly* reported in its July 1904 issue,

> when on the second day F.E. Stanley dashed up to the line in 28: 19 2/5, showing what seven [sic] horsepower can accomplish when it is put where it will do the most good. . . . Mr. Stanley got a splendid welcome and was induced to run his car up the skids to the platform of the Summit Hotel where it was photographed repeatedly with one of the railroad locomotives as a background.[6]

A red 1903 Stanley (which actually had a six-h.p. engine) was the racing car used that day in the first-ever 1904 "Climb to the Clouds" race. That event was staged to draw attention to a tour through the White Mountains, organized with the help of participating car manufacturers and well-known automobile personalities of the day to bring to public attention the poor condition of America's roads and to demonstrate that the automobile was a viable, multidimensional vehicle.

F.E. and Augusta Stanley drove a black steam car during the 1904 White Mountain tour itself. It was nicknamed "King of the Road" by wealthy New England industrialist and automobile enthusiast Charles Glidden. Stanley's car had deigned to pass all the other cars, including Glidden's, on the tour's first day. In exchange for the title, Glidden arranged for Stanley's car to remain behind his own for the rest of the tour. (In subsequent years, thanks to a trophy provided by Glidden himself, this popular event would become known as the "Glidden Tour.")

Other races and demonstration events followed, including the Giant's Despair Hill Climb at Wilkes Barre, Pennsylvania, and an equally famous hill climb outside Dublin, Ireland—all of them calling attention to the versatility, speed, and climbing ability of Stanley automobiles.

The Stanley Racers in Florida: 1906–1907

The Stanleys' greatest racing successes during these years—as well as their single great disaster—came not, however, on the roads of their native New England. They took place far to the south, on the smooth white sands of Florida's Ormond-Daytona Beach, where from 1903 to 1910 a series of automobile racing tournaments brought Florida and the automobile to the attention of the nation and the world.[7] In 1906 and 1907 they brought the Stanleys attention as well.

Stanley involvement actually began in 1905. That year Louis Ross drove an experimental tin-covered steam car powered by two separate Stanley engines over the one-mile course in the amazing time of 38 seconds. Ross's car was quickly dubbed the "Woggle Bug" because of its construction: two engines were hooked to each wheel end of the rear axle shaft, causing the car to "woggle." Though thought remarkable at the time, Ross's record lasted only a single year.

Neither of the Stanleys witnessed Louis Ross's triumph at Ormond, though F.E. reportedly helped Ross build his car—a sign that such racing had already captured his attention. Ross's success proved contagious. In 1906, F.E. Stanley accepted the invitation of personal friend and race promoter Charles F. Hathaway to bring a Stanley racer of his own to Florida. Hathaway, a resident of Somerville, Massachusetts, had been wintering at Ormond for several years, and in 1902 had demonstrated the feasibility of beach racing by covering a five-mile course, which he laid out himself, in a 10-h.p. stock Stanley Steamer at a rate of 43.39 mph. A year later, in February 1903, the first organized, officially timed race meet was held.

The Stanley Rocket, which F.E. shipped by train from New York City, startled the Florida racing community because of its canoelike appearance. The car's light wood body (blunted at one end, much like a canoe fitted with engines) had been manufactured to F.E. Stanley's specifications by the J. R. Robertson Canoe Factory of nearby

Auburndale, Massachusetts. According to Raymond Stanley, F.E. was so intent on creating an aerodynamic vehicle that he actually tested the wind resistance of different canoes by having them towed on a trailer attached to a spring scale through the streets of Newton. Stanley's driver, Fred Marriott, told the story a bit differently: that F.E. tested the shape of different canoes on windy days on top of the factory building in Watertown.[8]

F.E.'s Rocket Racer, with its small but powerful 30-h.p. engine mounted on the rear axle, quickly quieted the skeptics. First, the Stanley set a world's record for the five-mile event on January 24, at 107.784 mph. On January 26, 1906, Marriott broke the two-miles-in-one-minute record in the morning, and then set a land speed record for the entire event—one that held until 1910—at 127.659 mph in the afternoon. The morning race won the Stanleys the Dewar Cup.

Marriott, head of the repair department at the Stanley factory and a former bicycle racer, had joined the Stanleys in the early 1900s. Prior to 1906 his experience racing Stanleys had been confined to a race or two at the Readville track and a few hill-climbing contests.[9] Nevertheless, on the Ormond-Daytona Beach beach he soundly beat his gas-powered competitors.

"It was a great Stanley day," Augusta Stanley recorded in her diary on January 26,

> —as Fred drove the racer a kilo in 18 1/5 sec.—and a mile in the wonderful time of 28 1/5 sec—a mark no one has thought could be reached. Frank's genius has been recognized—and his judgement found to be good in letting Fred run the car.[10]

F.E. himself could scarcely contain his excitement in sending off a series of brief telegrams to his brother in Denver. F.O.'s response was short and very much to the point: "Wonderful, Wonderful, Wonderful, is All I Can Say."[11]

F.E. Stanley and Fred Marriott returned to Ormond the next year with an even more finely tuned car, determined to break their own record in the mile race. "There was never anything like it; that car was as smooth as velvet," Marriott recalled some years later. "We had made some trial runs, and we knew that we had not even scratched the surface to what she could really do!"[12]

On the morning of January 25, 1907, Marriott found the beach course rough and problematic, but he was determined to proceed. "We knew what we were doing," he continued, "—this time all they'd see would be a streak."[13] On the third trial of the day, with only his head visible in the low-slung machine, Marriott retreated several miles down the beach. Turning his red racer around, he steadily gathered speed in order to cross the starting line with a full head of steam and a wide-open throttle. Then it happened. Marriott hit a ripple, or gully, in the sand.

Eyewitness Glen Curtiss, who was standing astride his motorcycle near the starting line ready to race once Marriott's trial concluded, succinctly described what quickly became one of the most famous—and mythologized—accidents in automotive history:

> The slight depression in the course gave the car (which was provided with light springs) a toss-up. The sudden application of power assisted in raising the fore part of the car. . . . The floor then acted as an aeroplane—the car glided, with the rear wheels only on the beach. It then swerved sidewise, and when the front wheels again came in contact with the ground, it was headed toward the sea, the wheels of course went down [collapsed] and the car rolled over and over, breaking to fragments. The boiler kept on going, and rolled several hundred feet farther than the balance of the car, the escaping steam giving the appearance of a meteor rushing through the surf.[14]

The next day, the *New York Times* reported the event in the kind of dramatic terms that would characterize most future accounts, using a series of graphic similes with telling effect:

> When the car broke in two, it dropped the boiler as it did Marriott. The shell of the racer is like an inverted canoe, and as thin as bark. The shell was torn into splinters. One of the four bicycle-like wheels was partially intact but all that remained of the others were a few bits of twisted wire where spokes had been. The tubing was broken like pipestems. The debris was thrown into two piles, over which hundreds of amateur photographers hovered like seagulls and many souvenirs were carried away.[15]

That evening, Augusta's diary had a very different story to tell:

Truly this is Black Friday. I can hardly write I am in such a nervous condition and it is all so dreadful. Oh! Why did we come down to this horrible place? . . . I was in the upper piazza of the [Florida East Coast Automobile Association] club house with several other people. Soon they said, "he's coming"—and we got up to look and saw the car go into water as it looked a cloud of steam. The car was dashed to atoms—and Fred inside. Doctors went, brought him to the club house then took him to the Ormond [hospital]. They think he will live—as no bones are broken. He looked so dreadfully—pale and the bloody face—I can never forget it.[16]

The wreck of the Stanley Racer, Ormond Beach, Florida, January 25, 1907. From the collection of the Stanley Museum.

Marriott survived. But in the aftermath, Francis Edgar Stanley decided that the Stanleys would never again risk the lives of employees in such a dangerous sport. That decision has usually been attributed to the influence of Augusta, who until then had been as enthusiastic about automobile racing as her husband.[17] Her intervention came quickly. The January 31, 1907, issue of *The Automobile* quoted F.E. Stanley as stating that he had "no idea of resurrecting his famous steam sprinter . . . that the worth of a single fast mile or two has depreciated to such an extent that it is no longer worth while to build a car for this single purpose." Moreover, the story continued,

Mr. Stanley intends to return the Dewar trophy to Sir Thomas Dewar, the donor, and suggest to him the advisability of offering it in a race for a longer distance, at least ten miles, and perhaps more.[18]

The decision not to race for speed marked the end of an era. In the years that followed, Marriott's accident, and the details surrounding it, would become elevated to the realm of myth and legend, including the long-repeated story that shortly after crossing the starting line the Stanley "Freak" racer had reached the incredible speed of 197 mph.

F.E. Stanley would later estimate that Marriott's exact speed, at the time of the crash, was 150 mph, and that the car's front wheels were off the ground for only 103 feet. Under such circumstances, and with clear evidence of what might have happened to their driver, the determination of the Stanley brothers to abandon speed racing was perhaps as predictable as it was humane. From a purely technological perspective, however, it was also unfortunate. Susan Davis, author of *The Stanleys, Renaissance Yankees*, notes that their decision marked "a significant step toward the demise of the Stanley Steamer, and indeed of the steam car itself. It served to halt basic research and development in automotive steam technology."[19]

From Racing to Automobile Production

Between 1906 and 1908, F.E. Stanley and the Stanley Motor Carriage Company continued to refine their cars and introduce new models—all of them with the distinctive Stanley "coffin-nose." These included the sporty H and K models, a series of light, high-performance vehicles manufactured from 1905 to 1908, designed for those to whom speed and balance mattered.[20] Much of this nimbleness and maneuverability was gained by the simple expediency of moving the boilers forward over the front axle. The year 1905 was one of transition for the Stanley Motor Carriage Company. It saw the Stanleys manufacture the last of their horseless-carriage, tiller-steered cars and the first of their famous coffin-nosed vehicles. It also saw the first 20-h.p. engine.

One variation of the H series, the 1,600-pound Model H-5 "Gentlemen's Speedy Roadster," was clearly aimed at those who had read about the Stanleys' victories at Ormond Beach. Or, as the company's 1908 catalog explained, "for those who wish to hit a speed of 65 to 70 miles an hour on a good, safe road, without going to the expense of importing a $10,000 machine with its noisy cylinders and high expense and maintenance."[21] For the less speed-conscious, there was the Model F five-passenger touring car manufactured from 1906 to 1908, with its 100-inch wheelbase. It used a 20-h.p. engine and weighed 1,850 pounds. (The Model F was the Stanley sold in 1907 to the Osborns of Loveland for use in their new auto stage line.)

By 1908 the Stanleys were offering even more choice. In addition to the Model F, there was the Model J Limousine, a five-seater for town and suburban use, and the Model M, a large, 2,100-pound, five-passenger touring car. The Model M was the first Stanley touring model to utilize the powerful 30-h.p. engine developed for the racer. Also listed for the first time in that year's catalog was the Model K limited edition Semi Racer, which had been displayed in 1907 on the beaches of Florida. Intended for the open road, "The Model K, our semi-racing car," the catalog read,

is the fastest stock car in the world. It is intended primarily as a stock car for track and hill racing, and is geared to a very high speed. It is entirely practical for ordinary road work, except that it is unnecessarily powerful and fast for any such purpose. . . . We are planning to build only a limited number of these cars, and it is doubtful if an order placed later than February first can be filled this year.[22]

Only 25 of these cars, each costing $1,800, were ever built.

Cars—and Roads—in Colorado

While F.E. was racing in the East, creating demand for Stanley automobiles, F.O. remained in Colorado, continuing to improve his health while carefully laying the groundwork for several major new projects of his own. Though those plans clearly included a new hotel, Stanley first made his presence felt as an advocate for what he knew best: automobile transportation and the roads that made it possible.

Stanley Motor Carriage Company offices in Denver, 1910. From the collection of the Stanley Museum.

For all the enthusiasm over the new road up the Big Thompson, the roads leading to and from Estes Park left a great deal to be desired and in many cases were roads in name only, barely passable in some seasons by stage and wagon, at best a trial and tribulation for an automobile. What was true of Larimer and Boulder Counties was true generally not only of Colorado and the West but also of the nation at large. Throughout most of the nineteenth century, innovation and investment in the field of transportation had been largely restricted to railroads and to vessels plying rivers and canals, leaving America's roads outside towns and cities little better in 1900 than they had been a century before. Decent roads, as the Stanleys had long been aware, were a prerequisite for the automobile. As F.E. wrote to Augusta in France in June 1897, automobiles "will be seen . . . when the roads are fine."[23] Whether in the East or in Colorado, the nation's roads needed public champions.

By the time the Stanleys arrived in Denver in 1903, automobiles— gasoline, steam, and electric—were to be seen regularly on city streets. As early as May 1, 1900, William B. Felker, Denver's first automobile dealer, was advertising the immediate availability of a $750 Locomobile ("The Famous Steam Wagon. Cheap to buy. Cheap to run. No noise, odor, or vibration") at his Felker Cycle Company display room on 16th Street.[24] Felker, a former bicycle salesman, not only sold cars and then threw in free driving lessons, but publicized them.

In August 1901, together with C. A. Yount, Felker became the first driver to ascend Pikes Peak in an automobile. He easily surpassed the record set by the Stanleys' old friend, John Brisben Walker, who the previous September had quit at 11,000 feet only to announce that the summit could be reached and that it "would be a glorious experience."[25] Felker did not share Walker's enthusiasm. "I don't believe we could do it again," he told the *Denver Times*. "I can't tell you some of the risks we took and the dangers we constantly encountered. In the first place, the wagon road—that is the road we took—hadn't been used for two years."[26] Felker's statement was a premonition of further dangers ahead. In 1907 he was killed in a racing accident at Overland Park.

Though it required the use of dust coat and goggles, Denver's relatively flat, dry, open terrain was almost perfect for the motorist.[27] By 1902, Denverites owned some 200 automobiles. A year later, at a time when 11 automobile dealers were listed in the *City Directory*, they were being regularly exposed to races and exhibitions at Overland Park and elsewhere. Among the events most remembered was the race held in 1905 in which a Stanley driven by George Herring, who had removed the front seat and was sitting directly on the floorboard, beat a much heavier and more expensive Daimler.

But that was in Denver. Outside the city the condition of the roads, especially in the mountains, made automobiling of any kind problematic. When William Felker and four other drivers participated in the "first automobile run ever made" between Denver and Longmont in early October 1901, the Denver press pronounced the "condition of the roads . . . something awful, the machines and chaffeurs [sic]—mark the word—getting the worst shaking up of the experience." The return trip, made at night, was so harrowing that "not a chaffeur [sic] has so far opened his heart to tell of that night drive."[28]

The Good Roads Movement

Decent roads had long been a major concern for many Coloradans. The question was not whether they were needed, but who should build and pay for them. Early legislation, dating back to territorial days, supported the premise that roads were a local necessity or convenience and that the responsibility for building and maintaining them belonged to the county. For a time, Colorado's county commissioners were able to shift that burden to others by encouraging the chartering of toll roads, which allowed private individuals or companies to provide what counties were unwilling or unable to. The first real wagon road to Estes Park, in fact, had been the toll road built in 1875 by Alexander MacGregor and his Park Road Company.

Where counties did take the lead in road building and maintenance, poll taxes were levied to provide the funds. Such monies, however, were never sufficient, particularly along the Front Range where roads were typically used to get widely scattered farmers to and from town and market. In the absence of a sizable concentration of voters to lobby for them, mountain roads were often funded largely as an afterthought—much to the consternation of places like Estes Park.

All this began to change with the new century and the coming to Colorado of the "Good Road Movement," an organized effort originally inspired by the nation's bicycle enthusiasts. Its first convention was held in Denver in October 1900. Five years later, in 1905, the Colorado Good Roads Association was formed.[29] When the new organization met at the Chamber of Commerce building in Denver a year later, from December 4 to 6, 1906, its first vice president was Freelan O. Stanley.

The seriousness of the Good Roads Conference of 1906 is suggested by its roster of invited delegates. They included the governor of the state, the state engineer, a commissioner and surveyor from each county, the mayor of each city and town, and representatives from chambers of commerce and the various driving and automobile clubs. The agenda was devoted to questions of road building and how best to distribute the expense between state and local municipalities. There was also a call for formation of a state highway commission. Such an agency could be found, it was pointed out, in 28 states, but not in Colorado.[30]

Though F.O. Stanley attended the meetings, which took place a month before Fred Marriott's disaster on the beach at Ormond, there is no record in the proceedings that he took to the floor to register his views. He did not have to. Frank L. Bartlett, president of the Colorado Automobile Club and the organization's founder, left no doubt in anyone's mind where automobile enthusiasts stood—or just what they believed the future held in store. Despite the fact that in 1906 there were only 2,000 automobiles in the entire state, Bartlett was emphatic:

> The automobile is no longer a rich man's fad. . . . The automobile is to-day the greatest factor of modern times for health, education and morality; they keep our people out in the air and sunshine away from evil influences, and our young men and boys and even our girls are acquiring a rapid education in mechanics and engineering which never would be obtained by attending dances, playing cards or driving the family horse.[31]

F.O. Stanley shared Bartlett's enthusiasm over the automobile and its future. He was equally concerned about the need to focus state government on the responsibilities of road building and maintenance. Two years before, in 1904, Stanley had discovered at first hand just how difficult it could be to upgrade the mountain roads of Colorado to modern standards.

That spring, after some effort, he had managed to raise enough funds from the hotel-keepers of Estes Park, businessmen in Lyons and Denver, and officials of the Chicago, Burlington and Quincy (or Burlington Railroad) to hire a foreman and five crews to install new bridges and generally improve the old wagon road from Lyons to Estes Park with the hope that when completed, it would be taken over by Boulder County. "We don't ask them to make the road," the *Lyons Recorder* had pleaded at the time, "but to just accept it when it is finished. Mr. Commissioners, won't you PLEASE do this much for the people of Lyons?"[32]

Though the new road from Lyons to Estes Park still left much to be desired as a "drive-way" for heavy-duty autos, Stanley and the others were able to put it "in better shape than it ever has been before." Unfortunately, the expectations of F.O. Stanley and the people of

Lyons went unmet, for the commissioners of Boulder County did not come forward with the hoped-for support. It was a lesson in the realities, and politics, of road building that Stanley may well have shared with his fellow conferees in 1906.

By then, however, F.O. had new plans nearing completion. On March 7, 1907, just three months after the Good Roads Conference adjourned, Stanley, returning from a trip to Chicago, announced that he had made arrangements with the Burlington Railroad to establish an automobile line to travel over a new road from Lyons to Estes Park at a total cost of $50,000. Moreover, the *Lyons Recorder* reported, "Mr. Stanley says . . . the money is all raised for building and equipping the road."[33]

News of such a project naturally commanded attention. Lyons and Loveland had contended for years about which town was, or would be, the major "gateway" to Estes Park. The residents of Lyons, Longmont, and Boulder, the towns closest to Denver, were particularly concerned about the recently completed road up the Big Thompson (whose "perfection" had been openly praised by a delegate from Fort Collins at the December meeting). They understood that easy access to Estes Park from the new Colorado and Southern depot and commercial establishments at Loveland posed a distinct threat to their own economic interests. When Stanley came forward with his plans, he thus encountered immediate enthusiasm and support.

Reconstructing the Lyons Road

Stanley was premature with his assurances. The Burlington's involvement with projects such as this had been the subject of newspaper speculation since at least April 1903.[34] But when the *Longmont Ledger* announced further developments on March 22, 1907, it was to inform its readers that the new road would be built not by the Burlington but by a public-private partnership between the State of Colorado and F.O. Stanley of Boston and Estes Park.[35] Stanley had little difficulty securing the necessary financing, which totalled some $15,000. Pledging $5,000 of his own money, he persuaded the state to appropriate $3,250. Private subscriptions raised the rest.[36] The incentive, Stanley told his partners, was a new assurance from the Boulder

Stanley Steamers on the North St. Vrain road. Courtesy Estes Park Area Historical Museum.

commissioners that once completed, "the road will be turned over to the county which will keep it in repair and be responsible for all traffic going over it."[37]

Abner Sprague of Estes Park did the initial survey work. To supervise the actual construction, Stanley employed 60-year-old John B. Hall and his 28-year-old, son Charles Byron Hall, of Lyons. The elder Hall, a native of the Shetland Islands, was a good choice for the job. A resident of Lyons since 1882, Hall and his family lived east of Welch's where the road to Estes Park left the river to ascend Rowell Hill, and where much of the important work on the new project was to take place.

John Hall was intimately familiar with the task before him. He had been employed by F.O. Stanley two years before, in the late fall of 1904, to make a reconnaissance of the Little Thompson River between Muggins Gulch and Lyons with an eye to locating a better route for a road to Estes Park. His subsequent report suggests the difficulties faced by anyone interested in mountain road building in turn-of-the-century Colorado.

Hall and a companion spent two full days inspecting the canyon, hiring a team and wagon "to take us to the upper end of the canyon and meet us in the evening." His findings, as he had told Stanley in a letter written to Denver on January 17, 1905, had hardly been encouraging:

> Well, about The Little Thompson Road, we surveyed the canyon through and found the distance that we had to follow the bed of the Thompson, to be seven miles and a quarter; from the Thompson to the St. Vrain bridge, three miles; from the St. Vrain bridge to Lyons, three miles, making a total of thirteen and a fourth miles (13¼ mi).
>
> We found the canyon very, very rough and in most places very narrow, leaving no place for the road bed except by blasting. There are very few places where there is any soil left in the canyon. It has all been washed away and nothing left but the bare walls of the canyon; so if ever a road should be built there, the grade would have to be hauled in some places, a distance of over two miles.
>
> There are falls, in one place, forty feet high and another place where the canyon is so narrow that a man can jump across the stream, twenty feet above the water.

We made careful calculations, to see how many bridges it would take for the seven and a fourth miles and we thought it would take sixty. When I see you I can tell you more about it. You asked me to make an estimate of what I thought it would cost, but I cannot give you any figures on it, but I will say, the cost of putting a good road through would be enormous.[38]

Hall charged Stanley $16 for his services, $6 of which was for the horse, wagon, and driver. He concluded by telling Stanley to let him know what he wanted done.

F.O. Stanley was not discouraged. Locating a feasible roadbed in the mountains was simply a matter of perseverance and problem solving. His solution was to call upon the services of veteran surveyor Abner Sprague, who had found a way to put a road through the Big Thompson Canyon connecting Loveland, the next town to the north of Lyons, to Estes Park, over terrain almost as difficult as what Hall had described. Sprague, once again, found a way.

Though the Halls apparently had some initial difficulty in hiring the five crews they needed because of the strong demand for labor at the quarries in and around Lyons, work began in mid-April. Unrealistically, the Halls promised to have the job completed by June 1, in time for the beginning of the tourist season.[39]

Following Sprague's survey, the Halls built what in effect was a new road, beginning at the point where it entered the foothills above Lyons and continuing to its connection with the existing road at Little Elk Park, a quarter mile above the Meining ranch (at what is now Pinewood Springs). If the papers of the day are to be believed, the Halls did even better than asked. Though Sprague's specifications called for a road "no less than fourteen feet wide," one that would "give ample room for the machines and vehicles to pass each other,"[40] the finished road was 18 feet wide, with "plenty of room to pass anywhere."[41]

To achieve the grade and width required for "a first class automobile road," major portions of the existing road needed to be reconstructed and upgraded. Several new sections were also necessary, including one through Welch's resort. This bypass made it possible to redirect traffic along the creek and away from Rowell (or "Roll Over") Hill, whose 2,200-foot gain in a matter of little more than two miles had terrified travelers for years, producing more than its share of coach and wagon accidents. This new one-mile section was so critical to the road's success that Stanley himself personally negotiated the easement with Billy Welch, at a cost of $3,000.[42]

The other major section of new road, some two-and-a-half miles in length, lay along a mountainside strewn with rocks and boulders. This required blasting, after which "the side [was] built up with rock for a good base, then finished by hand work."[43] As the *Longmont Ledger* subsequently explained to its readers,

> Those familiar with the road which leaves Little Elk Park to join the Little Thompson will remember the deep gulch which the old road used to compel us to go down and then up. Now a fine grade nearly level leads around the side of the mountain, and the road up the Little Thompson is in pretty good shape. This gulch is called Rattlesnake gulch.[44]

The Halls were almost as good as their word. By late June the road was sufficiently complete to allow Stanley to make the drive from Lyons to Estes Park.[45] Two months later he notified the commissioners of Boulder County that the road to the north line of the county was ready for their acceptance.[46] To improve comfort and safety on the new North St. Vrain road, Stanley announced in November his intention to route a telephone line from Lyons to Estes Park that could be connected, as needed, to individual automobiles. "This feature," the *Lyons Recorder* assured its readers, "will be a very valuable arrangement in case of a breakdown of any machines on the roads, which will enable the drivers to inform headquarters of their difficulty at once."[47] (Such a "Feature," it might be noted, suggests that Stanley had in mind a concept for what we now know as highway call boxes.) At about the same time, Stanley constructed a series of concrete reservoirs along the road where steam cars could stop and take on water for their boilers.

The reconstruction of the road up the North St. Vrain canyon marked F.O. Stanley's first direct civic investment in the future of northeastern Colorado. As the *Longmont Ledger* told its readers that August, "This road was built by Mr. Stanley, who deserves a great deal more credit for the enterprise than he will get."[48] Fortunately,

STANLEY 9-PASSENGER MOUNTAIN WAGON.

These cars will be used for transportation to and from THE BELGRADE. Also other automobiles for hire.

N. F. STANLEY, MANAGER, Waterville, Maine

After June 1st, Belgrade Lakes, Maine

The Stanley Mountain Wagon. From the collection of the Stanley Museum.

getting the "credit" did not rank high on F.O. Stanley's list of priorities. Getting the job done did, however. Once the work on the North St. Vrain road had been completed, John Hall and a number of his workers moved on to Estes Park to help with the construction of F.O. Stanley's big new hotel.

Chapter 7

The Estes Park
Transportation Company

Since April 1903, fully two months before F.O. Stanley's historic trip, there had been rumors about the introduction of an auto stage line from Lyons to Estes Park.[1] Such rumors surfaced again four years later, at the time Stanley began to raise funds to reconstruct the North St. Vrain road. They were only rumors. But the news was greeted to the north in Loveland with consternation and resignation. "There is nothing for Loveland to do now," the *Loveland Reporter* advised its readers on February 28, 1907, "but continue advocating, or to go to work and build an electric line from here to the Park."[2]

Despite such pessimism, the situation soon took a dramatic turn. That summer, to the surprise of everyone, it was Loveland—not Lyons or Longmont, let alone Boulder or Denver—that first put in operation an automobile stage line to Estes Park making use of Stanley Steamers. Ironically its owner was not F.O. Stanley.[3]

Rather, it was David Osborn and his three sons—Will, Otto, and Estes—who pioneered automobile transportation in the Estes Park region when they formed and began to operate the Loveland–Estes Park Transportation Company. During the summer of 1907 the Osborns used three five-passenger Stanley Model F 20-h.p. touring

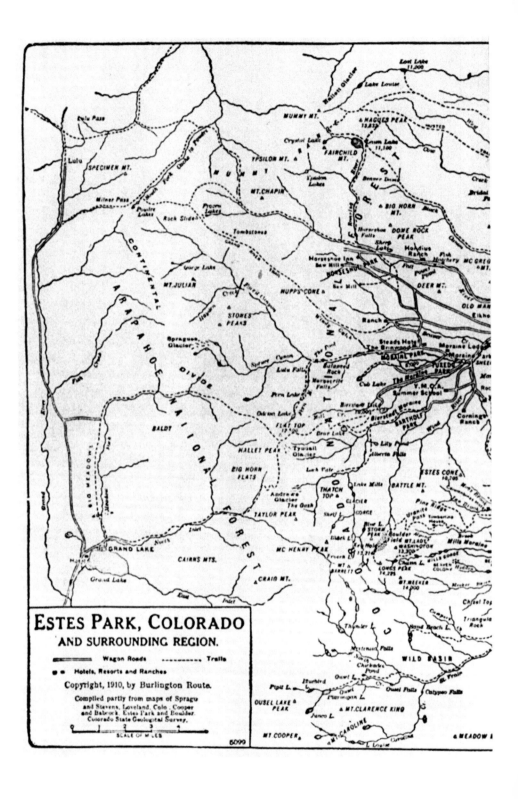

ESTES PARK, COLORADO
AND SURROUNDING REGION.

Wagon Roads — — — — Trails

●● Hotels, Resorts and Ranches

Copyright, 1910, by Burlington Route.

Compiled partly from maps of Sprague
and Stevens, Loveland, Colo., Cooper
and Babcock, Estes Park and Boulder,
Colorado State Geological Survey.

SCALE OF MILES

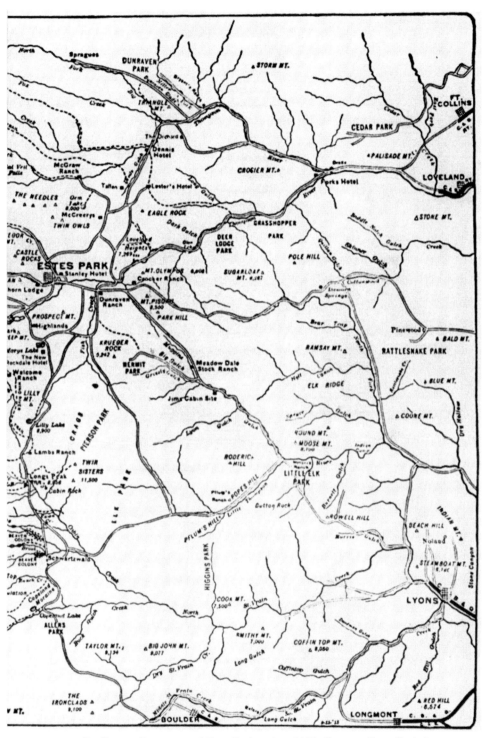

Burlington Route map of Estes Park region, 1910. Courtesy Estes Park Area Historical Museum and the Burlington Northern and Santa Fe Railway.

cars, and charged a fare of $3.50 for the daily three-hour trip ($6.00 for the round-trip, slightly more if the traveler's ultimate destination was Moraine Park). The company was incorporated the following year, on November 24, 1908, with capital stock of $50,000.[4]

The Osborn enterprise, headquartered with garage and offices at 432 Cleveland Avenue in Loveland, was helped immeasurably by the announcement as early as March that its major competition, George and Ben Johnson's horse stage line, would not operate during the coming 1907 season. The Colorado and Southern had refused "to deliver passengers [to waiting coaches] by the Neville switch on the Arkins branch seven miles west of Loveland." According to the *Loveland Reporter*, "The stage line in the past has not been a very paying proposition." Without this "concession" from the railroad the Johnson brothers simply were not going to attempt to compete with the horse stages based at Lyons.[5]

Aided by the Johnsons' withdrawal from the transportation business, the Osborn line was an immediate success. That summer it carried to and from the park an estimated 3,000 people. The following year the Osborns added three nine-passenger Stanley Steamers to the route, allowing them to transport as many as 100 passengers a day. (By the time they sold the business in the spring of 1916, their fleet would include as many as 18 Stanleys.)

Though the published schedule promised a three-hour trip, automotive speed records on the Big Thompson road, as elsewhere, were made to be broken. "Will Osborn, of Loveland, made the run in an auto from Loveland to Estes Park Friday in an hour and 45 minutes," the *Longmont Call* noted on August 24. "It is 35 miles all up hill."[6]

Their schedule called for two trips a day. Going west, the auto stage left Loveland at 8:30 A.M. and 1:00 P.M., arriving at Estes Park at 11:30 A.M. and 4 P.M. Only the afternoon trip went on to Moraine Park, where it arrived at 4:30. For the return trip, travelers could leave Moraine Park at 8:00 A.M., and Estes Park at 8:30 A.M. and again at 1:00 P.M. Passengers were each allowed one piece of hand luggage not to exceed 20 pounds; the transfer of other luggage and freight—and many vacationers brought with them considerably more—was accomplished by special arrangement with the company. The chief advantage, of course, was speed. As newspaper advertisements reminded potential customers, "This automobile service reduces the stage time from 6½ hours

Stanley Steamers in the Big Thompson Canyon. Courtesy Estes Park Area Historical Museum.

to 3 hours, and provides double service in each direction." By 1915 the time it took to negotiate the 32 miles had been reduced to two-and-a-half hours.7

During the decade that followed, travelers alighting at the Colorado and Southern depot at Loveland became used to a familiar sight. There before them was a neat row of gleaming red automobiles, with their drivers calling, "Take the Stanley Steamer to Estes Park." It was an allure that most vacationers bound for the mountains were hard-pressed to resist. The cars often traveled up the narrow-walled canyon in caravan fashion, weaving their way through the scenic wonders of the Narrows at the mouth of the Big Thompson, past a number of named rock formations.

From there it was up the winding, one-track road to the Forks Hotel (at what is now Drake), where the passengers alighted for lunch and the cars replenished their water supply by siphoning directly from the river. For most of the journey the curves were sharp and treacherous. The road crossed and recrossed the Big Thompson, the roadbed in places only a foot or so above the river, making periodic floodings and washouts inevitable. Meeting an oncoming car, an increasingly frequent occurence, usually forced one of the vehicles to back up to a spot in the road wide enough for passing.

Every trip became a potential adventure. During the first five years of operation, the Osborn steamers lacked tops, windshields, and side curtains, making the journey even more exciting. The initiated came prepared with goggles and slickers or capes that buttoned to the neck. Unprepared tenderfeet all too often arrived at their destination wet, dusty, or both. "Coming with Derby hats and high-wing collars, spats, and wearing neatly pressed suits," one experienced traveler noted with scorn, "you can well imagine their appearance when they arrived at their destination over dusty roads or through rainstorms."8

With the remarkable torque made possible by direct drive and without a need to shift because of the lack of transmission, the Stanley Steamer was well adapted to the sharp curves, steep hills, and hard surface of the Big Thompson road. It performed effortlessly, even over the particularly long, precipitous grade just beyond the Forks Hotel known as "The Rapids." This section of the road was so steep that it slowed most gasoline cars almost to a stop. One automobile historian, in fact, credits The Rapids with being largely responsible for the use of steam rather than gasoline cars between Loveland and Estes Park. "It was not until about 1917," he notes, "when greatly improved roads and much better gasoline cars were made that the gasoline cars climbed this famous hill . . . at a speed comparable to that of the Stanleys."[9]

The Stanley Mountain Wagon

It was precisely the challenge to get passengers from the railheads at Lyons and Loveland to the resorts of Estes Park, over steep mountain roads like the Big Thompson and North St. Vrain, that encouraged F.O. Stanley to design the celebrated nine-passenger Model Z Stanley Mountain Wagon. It was first introduced as a prototype in 1908. Refined on the basis of experience between 1911 and 1917, and enlarged into a long, sturdy 12-seater, the Mountain Wagon, with its high torque, low gear ratio, 136-inch wheelbase, and 30-h.p. engine, proved an ideal vehicle to haul large loads of passengers or freight over mountain roads, and as such revolutionized tourist travel, particularly in places like Colorado.

Though there was also a flatbed Stanley Express Wagon, built on the same chassis without seats, most resort owners found the standard version of the Mountain Wagon perfectly adaptable to their needs. By removing the rear seats it was quickly convertible into a roomy baggage wagon, with inside body dimensions of about 44 x 104–inches. Detachable sideboards were furnished for use in baggage service. By about 1912 the Mountain Wagon came equipped with top, windshield, and side curtains, greatly adding to the comfort of the passengers.

The Stanley Motor Carriage Company's 1917 brochure described the Mountain Wagon, that by then carried a price of $3,199, as a car which could do no wrong:

There is no risky rushing at hills and water bars, no dangerous taking of curves at high speed, and no noisy racing of the motor. The abundance of reserve power always at the command of the operator enables him to pick his way up the rough, stony hill, and to slow down almost to a stop over water bars and around blind curves. There is no clutch to work constantly at every turn. There is no change speed lever, the effort to work which is multiplied so greatly on bad roads and changing grades. And above all there is no keeping the mind constantly on the alert to anticipate these conditions which the operator knows may come up at the most unexpected or critical moments. The physical effort to meet these conditions, with the internal-explosive car, is great enough, but it is exceeded by the nervous effort of constantly looking forward for them. . . . Therefore the Stanley Mountain Wagon can, in fact, be driven with far less mental anxiety than any other make of car.[10]

For resort owners and freight operators in places like Estes Park there was an added incentive: "because the expenses of running them, especially as to tires, are so low . . . [they] leave the owner a good margin of profit."

Stanley Mountain Wagon in front of the Chamber of Commerce office, Estes Park. Courtesy Estes Park Area Historical Museum.

The company was largely correct in its claim that the Mountain Wagon operated without vibration or noise. It could, however, make plenty of noise, for all Stanleys were available with a whistle that was shrill and piercing. Its effect could be telling. "When we passed a man fishing on a bridge and the driver gave this whistle," one passenger recalled of a trip up the Big Thompson, "he scared the man so that he jumped right over into the river!"[11]

Steam cars were occasionally, however, involved in accidents of a more serious nature. Within a two-month period during the summer of 1908, for example, the Longmont papers reported two potentially tragic incidents, both on the same six-mile stretch of the Big Thompson road east of Estes Park. In the first, Otto Osborn, returning to Loveland with an empty vehicle, suddenly encountered a fully loaded steamer coming up the canyon in the other direction, which "very nearly pushed it into the Thompson." "Both chauffeurs," the *Ledger* reported, "were running like blazes trying to make up lost time. No one killed and no one hurt very bad."[12]

The second accident, again involving one of the Osborns, nearly ended in serious injury. It occurred when two cars, running together westbound toward Estes Park, ran into one another after the first auto blew a cylinder and suddenly stopped. The second car, "running fast and very close, ran into the forward machine at full speed. If the forward car had not lodged against some big logs it would have turned turtle into the Big Thompson, and probably some one might have been hurt or drowned, as it was loaded with women and babies."[13]

Despite such episodes, the Stanley's superiority in navigating the roads into and around Estes Park was almost universally acknowledged and acclaimed. Beside its use at F.O.'s Stanley Hotel, the Stanley Steamer was the automobile of choice at such resorts as the Elkhorn Lodge, Lester's Hotel (the old Rustic), the Brinwood in Moraine Park, the Columbine Lodge and Enos Mills's Longs Peak Inn in the Tahosa Valley, and at the encampment of the Western Conference of the YMCA (YMCA of the Rockies). A number of local and summer residents also owned Stanleys, including the Chapmans of Moraine Park, and Milton Clauser, whose summer home to the east of the site of the future Stanley Hotel was hung with barn doors so that his 1903 Stanley CX could be brought directly into the living room to rest in front of the fireplace.

Wreck of a Stanley Steamer on Pingree Hill, west of Fort Collins, and north of the town of Rustic, March 1910. Courtesy Fort Collins Public Library.

F.O. Stanley was very much aware of what the Osborns were doing, and was undoubtedly involved in some way in David Osborn's purchase of his Model F touring cars. Stanley could not help but be impressed by his success. Lyons and Longmont, on the other hand, were justifiably worried about the loss of competitive advantage to Loveland. Relief came with the announcement in early February 1908 that Stanley intended to put into operation his own auto stage line up the North St. Vrain road to Estes Park. The line would begin at Longmont where it would connect directly with the Colorado and Southern. "The next summer," the *Longmont Call* predicted with obvious anticipation,

> will see a large percent of the traffic which has gone by way of Loveland and the Thompson Canon, diverted to the new line. This will place Longmont where it belongs as the natural gateway to the scenic grandeur and beauties of the finest, and what is destined to become the most popular summer resort in the entire Rocky Mountain region.[14]

On June 16, 1908, F.O. Stanley incorporated the Estes Park Transportation Company (not to be confused with the Osborns' Loveland–Estes Park Transportation Company) with a capital stock of $15,000, divided into 150 shares.[15] Its managing directors were Oscar Peter Low, who had recently arrived in Colorado from Junction City, Kansas; Milton Clauser, supervisor of Manual Training for the Denver public schools,[16] and F.O. Stanley. Low and Clauser were involved in day-to-day operations: Low looked after the office and garage at Longmont, Clauser did the same at Estes Park. Two others were also part of the new management team: Byron Hall (John B. Hall's son), who was hired to supervise operations near his home at Lyons; and L. C. Larson of Longmont, whose job as general manager was to "look after the road." At about the same time, Stanley reportedly purchased and then shut down one of the old horse-driven stage lines.[17]

Though it was originally announced that operations would begin by May 15,[18] the first of the Stanley machines did not reach Denver and Longmont until the first week in June. The inaugural trip over the route to Estes Park to be used by the new line took place on Thursday, June 11, when a run up the North St. Vrain road was made by two automobiles, one driven by manager Larson, the other by Boyd Wallahan, one of the line's new drivers. Each car contained eight notables, though F.O. Stanley himself was not among them.[19]

Service began with six Model Z Mountain Wagon passenger cars and one express car, with their distinctive red bodies and yellow undercarriages. Two cars each were stationed at Estes Park and Lyons. Two more were stationed at Longmont, where the express car was also kept. The schedule of Stanley's new company, which quick-

Stanley Steamers at Lyons. Courtesy Estes Park Area Historical Museum.

ly obtained a government contract to haul the mail, called for a single three-hour trip each day, leaving Longmont at 10 A.M. and arriving in Estes Park by way of Lyons at 1:00 P.M. The return trip left Estes at 2:00 P.M.[20] At $7.50 the fare was $1.50 more than the Osborns charged, but Stanley blunted its impact by announcing in mid-June that 60 cents of each fare that year would be used for road improvements in Boulder County.[21]

From the beginning, special efforts were made to match departures and arrivals with the schedule of the railroads. At the Lyons end of things Stanley had made arrangements the previous November with Burlington officials to move the arrival time of the morning passengers from Denver forward an hour, from 11:30 to 10:30 A.M. Stanley guaranteed to "have them in the park at 12 o'clock for a big dinner."[22]

By mid-June the *Longmont Ledger* was convinced that Stanley's new line had brought Longmont and Lyons at least even in their contest with Loveland. "We can't see how Loveland has a cinch on Estes Park like some people say it has," editor Charles Boynton wrote on the 19th:

> As many tourists come into the Park and go out by way of Lyons and Longmont as by way of Loveland. If you don't think so, go to the junction at the Dunraven [ranch house, where the roads

Steamers and horses on Elkhorn Avenue, c. 1907. Courtesy Estes Park Area Historical Museum.

from Lyons and Loveland converged] and keep track of them for an average month and you will find out.[23]

In anticipation of his new transportation venture, Stanley purchased three lots on Elkhorn Avenue in December 1907, for which he paid Homer E. James $1,000 (a sign of how much village real estate prices had grown in little more than two years).[24] But until the garage and office that were to serve as headquarters could be completed, the Estes Park Transportation Company was forced to share the tent garage that the Osborns had put up that spring.[25] Today's visitors to Estes Park will have little difficulty identifying the original buildings of the transportation company, which, enclosed, now house the Park Theatre Mall. The Osborns' permanent garage, which by the summer of 1915 consisted of a 130 x 50–foot brick building with concrete floor and plate-glass front, was located on three lots farther to the west on the north side of Elkhorn Avenue, near Fall River.[26] The rear and roof structure of that building also still exists, though new storefront facades have long since masked its original identity and purpose.

O. P. Low sold his stock in the transportation company to Byron Hall and C. N. ("Casey") Rockwell in 1912 because his wife's health required her to seek a lower elevation.[27] Four years later, on May 1, 1916, Stanley sold the entire company. Its new owner was Roe Emery, a relative newcomer to Colorado, who simultaneously bought the Osborns' Loveland stage line, merged the two, and then absorbed both into his newly incorporated Rocky Mountain Parks Transportation Company.

Steamers on Elkhorn Avenue, 1908–1909. Courtesy Estes Park Area Historical Museum.

Received in the transaction were 20 12-passenger steamers and six trucks for hauling freight.[28] Ten days later, on May 11, it was announced that Emery had also purchased Grant Glover's Fort Collins–Estes Park Transportation Company together with its fleet of Stanley Steamers. The reported price was $5,000.[29]

Roe Emery, like F.O. Stanley, was a transportation pioneer. Having already introduced buses to Glacier National Park, with the encouragement and help of Louis Hill of the Great Northern Railroad, the onetime Wyoming rancher had come to Denver in 1914 at the invitation of the Burlington. Cooperation with the major railroads was key. By the spring of 1917, Emery had obtained their official designation as "authorized carrier . . . to the Park," had reequipped his line with a fleet of modern, 10-passenger touring cars, and was operating daily trips from Denver, Longmont, Lyons, Loveland, Fort Collins, and Ward. The cost of it all, the *Boulder Daily Camera* reported in May 1917, was $200,000—a "small fortune."[30] Success immediately followed. Over the next three decades, through the promotion of highly popular "circle tours" beginning and ending at Denver, Emery would build a small transportation and hotel empire, one that eventually included the Stanley Hotel.

Estes Park Transportation Company's headquarters on Elkhorn Avenue. Courtesy Bill Van Horn.

"All I did," Emery remarked late in life, "was to give people a chance to look."[31] Emery's statement was an accurate, if modest, one. It was also a statement with which F.O. Stanley would have emphatically agreed. Their relationship nonetheless got off to a somewhat awkward beginning. Emery almost immediately junked the Stanleys he had purchased and replaced them with gasoline-powered mountain wagons built by the White Motor Company of Cleveland. What appeared at the time as something of a gratuitous insult had, it turned out, a rather more benign explanation. Years later Emery revealed that the decision had little to do with Mr. Stanley or his steamers. His silent partner in the Rocky Mountain Parks Transportation Company was Walter C. White of the White Motor Company.[32]

The substitution was nonetheless ironic. During the first decade of the century, the White Motor Company, until 1906 the White Sewing Machine Company, like the Stanley Motor Carriage Company, had been a pioneer in the steam automobile business. By 1910, however, White, correctly anticipating the future, had abandoned steam in favor of gasoline.

The Estes Park Transportation Company, like its counterpart in Loveland, was very much a financial success. In 1928, Stanley recalled with pride, "I received about $22,000.00 for what cost me only $10,000.00, and the purchase price was based on an inventory of actual property value, nothing being added for good-will, and we had declared a dividend each year."[33] The auto stage line, Stanley might have added, was also his single most profitable Colorado business venture.

F.O. Stanley made one additional investment in regional transportation. In 1912 he helped finance construction of the Bunce School road from Peaceful Valley to Allenspark in order to facilitate the transportation of tourists from the railroad depot at Ward to Estes Park. By 1914 that route was being traveled by Stanley Steamer automobiles belonging to the Ward–Estes Park Auto Line, which connected at Ward with the Denver, Boulder, and Western's famous "Switzerland Trail of America." This narrow-gauge railroad, completed in June 1898, was one of the marvels of Western engineering. Beginning at Boulder it brought vacationers up Boulder and Four Mile Canyons, past the old mining towns of Crisman, Salina, Wall Street, and Copper Rock. At

Sunset the railroad branched—one branch went to Nederland and Eldora, the other, by zig and zag, came up a 6 percent grade and into Ward.

Art Lee, who drove five-, nine- and twelve-passenger Stanley Steamers for his father out of Ward during the summers of 1914 and 1915, recalled in a single phrase how perfectly adapted those automobiles were to the largely unimproved mountain roads over which he traveled. "They'd climb a tree," he wrote, and "with a full head of steam."[34]

The trip from Ward to Estes Park to which he referred was well promoted. Passengers were promised a journey that took them

> through Peaceful valley, a perfect dream of beauty; through Allens park, by pretty little Fern cliff, past the door of Copeland Lake Lodge, along the bank of the North St. Vrain, in the midst of tall pines, close to the foot of Longs peak, Mount Meeker and Lady Washington through Elkanah valley, by the gateway of Hewes-Kirkwood resort, the Columbines, Long's Peak Inn and the Rockdale hotel and down the Big Thompson valley and into the village. . . . The great variety of scenery offered by this trip is unequalled.[35]

The morning train to Ward left Denver at 7:50 A.M. and Boulder at 9:15 A.M., arriving at 12:05 P.M. Fifty-five minutes were allowed for lunch, and by 3:45 P.M., passengers were in Estes Park, having traveled a total of 88 miles. The total cost of a round-trip ticket from Denver to Estes Park by train and car was $9.60. Like the equally celebrated journeys by the Stanley Steamer from the railheads at Loveland and Lyons, the trip from Ward to Estes Park was for many summer visitors an adventure long to be remembered.

CHAPTER

8

The Stanley Hotel

The Stanley Hotel. Courtesy Denver Public Library, Western History Collection.

A pleasant surprise awaits them, for the new Hotel Stanley, where they will be domiciled, instead of being in the class ordinary of mountain hostelries, is simply palatial, equaling anything of its size in the world.

—*Rocky Mountain News*, June 13, 1909[1]

The major reason that F.O. Stanley took such an interest in rebuilding the North St. Vrain road, and then pushed the Halls and their workers to complete the project so quickly, was that by the late winter or early spring of 1907, his plans to build a new luxury hotel in Estes Park were virtually complete. The challenge then facing him was an obvious one. If he was going to build America's first modern resort hotel not directly accessible by railroad, he would need good roads to get there. By 1907, F.O. Stanley had been in Colorado long enough to know that the former would simply not be possible without the latter.

The first public indication of his intention came on January 25, 1907—almost two months prior to the news that "all the preliminaries are perfected for building the new auto road from Lyons to Estes Park"—when the *Longmont Ledger* announced on "good authority that F.O. Stanley, of the Stanley Automobile fame, is planning to build a $200,000 hotel at the head of Big Thompson Canon, as it enters Estes Park."[2]

Stanley chose his site with care, a quarter section north and east of the growing village, which shared much the same view of the Front Range as the one he enjoyed from his own porch half a mile to the west. The property, containing 160.4 acres, was part of Dunraven's Estes Park holdings, and must have been coveted by Stanley well before he reached his final understanding with Burton Sanborn.[3] Site and setting were integral to what F.O. Stanley had in mind: a large, luxurious hotel built in the tradition of the classic resorts of his native New England, with the outbuildings and amenities necessary to make it the first complete summer resort in northeastern Colorado.

Taking his inspiration once again from the grace and dignity of Georgian Colonial Revival architecture, Stanley designed a series of beautifully proportioned structures that are as arresting today as they were nearly a century ago, though their original mustard-yellow color has long since given way to white. Set in a crescent pattern across a hillside framed by the Twin Owls and Lumpy Ridge to the north, the wooden buildings of the Stanley Hotel, with their red hipped roofs and dormers, seem to rise effortlessly from the ground on their cement and stone foundations, individually and collectively at peace with their rugged mountain surroundings. "The delight in contrast between the highly organized Georgian facades and the raw power of nature exhibited without contest in hill and rock and mountain beyond is exquisite."[4]

When it came to architecture, Stanley considered himself something more than a talented amateur: the original conception, design,
and preliminary plans for the new hotel were unmistakably his own.[5]
Architects, however, were necessary for such major projects. For his
hotel in Estes Park, Stanley selected T. Robert Wieger of Denver,[6]
though many of the details about the role he asked Wieger to play,
and the working relationship that developed between owner and
architect, remain obscure.

Without the original architectural blueprints, it is tempting to
underestimate the extent of Stanley's reliance on others. But given the
magnitude of the undertaking, Stanley needed help. Despite his
involvement with the building of the Hunnewell Club in Newton, he
needed someone to engineer for stress and strength, someone who
knew how to build large structures able to withstand wind, cold, and
other conditions of the mountains. That Stanley should call on the services of Wieger, or someone very much like him, was logical.

Wieger was critical in at least one other respect as well: he introduced Stanley to the contractor whom Stanley hired to oversee the
construction of the main hotel, the casino, and the other buildings as
well. During 1903 and 1904, Wieger had designed houses for Frank
Kirchoff, owner of Denver's large Kirchoff Lumber Company.
Together, Kirchoff and Wieger, contractor and architect, working as a
team, then chose the subcontractors, most of whom, with the exception of the painters and apparently the electricians, were based in
Denver.[7] Once the plans were drawn and the contracts let, however,
Wieger remained very much in the background. Wieger made but one
documented visit to Estes Park during this period. That occurred on
July 2, 1909—shortly after the formal opening of the hotel—when he
registered at the Elkhorn Lodge for a visit.[8]

For day-to-day supervision throughout the many months of construction, Stanley relied almost exclusively on Kirchoff and his on-
site foreman, Al Roenfelt, a 23-year veteran of the construction
business, as well as on his Estes Park friend, English architect and
photographer Henry Rogers. Rogers actually drew up the plans for
the Casino (or Stanley Hall, as this music and entertainment building is now called),[9] and exercised enough authority on F.O.
Stanley's behalf to make decisions that at least some of the workmen found unpopular.[10]

The contract to excavate the hotel was given to Byron Hall. Ground was broken for the 217 x 107–foot main hotel building in the fall of 1907. By October 25 a crew of 32 men were at work,[11] and by the time their labor was suspended for the winter the hotel's foundation, cut into the hillside, was partially complete and the steel frames in place.

While some of the Denver subcontractors brought their own helpers, Roenfelt hired widely. During the next two years, workers poured into Estes Park from Longmont, Lyons, Loveland, Greeley, and Boulder, as well as Denver, swelling the town's population, straining available accommodations, and forcing some to live in tents. Even these were in short supply. When one Henry Zeller quit his job at the hotel and left to visit his parents back in Michigan, "He sold his tent to the Boston painters."[12]

Kirchoff and Roenfelt also hired a number of local residents—Frank Grubb, Carl Piltz, Johnny Adams, Lige Rivers, David Usher, Dolly Gray, and Matt Mulmberg among them—all of whom were no doubt delighted to find well-paying jobs out of season. There were so many new faces in the park by the end of October 1907 that Charles Lester, manager of Dunraven's Estes Park Hotel, reported, "324 people [are now] getting mail at the Estes Park postoffice and the population of the town is about 500."[13] Estes Park would not see such a demand for labor again until the coming of Roosevelt's WPA and the Colorado–Big Thompson project in the late 1930s.

The winter months of 1907–1908 brought most of the work to a stop. But at noon on Thursday, May 12, 1908, Kirchoff and Roenfelt, together with a large workforce, were back on the job. Their payroll quickly reached $600 a week for carpenters alone.[14] It was now spring and the work proceeded quickly. By the end of May, the steel framing had been completed and the Denver plumbers were at work. By June 8, construction of the third story had begun. A month later the first wagonloads of finished lumber for floors and siding began to arrive from the Kirchoff Lumber Yard in Denver.

Lumber used for framing and sheathing, on the other hand, was cut locally, either at Bierstadt Lake, where the Reverend Albin Griffith and his sons had erected a sawmill on land leased from the Forest Service, or in Hidden Valley, where Stanley himself had a mill run by Walter Fulton.[15] During the summers of 1907 and 1908, one of the Griffiths recalled, some 270,000 board-feet of lumber was cut at Bierstadt Lake,

The Stanley Hotel under construction, 1908. Courtesy City of Greeley Museums, Permanent Collection.

which were then brought out by team and wagon over a crude logging road leading down through Hallowell Park to Homer James's small planing mill just west of the village on Fall River. After being surfaced to size, the lumber was taken by wagon to the hotel site.[16]

For the first time since 1902, Flora and Freelan Stanley spent the winter of 1907–1908 in Newton, a sign that F.O.'s health had fully returned. They returned from Boston on Friday, June 2, 1908, and before long F.O. was spending most of his time at the hotel, where he had already picked out his room.[17] He was an exacting builder, and one can only imagine the slender, gray-bearded, well-dressed Mr. Stanley gingerly picking his way among workers and piles of materials to offer suggestions and advice, both of which were intended to be taken seriously.

Fortunately the Estes Park correspondent of the *Longmont Ledger*, with occasional help from the *Loveland Reporter* (which often simply reprinted what the *Ledger* had to say), has left an almost day-by-day record on the progress of the hotel's construction as well as bits and pieces of other news that gives the project a human dimension. Note the confusion over the new hotel's name—a confusion that F.O. Stanley would shortly be called upon to resolve.

Henry Zeller took seven carpenters to Bear Lake Saturday noon, returning Sunday evening. Result: 17 trout for 8 men, cost $1.50 each. They set a big tree on fire and had to cut it down to put the fire out at 2 p.m.[18]

• • •

Miles Sautter is a new lumber jack at the Hotel Stanley. Miles is from Longmont. We like to see the Longmont boys get in on this deal. It is their own fault there are not more of them here.[19]

• • •

Ye correspondent fell three stories at hotel Stanley Friday noon. No it didn't hurt much. You see we lit in a sand pile.[20]

• • •

Frank Kirchoff is coming up from Denver to-day (Wednesday) to again look over the hotel. Frank is the contractor.[21]

• • •

Mr. Rogers' horse fell down with him and broke his collar bone. We mean the collar bone of Mr. Rogers, not the horse.[22]

• • •

The big Flag pole for the Stanley arrived Saturday night.[23]

• • •

Mr. Albert Roenfelt, the Dunraven foreman, surely is going to take a great fishing trip. He dug a half gallon of worms Friday night.[24]

• • •

Several new stone masons came up from Denver Thursday to build a retaining wall around the new Dunraven.[25]

• • •

There was a big bunch of Denver visitors at the Hotel Friday. Now is the time to see the building, as it is all finished on the outside and shows up fine.[26]

• • •

The Joslin Dry Goods Co. of Denver had a man up here last of the week figuring on carpeting the Dunraven.[27]

• • •

Mr. Stanley left Monday for the east for good. He started last week but after getting to Denver, he returned to the park and canned a man.[28]

• • •

Mr. Roenfelt, the Dunraven foreman, says if us boys will all be good he will give us a week off on Christmas so we can go to our homes (ours in Longmont) and eat turkey and spend some money. All right, Mr. Roenfelt, we'll try to?[29]

• • •

Leonard Ramey unpacked all the kitchen utensils at the Dunraven Friday.[30]

• • •

Al Roenfelt sits up all night lately. No, he is not afraid some one will steal anything. He has the toothache.[31]

In early July 1908, with lathing and plastering on the hotel and concrete work on porches and sidewalks about to begin, Stanley laid a half mile of temporary water pipeline from the village limits to the hotel site. The shingling, which began on July 21, took six days for a crew of 13 to complete. ("At that rate," the *Ledger* summarized for its readers, "it would have taken one man 78 days or about three months."[32]) On August 14, with crews now putting in nine-hour days, it was reported that "plastering, lathing, and painting are going on at the hotel in fine shape."[33] By the 27th the siding was being put on, and before the month was out, Roenfelt was confidently taking bets that the carpentry work would be done by the end of the year.[34]

His prediction was on target, for by the time the first bad weather of the season arrived during the third week of October 1908, all the remaining work on the hotel itself was on the inside.[35] "Two loads of lumber, mostly finishing and flooring, arrive every night from Lyons for the new Dunraven," the Ledger reported on November 6. The next day, 52 heavy bathtubs arrived by horse-drawn wagon over Mr. Stanley's new road.

On September 30, 1908, with the work on the hotel well advanced, F.O. Stanley personally laid out the site of the first of the other buildings, the 44 x 96–foot Casino some 500 feet to the east, with the intention of having it plastered and lathed before the coming of cold weather.[36] By October 9, ground had been broken and by the middle of the month Carl Piltz, the veteran Estes Park mason, had completed the foundation, allowing the carpenters to begin framing.[37]

That foundation, like the one for the hotel itself, illustrates the practicalities of turn-of-the-century hotel construction, where speed of completion was important and expensive blasting was to be kept to a minimum. While both buildings have basements, they were excavated only to the extent that the rock could be easily broken up and removed. Where there were great boulders and rock outcroppings, those areas were simply left partially or wholly alone. Like the rest of the basement, the unexcavated areas were then timbered over with floor joists, making allowance for a low crawl space in which the stumps of some of the original trees can still be seen today.

On October 7, 1908, groundwork and excavation began "for a large building north of the hotel called the servant's quarters." The site for the icehouse to the south and west was also surveyed. A few days later it was reported that Stanley had crews working simultaneously on the new garage and machine shop (the Carriage House) to the east of the Casino, as well as on a large reservoir on the hill behind the hotel to serve as its water supply. Work was also begun on the approach road up the hill from the village. This outdoor labor continued into December, with construction of the laundry adjacent to the hotel building begun at mid-month. Progress was, in fact, so expeditious that by year's end, with the exception of the Manor House, Kirchoff and Roenfelt had the entire project well under way.

The building of the 32-room Manor House, a scaled-down replica of the main hotel, containing its own dining room, kitchen, parlors, billiard room, and heating, on the other hand, was still a year away. Work did not begin on that structure until October 1909, four months after the main hotel opened in June. It is nonetheless probable that the Manor House was part of Stanley's plan from the beginning. It occupies a convenient site adjacent to the main hotel building that would otherwise have been used for the Casino, and it completes visually and aesthetically the sweep of buildings that F.O. Stanley's artistic sensibilities would have dictated. The success of the hotel's first season encouraged Stanley to move ahead quickly with its construction so that it would be ready for occupancy by the summer of 1910.

Reported estimates of the final cost of Stanley's hotel project vary widely, from $150,000 to $1,000,000, with $500,000 being the most probable.[38] Unfortunately for the purpose of historians, Stanley kept few if any records. Old-fashioned when it came to money transactions, he preferred to settle his bills on a cash basis.

Labor difficulties on the hotel project were apparently minimal. Though there was a strike in late November 1908 ("Results: Everybody at work and happy and no scabs in the bunch"[39]), it was so minor and short-lived a disruption that the press never bothered to report the cause. To the extent that there were problems, they not surprisingly involved the vagaries of mountain weather. On the night of Sunday, November 19, for example, with the framing of the Casino well advanced, a "hard wind" toppled the entire structure. "Bill Ramey and ye correspondent had a hard time putting it up," the *Ledger* complained. "Now we will have to do it all over again."[40]

The only serious controversy involved the hotel's name. Early newspaper reports referred to the "big hotel" alternately as the "Stanley" or the "Dunraven," causing so much confusion that in August 1908 the *Ledger* was forced to address the issue directly. "We have been making a mistake all summer by calling the new hotel the Stanley," it told its readers. "It is the Dunraven. So we will call it the new Dunraven in the future."[41]

The "Dunraven," however, a name that in some quarters lingered well into January 1909, did not sit at all well with the residents of Estes Park. "If it was left to the people of the Park to name the new Hotel," the town's new summer paper, *The Mountaineer*, editorialized on August 13, 1908,

> it would be called "The Stanley." The name Dunraven does not call up pleasant memories. About the only thing Dunraven suggests is a land-grabber who tried to convert the Park into a game preserve for his own use. Mr. Stanley's name will always be associated with the upbuilding of the Park, making it a place delightful for all the people. Give the splendid structure a fitting name.[42]

F.O. Stanley was clearly sensitive to the issue, and offered a prize of $10 "to the person suggesting the most appropriate and fitting name."[43] It was not necessary. As the *Loveland Reporter* explained on October 15, "Mr. Stanley had intended to name the hotel the Dunraven, but a petition signed by nearly every one in the park was presented to him this week asking that the hotel be named the Stanley, and he has acquiesced."[44] That petition, which ceremoniously

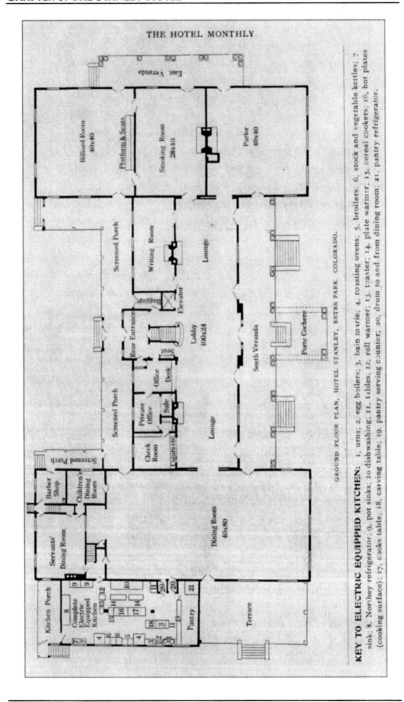

THE HOTEL MONTHLY.

GROUND FLOOR PLAN, HOTEL STANLEY, ESTES PARK, COLORADO.

KEY TO ELECTRIC EQUIPPED KITCHEN: 1, urns; 2, egg boilers; 3, bain marie; 4, roasting ovens; 5, broilers; 6, stock and vegetable kettles; 7, sink; 8, Norihey refrigerator; 9, pot sinks; 10 dishwashing; 11, tables; 12, roll warmer; 13, toaster; 14, plate warmer; 15, cereal cookers; 16, hot plates (cooking surface); 17, cooks table; 18, carving table; 19, pantry serving counter; 20, drum to and from dining room; 21, pantry refrigerator.

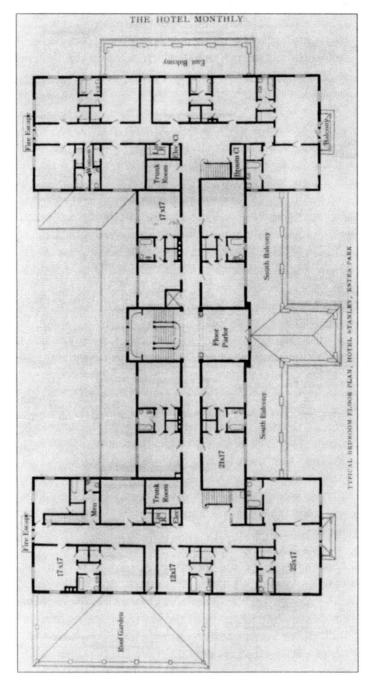

Stanley Hotel, floor plan. Collection of James H. Pickering.

arrived in the form of a buckskin inscribed with some 180 signatures, included the names of every other hotel- and resort-keeper in the park, as well as Burton Sanborn, architect Robert Wieger, and foreman Al Roenfelt. The petition, which for many years hung in the lobby of the Stanley Hotel, was simple and to the point:

> Mr. Freelan O. Stanley, Greeting: We, the undersigned, appreciating the good work you have done in Estes Park, hereby petition that the building which will stand as a monument to its founder, shall be called "The Stanley Hotel."[45]

That issue and others resolved, the Stanleys left for the east in mid-November, confident that the new hotel complex would be ready for the tourist season of 1909. Two months later, F.O. Stanley made one of his rare winter appearances in Estes Park. "Mr. Stanley is expected in from Boston, Mass., in a few days to accept the new Dunraven," the *Ledger* reported on January 15. "It will be ready to turn over to him the coming week."[46]

The hotel that Stanley accepted was stunning, even without the completion of its neighboring complex of buildings. To satisfy curiosity about a project whose progress he had reported for months and in such minute detail, editor Charles Boynton of the *Longmont Ledger* promised on several occasions to provide his readers with a full description of Mr. Stanley's hotel. When he finally got around to doing so, on Christmas Day 1908, Boynton took an unusual tack. Rather than simply describing the "monster structure" at the risk of understating Stanley's achievement, he chose to disaggregate it, interspersing his figures with bits of description and other information. Though perhaps exaggerating some of his numbers, editor Boynton clearly achieved the desired effect.

> To give you some idea of the immensity of this new hotel in the hills, we will give some of the figures connected with the work. The lathing consists of 32,500 yards. There were 36,500 yards of plastering. The reason there was more plastering than lathing is on account of the basement being plastered on the stone wall, which, of course, needed no lathing. It took 120 yards of sand, 2,200 sacks of cement, and a car of lime to do this work. It took

455,000 lath to cover the building, which at fifty lath to the bunch, required 9,100 bunches. There are five porches [on] this hotel. One on the northwest, one on the southwest, one on the east, one on the south, and one on the north, covered with Elaterite roofing.

There are two firescapes on the north side of the hotel, and one at each end of the building. There is a large elevator in the center of the building running from the basement to the attic. There are five fire places in this hotel to make cheerful the faces of the future guests.

It took 156,000 shingles to do this work, or 624 bales of 150 shingles each. It is eighty-eight feet from the top of the foundation to the highest point of the building. A large flag pole has been placed in the center of the roof. The bath rooms number twenty-nine in all, with of course just as many bath tubs. There are twenty dormers on the roof to give light for the long halls. There are twenty-five miles of telephone wire in the building with a telephone in each room and the office for central. There are six miles of gas pipe and plumbing pipe in the building, also one mile of picture molding.

This hotel has the largest and best equipped kitchen of any hotel in the west, Denver not excepted, the size being 24 x 52 feet. The dining room will also be of the best, size 40 x 80 feet. The children's dining room is a fine little room 12 x 14, the barber shop 12 x 12, billiard room 40 x 42, Main office 13 x 17, public office 13 x 15, parlor 40 x 42, writing room 17 x 35, smoking room 27 x 42, and the hotel lobby is 56 x 102. This includes all the rooms on the first floor. The second, third, and fourth floors are sleeping rooms and bath rooms. There are two big hot air furnaces in the basement to keep this building comfortable. . . .

This hotel is built in the shape of the letter H. The flooring is all of the hardest pine from the Bluff City Lumber Co. of Pine Bluff, Arkansas. There is a total of 345 acres of flooring on the four floors. It will require 20,000 lbs. of paint to fix this building up the way Mr. Stanley wants it. The siding is put on in the Boston Hip style. No corner boards. Every other board laps out across the end of the one put in before. It took 40,000 feet of siding to side up this building. Taking the basement and attic, together with the first, second, and third floors, there are in this hotel 466 windows, 378 doors, and 289 rooms. According to the time put in on construction of this hotel and the number of men employed, it would take one man twenty-one years, nine months and twenty-six days, providing, of course, that he could handle all the heavy timbers and steel by himself, that has been put into it. . . .

Last but not least, there have been driven into this building 596,718,916 nails, figuring kegs and nails to the pound.

"We don't mean . . . that Estes Park is out of civilization or any thing of that kind," Boynton concluded. "But when one considers that "Estes Park is thirty-four miles from Longmont and Loveland, the two nearest cities on the C. and S. [Colorado and Southern], and twenty-two long miles from Lyons . . . , of course it would look queer to some people why so big a hotel as that would be built up there."[47]

Boynton was quite correct in his assumptions about location. But he neglected to say anything about F.O. Stanley's vision and about the automobile and auto tourism that made it all possible.

Steamers awaiting the arrival of the druggists, Loveland, Colorado, June 1909. Courtesy Estes Park Area Historical Museum.

The Druggists Arrive

Epsom salts, syrup of Squills,
We are the boys that roll the pills,
Huckleberry horse, huckleberry cow;
Estes, Estes! Rah! Rah! Rah![48]

The winter of 1908–1909 had been unusually cold in the mountains. Snows lingered well into June to an extent "unparalleled in the history of Estes Park."[49] Nevertheless, by June 22 the Stanley Hotel was ready, as promised, for its first guests, the members of the Colorado Pharmacal Association, who had agreed to come to Estes Park for their 20th annual meeting. At 10:40 that morning, 125 visiting conventioneers ("as jolly a bunch of druggists as ever constructed a pill or reached for a bottle of soothing syrup") arrived with their wives at the depot in Loveland aboard the Colorado and Southern. The partying had begun early. As soon as the train left Denver, carnival horns, squawkers, and "souvenirs galore" were passed out—"everything known to man that would make a teething baby jealous."[50]

The special coaches were met at the Loveland station by F.O. Stanley and a fleet of 22 gleaming Stanley Steamers, accompanied by a bevy of "beautifully gowned ladies," positioned there to act as hostesses. Before piling into the waiting steamers, the attention of the druggists was directed toward two bear cubs that had been placed on exhibition in a nearby shop window. The bears, the new arrivals were informed, had been captured by one of the auto drivers on his way to Loveland earlier that day. The driver had managed to escape, but not before their mother had "chewed large chunks out of the rear tires."[51]

The druggists were clearly still in a holiday mood. One of their number was quoted as chortling, "How dry I am, how dry I am; nobody knows how dry I am," before he "broke off."[52] (What the teetotaling Mr. Stanley thought of such behavior the surviving record does not say.)

Stanley personally supervised the loading of passengers and baggage, and then the cars lined up for a parade, almost three city blocks in length. It included a band, Loveland's mayor, and officials from the Loveland Retail Dealers' Association. After traveling about ten blocks, the parade halted at the corner of Fourth and Cleveland. There

Mayor McMullen delivered a formal welcome from "Loveland, the gateway to Estes Park," "where the soil seems pleased at the chance to make a poor man wealthy, a rich man religious and a druggist happy."[53] On that note, the caravan set off for Estes Park.

Once in the Big Thompson Canyon, the reason for the bear cubs soon became apparent. At a particularly sharp turn in the canyon, the lead car stopped to examine a set of strange tracks in the road, only to be confronted by a man in a teddy-bear suit, purchased from Harry H. Tammen's popular curio store in Denver:

> At a signal the driver of the car, who had been supplied with a gun by the committee[,] fired at the "bear," which would fall over as if dead. The driver was too busy to stop, of course, and the next car would witness the same performance. It was a feature of the entertainment that caused a great deal of excitement. The driver never failed to explain that this was such a common occurrence that no one noticed it any more.[54]

> Twenty-two different cars stopped at the sight of the tracks and the same performance occurred. For multiplicity of lives this old bear had a cat dead buried and its obituary published in the monthly papers. It developed later that two well-known druggists of Denver were standing behind the rocks and pulled the string when twenty-two different shots were fired.[55]

That was not the only prearranged feature of the trip. Further up the canyon, "Two druggists were stationed along the river and as each car passed they were both seen to pull ten-pound trout out of the roaring stream."[56] After lunch at Frank Alderdyce's Forks Hotel at Drake, where the steamers took on water, it was on to Estes Park.

The next morning the association held its opening session in the assembly hall of the Casino—a building "of remarkable acoustic properties and of dimensions approaching a good sized auditorium"—where F.O. Stanley himself delivered the greeting. "Perhaps I should say, brother druggists," he told his audience,

> as I hold here in my hand a card I received some time about last January, and it says that this is to certify that F.O. Stanley is a

member in good standing of the Colorado Pharmacal Association.

Now, I have had during my life inspirations and hopes; I have thought many times that I might be President of the United States some day, but I never dreamed that I should be a druggist in good standing, and a member of the Association.

After quoting several lines of verse from William Cullen Bryant about ancient "rock-ribbed" hills, "venerable woods," "complaining brooks," and green meadows, Stanley concluded his remarks by wel-' coming his guests on behalf of "the whole of the Park," graciously mentioning by name three of his fellow hotel-keepers.[57]

The next two days were a mixture of work and play, with prizes awarded for catching the most trout and to the winners of various games. Mr. Stanley was a most attentive host. During the second session on Thursday morning, while the druggists were meeting in the Casino, he conducted their wives on "an auto ride through the park," stopping at the Elkhorn Lodge, the new fish hatchery on Fall River, Stead's Hotel in Moraine Park, the English Hotel, and the Rustic Hotel in the north end. One afternoon, "there was a ball game between the druggists and salesmen. No one knows who won, as [association president] Fred Shaw of Denver batted the ball into the middle of the Big Thompson and the umpire refused to make a decision."[58] Thursday evening featured a banquet (the "pinnacle of jollification") and a grand ball.

The new hotel impressed everyone. One of those most appreciative was Mrs. C. M. Ford, who the following month described her visit for readers of the *Rocky Mountain Druggist*. Though her account is not without errors of fact, it is surprisingly comprehensive.

The strongest impression on entering the Stanley is the spacious-ness of its rotunda and artistic elegance of its furnishings. The floor coverings throughout the house, whether they be Axminster, Oriental or body Brussels, are of the finest and most luxurious quality as well as the most artistic combination of colors and design. The harmonious blending of red Axminster on the rotun-da floor with the mahogany of the woodwork and furnishings are pleasing to eye and sense. Great mahogany pillars support the beamed ceiling, while the massive stairway in the background, with its magnificent proportions, restful landings and graceful curves, strongly suggests the comfort and conveniences above.

The salon at the right of the rotunda and in the front of the house would gladden the heart of a Frenchman of Louis XVI time. . . . The room is fifty feet square. The side walls are done in pale green panels, framed in old carved ivory. The carpet an apple Axminster. The grand piano and furniture, which is made up of all appropriate shapes in harmony with the motif, are of the prevailing mahogany, and when upholstered are in pale green silk. The many windows are curtained with cream grenadine and lace, and altogether the room gives one a cool, refreshed feeling very grateful on a summer day.

Next to the salon is the rest room,[59] a trifle smaller than its neighbor. If there was one woman in our party who did not break the seventh commandment when she saw this room the writer failed to find her. The beams in the ceiling, the woodwork and furniture is dark green oak, while the panels on wall and ceiling are golden brown burlap. The fireplace, large enough to hold a tree, is made of green brick. "They say" the Oriental rug in this room cost $9,000, but to me it seemed a crime to put a money price on it, so beyond measuring was its beauty. A Christmas in the rest room with just the nearest and dearest ones would surely be of historical value to any family tree.

Next to the rest room and still in the south end of the house is the billiard room, the distinguishing feature of which is a cork floor. The seats around the walls of this elegant room are upholstered in dark green leather, which, judging by the number of occupants, are particularly comfortable. There are six large billiard tables, all completely equipped. The space between this room and the stairway is occupied by a writing room containing every appliance that the heart could wish from blotters to desks. The only wonder is that automatic brains are not furnished to power the pen, so thoughtfully were all the wants anticipated in this gem of a room.

Then the elevator, which is always in order, and an attendant who shares its amiability.

The stairway, office, and cigar stand complete the back of the rotunda and is each perfect in its appointments.

The telephone room, which is part of the office, is worth more than a passing mention. Each guest room has a telephone connection, and the dear little lady who presided at the desk surely deserves all praise for courteousness, patience and skilled service.

The dining room at the north end of the house, like every other apartment, is perfect of its kind. A hundred feet long, seventy-five feet wide, with most elegant electric features, cut glass, silver and every known embellishment to please eye or taste. Unlike the usual hotel dining room the floor is covered with an elegant Axminster in soft brown colors, a tribute to the eye and ear of the guest.

The unobtrusive recess for the musicians is another evidence of the fitness prevailing. The jewels in the case were worthy of setting, too, for the numbers played were invariably well rendered and discreetly selected. We confess to being a little old fashioned in musical taste and don't like a steady diet of ragtime, or, as later authority has it, "popular music." Maybe some of us looked the part of a back number. So be it.

The kitchen we are willing to take on faith, but knowing that things new do not always, or even often, run smoothly, we were willing to judge from results, and everything that came to us was satisfactory. The wonder was that we had any service at all, but to the credit of the management, we were well cared for. The electric fixtures in the dining room, of wrought iron, are twelve in number. Each chandelier has six strong lights and the seventy-two when turned on make a brilliant picture.

The cooking, laundry work and heating of the Stanley is all done by electricity—another instance of the progressive spirit of the owner.

The floors above, of which there are two, are arranged with wide corridors and rooms on either side—and all "outside" ones—each having two windows; and arranged en suite of two with a connecting hall and bath room either of which rooms may be disconnected at the wish of the guest. Each room is beautifully furnished, with tinted walls and mahogany doors, the latter with fret work of white enamel.

The carpets on the first floor, of luxurious Axminster, match in colorings the wall tints, while the furniture is an exact replica of the doors.

Stanley Hotel lobby, looking east toward "the Parlor" (Music Room), right and "the Rest Room" (Piñon Room), left. Courtesy Estes Park Area Historical Museum.

Every bed in the house is the best make of brass, while the beds themselves are so comfortable and "homey" as to make one sleep like one of the seven.

The rooms on the upper floor differ only in the floor coverings, which are body Brussels. We are told the number of rooms is only ninety, which in the near future, we prophesy, will be all too few. . . .

The Casino, situated about one hundred feet to the right of the main building, is large and commodious and equally adapted for dance or assembly hall, as occasion may require. A bowling alley connected with the Casino leaves nothing to be desired in the way of indoor entertainment, while the golf links and tennis court for the open-air athlete are beyond adverse criticism.

The garage, prodigally supplied with Stanleys, has room to spare for tourists who wish to bring their own cars.

The stables, stocked with horses trained to mountain fastnesses and all matter of vehicles, await the pleasure of the guests.

Stanley Hotel lobby, looking west toward the Dining Room. Courtesy Estes Park Area Historical Museum.

What wonder this spot is magnetically drawing the fastidious of the country! And surely the day is not far distant when Estes Park and the Stanley will be in the itinerary of all foreigners who are seeing the best of our resourceful country.[60]

Only one event marred the hotel's opening. It occurred, on Saturday, June 26, the day after the druggists' safe departure. F.O. Stanley was in the new laundry overseeing final construction and the installation of machinery, when he was overcome by the fumes from a nearby gasoline engine that was supplying power to the building. Collapsing into unconsciousness, Stanley was carried to his room and physicians were summoned. Though "for a time his life was despaired of, . . . the desperate efforts of the attending physicians finally pulled him through." F.O. Stanley quickly recovered.[61]

Nothing, however, could diminish or spoil the immensity of Stanley's achievement. "Today is the most notable day in the history of the village of mountaineers," the *Rocky Mountain News* announced on

June 23, "for with the opening of the Stanley Hotel Estes Park takes first rank with any resort in the world."[62] The News was certainly correct. Accommodations for what the *Longmont Ledger* described as "the monied class of people"—by which it meant those who could afford $5 a day—had come to Estes Park.[63] The era of the storied Stanley Hotel had begun.

Brochure, Hotel Stanley. From the collection of the Stanley Museum.

9

The Infrastructure of Estes Park

F.O. Stanley had already taken care of the first and most critical part the infrastructure needed for his new hotel: a reconstructed road up from the Burlington railhead at Lyons. But of equal importance to the long-term success of the entire enterprise was the infrastructure of Estes Park itself. Even as the planning and construction of the hotel were going forward, Stanley, working with and through others, had begun to lay the foundation for Estes Park's future: the town's first bank, first water company, and first hydroelectric plant. Later he would be instrumental in securing Estes Park's sewer system and first public golf course. The first three of these projects were incorporated within the brief span of seven months in 1908. The others followed within little more than a decade.

The Estes Park Bank

By 1907 the need for a bank to serve an increasingly large number of hotels, shops, and other business establishments had become obvious. Though F.O. Stanley rightly gets credit for originating the idea

Estes Park, 1908. Photograph deposited by Sidney W. Sherman in a time capsule during the building of his house in the spring of 1908. The tent in the lower left corner is the temporary headquarters of the Osborns' Loveland–Estes Park Transportation Company. Courtesy George Hix.

for the Estes Park Bank,[1] most of the work organizing the third chartered bank in Larimer County was left in the hands of others. The work was done by 46-year-old Sidney Willis Sherman, who had come to Estes Park from Michigan for his health that year, bringing with him, it turned out, considerable experience as cashier of a national bank in Grand Rapids.

We know comparatively little about Sherman,[2] who during the next four years played a key role in helping Stanley and others address Estes Park's infrastructure needs. He was clearly bright and hardworking and, for a time at least, had the confidence of Estes Park's leading citizens—F.O. Stanley, Frank Crocker, Cornelius Bond, Howard and Homer James, and Sam Service among them. By 1913, however, he was gone. Having become very much a part of the community, Sherman abruptly disappeared from the Estes Park scene, leaving others to carry out the responsibilities he had so well assumed.

For a number of months after his arrival, Sidney Sherman, clearly acting with the support of Stanley and others, actively promoted the idea of a bank, both in Estes Park and in the valley towns. Of the 36 individuals who initially agreed to purchase stock and become share-holders, a surprisingly large number, 11, were residents of Loveland—a tribute to that success. Sherman succeeded so well that by early 1908 he had received enough commitments toward the bank's $12,000 cap-italization to call an organizational meeting. That meeting was held in Estes Park village on February 20, 1908, at the Hupp Hotel. By that date, 119 of the original 120 shares of stock had been subscribed.

F.O. Stanley, as a sign of his interest and commitment in the new ven-ture, subscribed for five shares at a cost of $500.[3] Since he was winter-ing in Newton, he did not attend the meeting that officially organized the bank and selected its first officers. His absence scarcely mattered. That afternoon his fellow stockholders, the majority of whom were Estes Park residents and businessmen, proceeded to elect him not only to the seven-member board of directors but also as the bank's first pres-ident—a sign of the esteem and respect in which Stanley was held by the leading citizens of his adopted town.[4] Although he informed his fellow directors by letter the next month that he would serve as a direc-tor but declined the presidency, they refused to take his "no for an answer."[5] In the end, "F.O. Stanley, President" graced the letterhead of the Estes Park Bank for the next 11 years.

Sherman, who had put up $2,000 of his own money to become the bank's single largest stockholder,[6] was hired as its first cashier at an annual salary of $1,200. The one-story, 20 x 40–foot brick bank built that spring was located on Elkhorn Avenue, directly across the street from the Hupp Hotel, on land that had been the site of Estes Park's first schoolhouse. The two lots had been purchased from the Estes Park Town Company on February 15, 1908, just prior to the bank's first organizational meeting, for a price of $800.[7]

Construction work on the new building began almost at once, the contract going to Guy Smith for $1,627, a price that included the bank's 6 x 8 x 9–foot reinforced concrete vault. Smith moved ahead quickly. By the third week in May he had the job completed, and the building was formally accepted by the directors at their meeting of May 26, 1908. An opening was confidently planned and announced for June 1. Then came an unexpected delay. The specially made polished oak, ground glass, and iron grillwork fixtures and the desks and counters failed to arrive on schedule. Though any delay was disappointing because of the approaching tourist season, the bank's directors took full advantage of the situation. On Saturday, June 6, they opened the doors of their new building for a dance to which everyone in town was cordially invited.[8]

On Tuesday, June 16, the Estes Park Bank was finally ready for customers. "The new Estes Park bank has been authorized to begin business," the *Longmont Ledger* announced two weeks later. "Now we can put our stray dollars in for safe keeping."[9]

The bank was a financial success from the very beginning, and dividends of 6 to 12 percent were paid to shareholders virtually every year from 1910 to 1930. Sound banks are relatively unexciting. The Estes Park Bank was largely that. It easily survived the most trying moment of its early years: a brazen robbery in October 1920 during which thieves came through the roof, blew open the safe, and made away with $700 in cash and $1,700 in Liberty bonds. The job was a thorough one, so much so that the Larimer County sheriff was left to conclude that "experts" had been at work.[10]

Estes Park Bank. The figure in the doorway is Charles Hanscon, a part-time employee. Courtesy George Hix.

The Estes Park Water Company

Stanley's participation in the Estes Park Water Company was more direct, as was his stake in its success. By the summer of 1908, as the construction of the hotel advanced, it was clear that the original water system leading from Black Canyon Creek laid down by the Estes Park Town Company in 1906 was inadequate. Though at the time it was intended to "supply the demand for at least five or ten years," no one could have anticipated how quickly the growth of the town would render the system obsolete.

At their meeting that July at John Manford's new Manford Hotel on Elkhorn Avenue, the Town Company's officers confronted this reality. They decided to replace the old main with a new six-inch pipe and to build a new reservoir in the Black Canyon.[11] But as Cornelius H. Bond and the other officers of the Town Company also recognized, the need to install the new main, and the need for even "more extensive improvements," required the creation of a public utility capable of dealing with this problem and future ones in ways that a real estate development company simply could not.

Two months later, on September 17, 1908, F.O. Stanley, together with four others—Bond, John Y. Munson, Howard E. James, and J. R. Anderson—met to organize the Estes Park Water Company with capital stock of $20,000.[12] (The authorized stock was subsequently increased to $100,000 in October 1921, of which $60,000 was ultimately sold.) The new company was incorporated under Colorado law on October 7, 1908. By that date Donald MacGregor had replaced Anderson as a director. Sidney Sherman, who had recently been installed as cashier at the Estes Park Bank, was chosen to serve as secretary. The incorporation papers made the purpose of the company clear. It was to

> furnish the residents of Estes Park water for domestic, irrigation and power purposes and to obtain said water rights by purchase, appropriation or any other legal manner, and to purchase, construct and own all necessary property, such as reservoirs, ditches, flumes, pipe lines and office buildings, for storing, and conducting said water to the residents of Estes Park.[13]

The Estes Park Water Company's first project demonstrated why Stanley, Howard James, and Donald MacGregor were so actively involved. To increase the holding capacity of the system, it began the construction of two new concrete reservoirs—one 30 x 30 feet on the hillside above James's Elkhorn Lodge, the other 20 x 20 feet, north of the new Stanley Hotel—linked by a four-inch pipe.[14] The entire system was based on the continuing availability of water from the MacGregor ranch and Black Canyon Creek, requiring Donald MacGregor's consent. The new storage facilities, it was anticipated, would add some 100,000 gallons to the available supply of water, and make immediately possible the distribution of 6,000 to 7,000 feet of new main throughout the town.[15]

F.O. Stanley's name appeared first on the official certificate of incorporation. He was its major and controlling shareholder, and his involvement with the Estes Park Water Company would continue for two decades.[16] In December 1928 the company was sold to a group of four prominent Estes Park residents, Albert Hayden, Ralph Macdonald, Frank Grubb, and Charles Hix, for $33,900, in order, it was reported at the time, to prevent "outside parties from securing a controlling interest" and raising water fees exorbitantly.[17] The "outside party" was a relatively new resident, 32-year-old Charles Salit, president of Denver's Ice & Storage Company. Salit had purchased land in Devils Gulch, settled in, and then attempted to set himself up in a new business by purchasing the water company. Operating through an agent in Denver, he sent out a letter offering to buy the 331 outstanding shares of the company's stock for $100 each.[18] It was this action, and the threat they believed it implied, that apparently caused Hayden and the others to come forward.

Their purchase was only a temporary measure. Within a month the new owners approached the town trustees with a proposal to sell the water company to the Town of Estes Park for $73,260. The offer was accepted following an election held on June 10, 1929, and paid for by the subsequent issue of $75,000 in bonds.[19] The transaction effectively brought to an end the "threat" posed by Charles Salit and validated the good business sense of Albert Hayden and his three partners, who appear to have been well rewarded for their public spiritedness.

The Estes Park Electric Light and Power Company

Because it was so critical to his plan for a new "all-electric" hotel, F.O. Stanley single-handedly established the town's first hydroelectric plant on Fall River. Once in place, that plant quickly became critical as well to the expanding needs of the village of Estes Park, and would remain so for the next four decades.

Stanley's decision to use waterpower as opposed to coal was deliberate and calculated, and involved the careful weighing of economic trade-offs. Coal in 1907–1908 cost $12 a ton, a considerable amount. Moreover, it had to be delivered to Estes Park over roads that, however "improved," still posed their own uncertainties and risks. From an economic point of view the use of waterpower presented a better solution, though it brought with it problems of its own, some of them lingering.

While there had been public discussion for years about the possibility of harnessing the rich watersheds of Estes Park for power generation, F.O. Stanley once again played the role of pioneer. Securing the water rights to Fall River, presumably those that B. D. Sanborn had purchased in 1905 before the Dunraven acquisition,[20] Stanley broke ground for the new plant on October 9, 1908. The site chosen was an 80-acre tract on Fall River below Horseshoe Park, just above the new fish hatchery, three miles northwest of the village. There surveyors had located a flat terrace, some 10 to 15 feet above and 30 feet north of Fall River, on which they constructed a one-story, concrete-floored, 28-foot x 26¾-foot wooden frame building, to house both turbine and generator.

On October 28, 1908, shortly after the contract for the plant's construction was awarded, the articles of incorporation creating the Estes Park Light and Power Company were signed by the four individuals who were to serve as directors: Freelan O. Stanley; John Y. Munson and Cornelius Bond, both principals in the Estes Park Town Company; and Sidney W. Sherman, cashier of the Estes Park Bank. The capital stock was set at $20,000.[21]

When news of the power plant, and the fact that it would provide electricity to light both the hotel and the village, began to circulate, the press was appreciative. "When the season opens in Estes Park next summer," the *Longmont Call* predicted in November, "visitors will hardly know the town. F.O. Stanley is certainly all right."[22]

Though details of the plant's actual construction are sketchy, Stanley sought expertise from the consulting engineering firm of Vail, Walbran, and Read, located in Denver. Byron Hall, Stanley's chief assistant in such matters, did much of the work. The rough lumber for both the original power plant building and the adjacent two-bedroom operator's cottage was probably cut, like much of the lumber for the Stanley Hotel, at F.O. Stanley's mill in Hidden Valley or at the Griffith mill at Bierstadt Lake.[23] The original color of both the power plant and the operator's house was mustard yellow, matching the hotel. The concrete foundations were painted red.

In its heyday the power plant in its natural ponderosa pine setting was well landscaped and manicured. Though the technology of the generating equipment demanded the attention of the operator on a more or less regular basis, he still had time to look after the grounds, making Mr. Stanley's power plant a pleasant place for tourists to stop during a visit to the fish hatchery or on their way up Fall River Road to Horseshoe Park and, later, to the new Rocky Mountain National Park.

The equipment that Stanley ordered was state-of-the-art. It consisted of a 200-kilowatt/2,300-volt, horizontal shaft Western Electric Synchronous Generator, powered by a Denver-built HUG waterwheel (of a Pelton type) and a slate-and-marble, brass-controlled switchboard. Water to drive the turbine came from an intake pipe located on the north bank of Fall River at Cascade Lake, an earth-and-log dam and diversion 5,300 feet upriver from the plant. From there the water moved through a buried 18- and 20-inch riveted steel pipe to a spot some 400 feet lower than its source. It was estimated at the time that the "minimum summer fall of the stream" would produce 400 h.p. of energy.[24] The original pipeline (the Hondius-Cascade Pipe Line) had been built by Pieter Hondius and Fred L. Clerc, who deeded it, together with the water rights and right-of-way across Hondius's land, to Stanley in November 1908.

The completion of the plant, which cost an estimated $69,000,[25] was a nip-and-tuck affair. There were formidable problems. Just getting the plant's big generator to Estes Park required that a team of horses be hitched behind the wagon so that the teams in front would not be literally pulled from the road on sharp turns. With less than two weeks to go before the druggist convention arrived in June—an event that had been booked and advertised since at least the previous

Fall River Power Plant. The original hydro unit, following the Lawn Lake Flood of 1982. Lew Dakan photo. From the Stanley Museum collection.

January—the generator and its turbine were still being installed.[26] To the relief of everyone, and no one more so than its owner, the lights of the Stanley Hotel were turned on for the very first time on the opening night of the convention. The "effect was marvelous," the *Loveland Herald* reported, "so numerous are the lights. They will be turned on at Elkhorn Lodge and over the whole city in a short time."[27]

Though most of the problems connected with the power plant came later, there was one serious early disruption. According to Laurence Thomson, whose father superintended the nearby fish hatchery, shortly before the hotel reopened after the pharmacist convention (Thomson gives the date as July 4, 1909), a good-sized rock became lodged in the final section of the intake pipe. When the operator went to open the pipe and start the plant that morning, Thomson recalled, the intake pipe buckled and then burst, throwing a stream of water directly into the power plant:

Fortunately, the windows had not been put in permanently and the doors opened out, so that the water just entered and rushed out. Of course, the plant couldn't be operated and the hotel was without electricity for lights and other uses. . . . I spent days trying to do what I could to get rid of the water so that the plant could be put into operation.[28]

It was equally fortunate that this event occurred after the departure of the pharmacists and before the Stanley Hotel opened again to receive its first regular summer guests.

The plant on Fall River was perfectly balanced and highly efficient, and though the electrical output was small, so too was the amount of water it used. Visitors were impressed at Stanley's achievement and the technology that made it possible. One of the more important and influential visitors was John Willy, the veteran editor of the *Hotel Monthly*, the leading publication of its kind in the world.

Willy, who began his term as editor in 1892, was for more than half a century the acknowledged barometer of the industry. Moreover he was particularly fond of Estes Park. Between 1888 and 1921, Willy made "seven or eight" visits, and after several of them, reported to his readers on the changes he observed in the local resort industry. Nothing he saw caused more comment than the Stanley Hotel and its "electrical service," which, he told his readers in July 1910, was "more varied . . . than any other hotel in the world."[29] The power plant itself, he added, was "one of the sights of the park."

When Willy returned to the subject the following month, it was to provide the best contemporary account we have of the hotel's all-electric interior—a world to which most guests were never introduced. Willy began with the kitchen and its "novelties":

The kitchen of Hotel Stanley is out of the ordinary. In describing this kitchen it is well to bear in mind that, not alone is the roasting, frying, broiling and toasting done by electricity, but that all the hot water and steam is produced by electricity generated by water power. Also it is well to bear in mind that the articles of kitchen equipment are, as a rule, but slightly changed in appearance from those we are accustomed to see; for the skill of the inventor has adapted electrical energy to serve the cookers in their old forms, except that he has done away with coal, wood, charcoal, ashes, gas and hot steam pipes, and made the kitchen for the workers.[30]

The detail that Willy provides could only have come from an industry professional:

> The greatest departure from the customary kitchen equipment, so far as appearances go, is the Range. In the Hotel Stanley kitchen . . . the roasting ovens have heating units at top and bottom, each controlled by a three-heat regulating switch, so that heat for quick, slow or medium cooking can be obtained at will by simply turning the particular controlling switch; and, too, the cooking can be done with scientific accuracy.[31]

Willy's account continues at a leisurely pace, with comments on the hot plates, controlled by three-heat switches; the carving table with its underneath heating units; the 20-gallon vegetable and stock kettles, each with its own three-heat, bottom-mounted heating unit; the battery of urns; and even the hotel's "automatic Egg Boiler (Wrought Iron Range Co.'s Victor) . . . equipped with three heating units."[32]

After touring the bake shop in the hotel's basement with its 120-loaf-capacity oven, Willy moved on to describe, in somewhat less detail, the electric system that provided steam and hot water for the laundry, kitchen, bathrooms, and other purposes—a system that gave the Stanley Hotel much of its claim to superiority and uniqueness. Here there were other Stanley firsts. Perhaps most significant was the laundry, "the only steam laundry in the world where all the power is electrically produced."[33]

Where John Willy's description of the hotel's heating system leaves off, an unnamed writer for *Electrical World* begins. The two-page account of the "Electric Steam Boiler and Water Heaters at Estes Park, Col.," which appeared in the December 1910 issue, intended for industry professionals, made the innovative nature of Stanley's contribution clear enough. The steam used for the washing machines and mangle, the writer carefully explained, was generated by a 95-kilowatt electric boiler constructed especially for the Stanley Hotel by the General Electric Company—"doubtless the largest similar apparatus ever built."[34]

Measuring six feet in height and three feet in diameter, the 95-kilowatt electric boiler was capable of bringing cold water to steam to the required level of 60 pounds of pressure per square inch in about 40 minutes. What made the boiler technically advanced were its insides, which consisted of 85 dead-ended tubes, arranged in rows, each about one-and-a-half inches in diameter and five inches in length. Each of these tubes, in turn, contained its own one-kilowatt, 110-volt heating unit. A small but critical feature of these elements was the fact that they were formed of special zinc link-fuses rather than lead ones, making them able to withstand the high temperatures inside the boiler.[35]

Such things were of great interest to F.O. Stanley. It was precisely in the attention that he gave to details such as these, many of which bear the mark of his own ingenuity and inventiveness, that Stanley's reputation as a technological pioneer rests.

Besides the steam boiler in the laundry, Stanley installed four additional heaters in his hotel complex to supply hot water to its buildings and to the laundry itself. A 600-gallon heating tank, located in the basement of the main hotel building, had enough capacity to provide hot water for 120 baths at one time, and also to pipe water "to small hot-water radiators in the private bathrooms, intended for emergency use on chilly mornings during the hotel season."[36]

The other heating tanks were smaller. A 200-gallon tank furnished "all hot water for washing and cleaning purposes in the kitchen," while a similar-sized tank in the laundry supplied "all the needs of that place, in conjunction with the steam boiler, besides furnishing hot water for the employees' quarters which are above." The fourth heating tank, with a capacity of 400 gallons, provided hot water for the baths and lavatories in the new "manor house," then under construction. That building, the author explained, "is smaller than the main summer building, and will remain open throughout the year."[37]

Stanley was pleased with his electric water-heating system, which he concluded was "an entire success" after a two-month trial. The "problem of hot-water supply has been completely solved," he told *Electrical World*. "Twenty kilowatts for the 600-gal. tank has proved ample. The laundry is delightfully cool, and the temperature of the steam boiler does not rise above blood heat, in spite of carrying 60 lb. pressure inside."[38]

As on other occasions, Stanley was more than willing to improve upon his success. Local demand for electricity from residents increased, and by 1913 he was faced with a choice of either enlarging the power plant or building a new steam plant at the hotel. By then, however, the price of coal delivered to Estes Park had dropped, and Stanley decided that a steam plant at the hotel made better financial sense. A new plant with fire tube boiler, tall metal smokestack, and whistle was constructed to the west of the main hotel building, north of the pond and icehouse. Once in service, it provided heat and hot water for the entire Stanley complex, decreasing the hotel's reliance on electricity from the plant on Fall River.

There were problems with the original power plant almost from the beginning. Throughout the first years of its operation, when Alfred Lamborn, manager of the Stanley Hotel, had oversight responsibilities over the hotel, the plant was plagued not only by inadequacy of equipment but also by winter weather, which so greatly reduced the flow of water in Fall River that service from the hydro unit was restricted to only a few hours a day.

There were other annoyances as well. One was the lack of meters to measure the use of electricity by subscribers. This problem, however, was by no means unique to Estes Park, and was easily overcome by the well-tested expedient of collecting revenue through the direct sale of lightbulbs. Another annoyance was the fact that electric clocks would not work in Estes Park. Here ingenuity provided no remedy. Like many early hydro plants, Mr. Stanley's power plant was simply unable to maintain a steady flow of electrical current.

The major problem remained the periodic lack of water in Fall River. In retrospect, Stanley's choice of a site for his plant had been less than ideal. In 1909, however, the Fall River location, which was both accessible and available, made good sense. Stanley had originally intended that his hotel would operate only during the summer months. Therefore it was only necessary to find a location that guaranteed sufficient water flow on a seasonal basis. But once electricity was available, the kerosene and gasoline lamps to which the residents of Estes Park and their visitors had grown more or less accustomed seemed unnecessarily rustic and old-fashioned. They too wanted the convenience of electric lighting and asked to tap into Stanley's new power supply.

F.O. Stanley proved obliging and generous. Initially the total demand for electricity was small, and though winters restricted service, the plant could accommodate customers on a more or less year-round basis. In the years before 1917, when the town of Estes Park was incorporated, Stanley even took care of the streetlighting needs of the village for free.[39] No one, however, could have anticipated the dramatic increase in demand which came in the next decade from the town's growing number of commercial and residential users, not to mention the demand caused by the building of outlying summer cottages. Had he realized such things, F.O. Stanley might have designed and sited his power plant differently.

Had the power plant been "located in the village," the *Estes Park Trail* noted in April 1924, "it would have ten times the water for operation over its present location, and if it was located where Loveland's new plant is to be located [at the mouth of the Big Thompson Canyon] it would have nearly twenty times the water for operation." Even in its present location, the *Trail* assured its readers, "the Estes Park water power plant 'is a decided success' and gives 'good service.'"[40] Such testimonials did not, however, bring an end to complaints.

In October 1921, in an attempt to improve hydro-generating efficiency, a second generator and turbine were installed at a cost of $17,000. Both of these new units were housed in a room approximately 16 x 15½ feet in size, which was added off the northwest corner of the original plant.[41] This 680-kilowatt General Electric generator and 900-h.p. Worthington Francis type turbine unit "was truly 'bigger than the stream,'"[42] meaning that its capacity was far larger than the source of water that turned the blades of the turbine. It could only produce power from May through September. But since the Stanley Hotel and the adjacent town of Estes Park were only fully occupied during the summer months, the new hydro unit provided an effective short-term solution to the power shortage.[43]

The problem of Fall River remained. By 1922, additional demands upon the system had become so pressing, and complaints about the "miserable service" in winter were again so great, that Stanley spent an additional $48,000 to raise the dam at Cascade Lake by five feet (to a height of 17 feet). This created more water storage capacity and thus increased the flow of water. He also put in a new 24-inch, wooden-stave pipeline wrapped with wire, and rebuilt the transmission lines between the plant and the village.[44]

Despite such efforts and the expense that went with them, the plant's problems lingered well into the 1930s, long after it had passed

Fall River Power Plant. The Fairbanks Morse diesel unit, installed in 1931. Courtesy Denver Public Library, Western History Collection.

from F.O. Stanley's hands into those of the Public Service Company of Colorado. Though demand continued to grow, no new attempt to improve winter service was made until January 1931. Then a 50-h.p. Fairbanks Morse diesel engine and 32-kilowatt generator were added for use when the water level in Fall River forced the plant to cut back operation of its two hydro units. To accommodate the new equipment, the power plant building was once again enlarged, this time by constructing a 20 x 15–foot addition on the western side of the original structure.[45]

The new diesel generator helped, but it too was insufficient. In February 1933 the level of water in Fall River once again made it impossible to run the two hydro units for more than a few hours a day. Even with the new diesel "in operation night and day," the Public Service Company could not meet demand. In desperation the company turned to the Western Conference of the YMCA and obtained permission to overhaul and put into service the old steam plant on their property.

The YMCA equipment mostly stood idle, used only for backup purposes since 1927 when the conference was connected to the Stanley Light and Power Company. The Y was then closed during the winter months, with only a watchman in residence; to reach the plant the company was forced to ask the National Park Service to break open the road with its big new rotary plow.[46] To operate the old YMCA plant, water had to be hauled in from the village, a distance of eight miles, and coal had to be trucked in from Lyons, a distance of more than 30 miles, underscoring the seriousness of the situation.[47]

The lessons of that winter were clear; by October 1933, plans had been developed to add a second diesel-driven generator by expanding the existing diesel room across the rear, or Fall River side, of the original power plant. Because of a recovering winter water supply and the financial realities of the Depression years, this 300-h.p. Fairbanks Morse engine and its 200-kilowatt generator were not actually acquired and placed in operation until 1938.[48]

Though no formal records of operation and cost were kept until 1916, the Stanley power plant, even with its successive alterations, never made much money. According to Byron Hall, who helped construct the original plant and served as its manager for more than 20 years, the income from subscribers during the early years did not cover taxes and the interest on Stanley's original investment, let alone the cost of operation and maintenance.[49] Each year F.O. Stanley simply made up the difference out of his own pocket.

Getting the original power plant built and keeping it in repair and operation were difficult. Equally, if not more, difficult, as it turned out, was securing another buyer. When the plant was finally sold on June 1, 1928, to Public Service of Colorado, F.O. Stanley and the entire Estes valley breathed a sigh of relief.[50] Though the sale itself hardly brought an end to the plant's problems, they were no longer F.O. Stanley's direct concern.

Over time the village of Estes Park would have developed and expanded its basic infrastructure to meet the ever-increasing demand of both residents and tourists. Thanks to F.O. Stanley's initiative, cooperation, and money, that infrastructure came sooner, and was substantially better, than the town would have put in place on its own. Yet when it came to taking credit for his efforts, Stanley habitually backed away.

Though F.O. had numerous opportunities to take credit himself, he used such occasions to deflect it to others and to find ways to celebrate the achievements of the community at large. In June 1910, for example, during a visit by the Rocky Mountain Hotel Association whose members had come to the mountains of Estes Park for their annual outing, the luncheon conversation turned to the quality of the roads in the valley itself. Stanley, asked to speak to the issue, chose instead to lecture the hotelmen about the "the harmony that prevails in the Park":

> You may hunt this United States all over and not find another place where all are working so harmoniously together. What is the result? Good roads. A fish hatchery that is one of the best in the United States, built and maintained by private subscription, the money mostly raised by the ladies in the Park. We have many other good things. You can take this as an example of what can be done.[51]

Though Stanley might well have mentioned that he himself had been one of the hatchery's largest single contributors, he did not. This was simply F.O. Stanley's way.

The host of the day, W. G. Edwards of the Rustic Hotel, did not, however, let Stanley's remarks pass without comment, making sure to point out to the newcomers just where much of this spirit of community cooperation originated. "He paid a glowing tribute to Mr. Stanley," the *Hotel Monthly* reported the next month, "who, he said, had not done a solitary thing which has interfered with any other hotelkeeper in the Park; and he has greatly benefited the Park by being in their midst."[52]

The Estes Park Sewerage Association

What Estes Park appreciated most about its most famous summer resident was the fact that when things civic needed to be done, F.O. Stanley was there to do them, always with money, and usually in some sort of leadership role. In September 1909, for example, the need arose for a new sewerage system. Stanley, Dr. Homer James, and Sam Service were appointed by the new Estes Park Sewerage Association to identify "the best route of the sewer." Once this was accomplished, Stanley located the new line in Stanley Meadows below the hotel,[53] an area now largely covered by Lake Estes. In 1935, Stanley formally donated this land to the town.[54]

Estes Park in 1909 was responding to a crisis. A lawsuit had been filed the previous year by the City of Loveland to protect the integrity of its water supply (*The People of the State of Colorado vs. the Hupp Hotel*) by halting "at once . . . sewerage from flowing into the Big Thompson." The hotel won in the county courts. But Loveland appealed, and by January 1911, even with the new sewer in place, the suit had reached the Colorado Supreme Court. That same month, no doubt as a signal to the court that the Estes Park community recognized the extent of its problem, Cornelius H. Bond, Carl Piltz, Benton R. Bonnell, Sam Service, and James W. McMullen incorporated the Estes Park Sewer Company, with capital stock of $5,000, divided into 5,000 shares.[55]

That same month, January 1911, Estes Park received help from its downstream neighbor. The Loveland City Council voted to purchase $500 in stock in the Estes Park Sewer Company toward the installation of yet another sewer system, estimated to cost about $3,000. The new system allowed sewage to be piped a half mile east of Estes Park to a ditch that would carry it to "a point farther north on the Stanley meadow." There the sewerage could be dispersed into a gravel bed and dry out. This ended the lawsuit.[56]

By September 1914, however, the issue of polluting the Big Thompson was back in full force, with several members of the Loveland City Council charging that "the ditch was never constructed [by Estes Park] as promised." A mass meeting of Loveland citizens followed, during which it was "officially reported that Estes Park will take such steps as Dr. Morgan [state health officer] recommended for proper sanitation and that a septic tank will in all probability be installed to receive sewerage at the outlet near the river. A private tank will be installed at Stead's hotel."[57]

It was an issue that would not go away. For some reason the promised septic tank was not installed, and by September 1915, Loveland was again aroused, this time with rumors about typhoid. Water samples had been taken and new charges of "negligence" raised. The system in Stanley Meadows was not working. A visit to Estes Park revealed that the bank of Fall River, "back of the Hupp hotel and extending to the Monroe livery this side of the bridge, is a veritable dumping ground and is a menace to the health of those who derive their water supply from the river."[58]

Citing a "breach of trust on the part of the Estes Park authorities" because "the city's subscription to stock in the Estes Park Sewer Co. was made on the understanding that it would protect Loveland from having the water polluted," there was talk of contributing funds so that proceedings could be immediately instituted "to carry the case thru the highest courts if necessary." The *Loveland Daily Herald* told its readers on September 23,

> It is probable that the city will take such action, and in view of existing conditions it is predicted that charges will be preferred against the sewer company which will involve practically all hotel proprietors and business men of Estes Park.[59]

Again there was a remedy: the construction of a second filter basin at a cost of some $2,000, and the installation of a septic tank. A meeting was held in Estes Park, presided over by Alfred Lamborn,

Stanley's manager. C. H. Bond was the chief spokesman for the sewer company. Bond explained carefully that the sewer outlet was a full 950 feet from the Big Thompson, and that his own analysis of the water suggested that Loveland's problem came not from Estes Park but from farther down the river, "right in the city's [Loveland's] storage and filter basins." Bond continued, "I was on the Loveland council when the water system was built," he continued, "and I contended then and have since that sooner or later they would have trouble with the water." Nevertheless, he concluded with accommodation, "we stand ready up here to do our share in making things right." A new septic tank "can probably be done at a moderate expense, but this is not an incorporated town and there are comparatively few here to bear the cost."[60]

In October 1917, when the system again needed to be expanded, F.O. Stanley met with the town trustees and gave permission to allow for the installation on his land of a larger Imhoff tank, of the type "being used at the government army cantonments and which is being installed at the army recuperation camp in Denver." The following April, the town fathers then asked Stanley to contribute $1,000 toward the $8,000 cost of its construction. Presumably he contributed.

The new system was built farther back from the Big Thompson in a bed of gravel "for perfect filtration." Its installation was doubtless hurried along by the fact that Estes Park was visited in January of that year by a Larimer County grand jury "to see whether or not the demands of the city of Loveland regarding the disposal of sewerage . . . are being complied with in this section."[61] They apparently left satisfied, for there were no indictments.

The Golf Course and Garbage Dump

On two more occasions before 1921, F.O. Stanley made his public presence felt. The first occurred in 1916. By that date it had become clear that the nine-hole golf course at the Stanley Hotel could no longer meet the needs of Estes Park residents and summer visitors. Another, larger course was needed. Stanley's response was to join forces with Frank L. Woodward and Thomas B. Stearns of Denver, two civic-minded men of wealth who also happened to be longtime

At the Rocky Mountain Hotel Association meeting, June 1910. The photograph was taken for Hotel Monthly. *Left to right: James Stead of Stead's Ranch in Moraine Park, Howard James of Elkhorn Lodge, F. O. Stanley and Alfred Lamborn of the Stanley Hotel, and W. G. Edwards of the Rustic Hotel. From the collection of James H. Pickering.*

summer residents of Estes Park.[62] The three men formed a syndicate and purchased 120 acres of land from Carl Sanborn for $20,000 for a new "model" 18-hole course.[63]

The property selected for the new course stood directly in front of the site of the old Estes Park Hotel and encompassed much of the same ground above Fish Creek on which the Earl of Dunraven had laid out a nine-hole course shortly after opening his hotel in 1877. Said to have been among the very first in Colorado, it was reportedly designed with the help of "a golf expert from Scotland."[64]

Once the purchase had been completed, Stanley and the others immediately placed responsibility in the hands of local golf enthusiasts. By November 1916, Joe Mills, Howard James, and Albert Hayden had organized the Estes Park Country Club, had sold $15,000 worth of stock to 30 residents, and were preparing to erect a log clubhouse "with monster fireplaces abounding" and lay out a new 6,000-yard, par 73 course to be ready for the 1918 season. Also projected were a café to be operated during the season and "facilities for tennis, dancing and many other amusements."

Golf at the Stanley Hotel. Courtesy of the Estes Park Area Historical Museum.

Though the supporting amenities were never fully achieved, the golf course itself was formally opened for play on July 4, 1918. That summer, and for many years, it hosted a number of well-attended tournaments with individuals and teams from the valley towns participating.[65]

Stanley's second public intervention during this period came five years later, in 1921. The town of Estes Park needed a place to dispose of its refuse, and once again F.O. Stanley came forward. This time it was to provide land "hidden from public view and yet accessible." Stanley's only stipulation was that the "town would take the proper care of the rubbish dumped."[66]

Stanley's motives were largely altruistic. It is true that the hotel needed access to a trustworthy sewerage disposal system, adequate enough to allay fears about pollution from residents along the Big Thompson and in Loveland. It is also true that the decision to allow Estes Park to use his land for that purpose cost him little or nothing. But the golf course transaction had little to do with the direct success of the Stanley Hotel. Moreover the money came directly out of his own pocket. Stanley, an avid bowler and an expert at pool and billiards, rarely played golf.

No civic good purpose seemed too small to attract F.O. Stanley's interest or energy. In September 1912, Stanley chaired a meeting called to promote a proposal for a new Fall River road over the Continental Divide, during which the conversation turned to the "real need of beautifying the village of Estes Park." After Stanley rose to speak, indicating that "the first and most important condition to be met was to keep the streets CLEAN," it was suggested "that a committee of ladies would be most influential in bringing about the desired conditions." F.O. Stanley promptly appointed a committee of five.[67]

Such gestures were not casual or perfunctory: they expressed Stanley's sense of stewardship. "I felt confident when the movement was started last fall at the meeting we had," he wrote from Newton on June 9, 1913, to Dorothy Schwartz of Estes Park, presumably one of the ladies he had appointed, that if we could get the ladies interested, that we should have a new era of cleanliness in Estes Park, and I am of course more than delighted to learn that the movement is so successful.

Nature has made Estes Park one of the most beautiful places in the world, and we should fall short of our duty and responsibility if we failed to make it the cleanest pleasure resort in the world. With the pure air and perfect water supply, we could make Estes Park as famous for health conditions, as it is for its scenery.

You may tell the good women of Estes Park that they can rely on me at all times for assistance in every reasonable manner, to aid them in continuing the work so well begun.[68]

You can "rely on me at all times": the respect that F.O. Stanley earned for such efforts, and for the attitude and sense of commitment they expressed, was enormous. It was so great, in fact, that his fellow citizens willingly made allowances for some of Stanley's well-known foibles—even when it came to his habit of leaving his car in the middle of busy Elkhorn Avenue (where by August 1923, parking was limited to two hours). "Everyone knew they had to detour around it," Bertha Ramey recalled, "because Mr. Stanley had the right to park wherever he wanted to."[69]

10

The Coming of Rocky Mountain National Park

The passage of this bill is the crowning result of one of the best organized and most efficiently managed campaigns ever conducted by Colorado people to obtain any benefit for the state.
—*Rocky Mountain News,* January 16, 1915[1]

The idea for what would become Rocky Mountain National Park began with a suggestion made at the October 1907 meeting of the Estes Park Protective and Improvement Association, an organization of landowners committed to promoting both conservation and recreation. The speaker on that occasion was Herbert N. Wheeler, newly appointed head of the Medicine Bow National Forest. Two years earlier the forest preserve had been extended south from Wyoming by President Roosevelt to embrace the wilderness west of Estes Park. Wheeler had recently established his Forest Service headquarters in the village, and residents were interested in having the opportunity to hear his thoughts about a subject of widespread—not to mention local—interest.

"If you want to draw tourists," Wheeler later repeated what he told his audience, "you should establish a game refuge where tourists can see the wild life."[2] Pressed for what he had in mind, Wheeler produced a map showing an area of over 1,000 square miles extending west from the village. F.O. Stanley may well have attended that meeting, for he was in Estes Park that month overseeing the construction of his hotel. Whether in attendance or not, he was in sympathy with the organization's goals and soon would be one of its most vigorous and active supporters.

The preserve idea, as might be expected, drew a positive response. Estes Park's residents had grown increasingly alarmed by the scarcity of big game and by the general mistreatment of wildlife and the wilderness by visitors. The Estes Park Protective and Improvement Association (EPPIA), initially founded in 1895[3] "to prevent the destruction of the fish in the rivers of the Park, the illegal killing of game, and the destruction of the timber by camp fires,"[4] was revitalized in 1906 with new bylaws and F.O. Stanley's involvement. The organization's concerns were well founded. By the turn of the century the local elk population, which had once drawn hunters to Estes Park from as far away as England, was virtually depleted. Other indigenous animals fared little better, for in response to the angry cries of ranchers the State of Colorado routinely paid bounties for the skins of mountain lions, wolves, and coyotes.

Local rivers and streams were equally in danger. There continued to be visitors, as well as residents, who thought nothing of demonstrating their fishing prowess by catching trout in as large a quantity as possible, and of any size. Fish, however, could be restocked, a cause that led in 1907 to the establishment of a good-sized fish hatchery on Fall River, made possible by a local subscription that raised $3,352 and to which F.O. Stanley himself contributed one of its three ponds.[5] In 1909 the association donated an additional $2,000 to build a house for its resident manager. Under the supervision of Superintendent Gaylord H. Thomson, the hatchery soon became one of the best in the state and a major attraction for tourists.

Absent from the meeting at which Wheeler spoke was Enos A. Mills (1870–1922), the owner of Longs Peak Inn. Mills was then serving as a lecturer for the Forest Service and already on his way to becoming Colorado's leading advocate for the wilderness. Hearing about Wheeler's suggestion, Mills wrote to inquire where the boundaries for such a preserve might be located. Wheeler's response clear-

F. O. Stanley at the Fish Hatchery on Fall River. From the collection of the Stanley Museum.

ly hit a responsive chord, and by October 1908 the *Loveland Reporter* indicated that Mills and Stanley were "actively working" together on the project. Of the "millionaire" Stanley, the *Reporter* specifically noted, "the idea of making the park a national one, involving greater benefits to state, district and incidentally himself appealed to him."[6]

Little more is heard about the Wheeler proposal until the June 1909 meeting of the Estes Park Protective and Improvement Association, when a committee of two, consisting of Enos Mills and Freelan Stanley, was appointed to study the matter further.[7] Their report was emphatically positive, for at its September meeting the Association voted unanimously to seek the creation of the Estes National Park and Game Preserve along the general lines that Wheeler had suggested.[8]

F.O. Stanley would continue to be an active member of the Estes Park Protective and Improvement Association during the years that followed. Having served as the organization's president in 1906, he was elected a director in August 1912 and again in 1913.[9] In August 1912 he hosted an association benefit at the Casino on behalf of "good roads and trails." It was subsequently reported, "About twenty-five couples took part in the grand march led by Mr. Stanley and Mrs. Lamborn [wife of hotel manager Alfred Lamborn] looking very beautiful as summer."[10] Two years later Stanley was appointed to yet another association committee, this time to look into ways of further protecting the purity of the town's water supply.[11]

Enos Mills, who left the Forest Service in May 1909, immediately made the cause of this new national park his own, authoring a forceful manifesto, which became his platform:

> Around Estes Park, Colorado, are mountain scenes of exceptional beauty and grandeur. In this territory is Longs Peak and one of the most rugged sections of the Continental Divide of the Rockies. The region is almost entirely above the altitude of 7,500 feet, and in it are forests, streams, waterfalls, snowy peaks, great canons, glaciers, scores of species of wild birds, and more than a thousand varieties of wild flowers.
>
> In many respects this section is losing its wild charms. Extensive areas of primeval forests have been misused and ruined; saw-mills are humming and cattle are in the wild gardens! The once numerous big game has been hunted out of exis-

tence and the picturesque beaver are almost gone.

These scenes are already extensively used as places of recreation. If they are to be permanently and more extensively used and preserved, it will be necessary to hold them as public property and protect them within a national park.[12]

In the next months, Mills turned to what he did best, writing letters and articles and giving interviews and speeches, all directed to building a broad base of public support. In time that coalition would include such powerful and influential organizations as the American Civic Association; the Sierra Club; the Colorado Mountain Club; the General Federation of Women's Clubs; the Daughters of the American Revolution; the Colorado legislature; the state Democratic and Republican organizations; the Denver Chamber of Commerce; business and civic organizations in Boulder, Larimer, and Grand Counties; and most of Colorado's newspapers. To the extent there was significant opposition, it came, predictably enough, from mining, grazing,

Charles Evans Hughes, Enos A. Mills and F.O. Stanley. Photo by Stuart Mace. Courtesy Enos Mills Cabin collection.

timber, and water interests who argued against "locking up nature" by restricting the amount of public land available for commercial use. Aided by the enthusiastic endorsement in January 1913 of Robert Marshall of the United States Geological Survey, the peripatetic Mills pushed himself to the brink of exhaustion by seeing to its conclusion a campaign that lasted a full six years, during which he made more than 300 appearances across the nation.

As a native of rural Maine, F.O. Stanley appreciated mountains, streams, lakes, and forests, and understood the importance of conservation and preservation. Though he seldom abandoned himself to the wilderness with the enthusiasm of Enos Mills, and made only one known attempt to climb a major mountain,[13] he and Flora were appreciative of nature. Stanley enjoyed it enough, in fact, that in June 1908 he purchased two bear cubs from Jim McCall and Byron Hall of Lyons, who had captured them after the death of their mother. Perhaps in imitation of Enos Mills, who in 1903 had exhibited two grizzly cubs, the famous Johnny and Jenny, at Longs Peak Inn, Stanley put his bears on display at his home in Estes Park, on one occasion bringing them down to a bazaar in the village "to help make a collection of wild animals."[14] The cubs were a way of proving to tourists, he is quoted as saying, "that the inroads of civilization have not yet obliterated all the original dwellers from their wild haunts in the fastnesses of the Rockies."[15]

That summer, at least one of those "tourists," the editor of the *Longmont Ledger*, on a day trip through Estes Park, made a point of visiting the cubs at the Stanleys' home "Rockside."[16] By the following April, however, the novelty of the thing had worn off. While Mills had shipped Johnny and Jenny to the Denver Zoo, where they were displayed for many years, Mr. Stanley gave his bears to Thomas Young, manager of the Dunraven ranch, "to look after."[17]

F.O. Stanley was ultimately a realist, which did not always place him with the majority. When the Estes Park Protective and Improvement Association took up a subscription in 1913 to underwrite the cost of reintroducing the elk by bringing a small herd from Yellowstone, F.O. Stanley seems to have been the only one to voice a reservation, albeit facetiously. Writing from Newton on March 20, 1913, he told Pieter Hondius, president of the EPPIA and the project's chief architect, "From what I learn about the elk, I am afraid Estes Park will be over-

Lyons, Colorado. Returning the elk to Estes Park. From the collection of James H. Pickering.

Elk in a Stanley Mountain Wagon. Courtesy Estes Park Area Historical Museum.

run with animals of that kind, and we may have to get Roosevelt up there to help reduce the number."[18] His voice, serious or not, was prophetic. Unfortunately, by the time most residents were willing to admit that Stanley had probably been right, Teddy Roosevelt was no longer available to come to their aid.

Whatever his initial skepticism, Stanley finally gave the project his active support. He doubtless contributed money, and when the animals finally arrived in Estes Park by way of Lyons, having been brought up the North St. Vrain road in Stanley Mountain Wagons equipped with special covered crates, he obligingly allowed the herd to be pastured behind the Stanley Hotel prior to its release. "One of the interesting sights for tourists in Estes Park, which will be new even to former visitors," the *Estes Park Trail* noted in June 1913, "is a herd of about twenty-five elk, which can be observed any day grazing in what has been rechristened the Stanley Elk Park."[19] What the *Trail* did not say was that the elks' stay in Stanley's pasture was not for the purpose of display, but rather to acclimatize the animals so they would know where to return for food should the winter prevent sufficient foraging.

The rapport that F.O. Stanley established with Enos Mills before and during the park campaign was undeniable. On most issues Stanley took Mills's side without question, even when doing so got him into trouble with others.[20] Mills, on his part, needed and appreciated Stanley's moral and financial support. Without his Forest Service salary, and forced to rely solely on what he earned at Longs Peak Inn during the short summer season and from his writings, Mills could not have waged his long campaign for the park without the support of others. In August 1912 the EPPIA gave Mills $400 to help "him defray some of the expense connected with the appearance of pictures and articles about Estes Park in many of the leading papers and magazines of the county."[21]

Though the surviving record is thin, F.O. Stanley surely helped Mills financially during this period as well. The one piece of evidence documenting his support is a letter from Mills dated September 6, 1910, in which he itemized his expenses. "My dear Mr. Stanley," it begins,

In giving publicity to the proposed Estes National Park and Game Preserve proposition I wrote upward of 2300 letters, made

42 addresses, sent out 430 photographs, wrote and mailed 64 newspaper and magazine articles.

I visited and made at least three addresses each in Greeley, Ft. Collins, Loveland, Longmont, Boulder, Denver, Colorado Springs and Pueblo.

In doing all this work I incurred the following expenses:

Hotel	92.00
Railroad	48.00
Stage	63.00
Photographs	84.00
Typewriting	12.00
Telephone	14.00
Postage	52.00
	365.00

The Estes Park Transportation Company donated four rides to and from Lyons; the Brown Palace Hotel, Denver, cut ten dollars off one bill; and I received the following in cash:

The Saturday Evening Post	25.00
The Denver Republican	5.00
J. A. Ferguson	15.00
	45.00

My expense account though only approximate is within a few dollars of the exact amount spent. Hence I am out $365.00

Less,	45.00
	320.00

Yours very truly

At the bottom of the letter there is a handwritten note: "recd 315.00."[22]

As the park campaign went forward, Stanley no doubt aided Mills in other ways. Like Mills, F.O. Stanley was a proficient letter writer as well as a sophisticated influencer of men. Evidence is again lacking, but it would be a fair assumption that Stanley used his Newton winters and his reputation as an automobile man to lobby on behalf of the national park by taking the park question directly to the congressional delegations of Maine and Massachusetts as well as to the eastern press.

Though it finally took three separate bills and five major revisions to get the measure through Congress,[23] the legislation creating Rocky Mountain National Park was signed into law on January 26, 1915, by President Woodrow Wilson. The 700-square-mile park that Marshall had recommended had been reduced to 358.5 square miles, far short of Enos Mills's original proposal. It was, nonetheless, a most significant victory. And it was Enos Mills who deserved much of the credit. F.O. Stanley's respect for Enos Mills and what he had accomplished is contained in the letter he wrote from Newton the day that Wilson affixed his signature to the park bill:

Dear Mr. Mills:

I am writing to congratulate you upon the passage of the Rocky Mountain National Park bill. What you have done in this connection has had more to do in accomplishing this result than what has been done by all the others together. I am satisfied that any unprejudiced person who has had as good an opportunity as I have had to watch the progress of this movement, will agree with me in this statement.

The people in Colorado, and in fact the people in the entire country, owe you a debt of gratitude for the untiring work you

Stanley Mountain Wagon belonging to Longs Peak Inn. Charles Tresner, driver, 1915. Courtesy Fort Collins Public Library.

have done in connection with the creation of this National Park.

Trusting you may live many years to see the results of your good work, and with the best of wishes for your prosperity and happiness, I am,

Yours very truly[24]

For Stanley, as for many others, Enos Mills was, as F.O. noted with emphasis in a letter of June 1915, *"The man that made Estes Park famous."*[25]

The official dedication of Rocky Mountain National Park took place beneath a banner slung between two pines in Horseshoe Park on the afternoon of September 4, 1915. In spite of the uncertainty of the weather, a sizable crowd of onlookers had slowly gathered all morning to be part of what clearly was to be a historic event. They came by automobile, buggy, bicycle, horse, and on foot. "Put pennants and banners on your machines and start early for the park," the Fort Collins *Weekly Courier* had told its readers. "Plan an organization for the affair so that others may know that Fort Collins is on the map."[26] For those who did not bring food, "a delicious box lunch" was provided by the ladies of the Estes Park Woman's Club, who also distributed small button souvenirs and made sure there was plenty of hot coffee, for the day was chilly and dour.

"After a concert by the Fort Collins band, which surrounded by pines and towering mountains, never sounded better,"[27] and a chorus of "America the Beautiful" from an assembly of local schoolchildren, the formal program began. The master of ceremonies, the chair of the "Celebration Committee" appropriately enough, was Enos Mills, already recognized as "father of the Rocky Mountain National Park." Using an impromptu podium, he read telegrams and introduced the visiting dignitaries, who included Colorado's new governor, George A. Carlson, Congressmen Edward Taylor and Charles B. Timberlake, and Assistant Secretary of the Interior Stephen Mather. Representative Taylor and Mills had arrived together in Longs Peaks Inn's new Stanley Mountain Wagon, bringing with them Mary Belle King Sherman, whose General Federation of Women's Clubs had been major supporters of the park bill.[28]

The program for the day had been distributed in advance, and of those listed to speak, very few apparently did not. One of them was

Rocky Mountain National Park Dedication

At Two P. M. September 4, 1915

Fall River Road, Estes Park, Colorado

PROGRAM

Coffee served, beginning at Twelve

Music, Fort Collins Band

America, by the School Children

Speeches at Two P. M. Limited to five minutes

Enos A. Mills, Chairman

Hon. S. T. Mather, Assistant to the Secretary of the Interior

Governor George A. Carlson

Mrs. John D. Sherman, Chairman Conservation Department, General Federation of Women's Clubs

Hon. Edward T. Taylor

F. O. Stanley

Hon. C. B. Timberlake

Hon. Thomas M. Patterson

T. B. Stearns

AMERICA

My country, 'tis of thee,
Sweet land of liberty,
Of thee I sing;
Land where my fathers died,
Land of the pilgrims' pride;
From every mountain side,
Let freedom ring.

My native country thee,
Land of the noble free;--
Thy name I love;
I love thy rocks and rills,
Thy woods and templed hills;
My heart with rapture thrills
Like that above.

Program: Dedication of Rocky Mountain National Park, September 4, 1915. Collection of James H. Pickering.

Enos Mills and F. O. Stanley at the Park Dedication. Left to right: government publicist Robert Sterling Yard; Mills; Stanley; Colorado Representative Edward T. Taylor; Mary Belle King Sherman, representing the General Federation of Women's Clubs; and Colorado Governor George Carlson. Courtesy National Park Service.

Freelan O. Stanley.[29] Mills "endeavored to induce" him, but Stanley, perhaps out of deference to his friend and collaborator, was "too modest to appear."[30] Instead he "told Mr. Mills to make a bow for him," and "Mr. Mills made the bow so nicely that he received a round of applause."[31] F.O. Stanley's presence that day, however, was duly captured on film, standing next to Mills and waving a small American flag.

To those unaware of their relationship and mutual respect the scene might well have seemed incongruous: the bewhiskered 63-year-old easterner, standing next to the ruddy-faced and much younger man of the West—as different in many ways as their two hotels. Yet sharing as they do a unique moment in time in what has long since become a famous photograph, one is tempted to see similarities as well. Age and background apart, the two men shared much in common: native intelligence and inventiveness, strength of character, a determination to reach their goals, and, of course, a common love of Estes Park. The day and the hour, however, belonged to Enos Mills.

Park Dedication, automobiles in Horseshoe Park. Courtesy Estes Park Area Historical Museum.

As Frank Lundy Webster of the *Denver Post* reminded his readers, "This was Enos Mills day in Estes Park . . . his dream of years finally brought to reality."[32]

Though the event was well reported in the Colorado press, references to F.O. Stanley are few. "It was given out," wrote Charles Boynton, editor of the *Longmont Ledger*, "that Mr. Stanley had counted about 100 autos and estimated that probably five persons averaged with each auto: so that 500 people were present."[33] The reference to Stanley and the automobile caused Boynton to reflect:

it brot [sic] back old time memories when we camped near the spot now made famous by this gathering, in 1885 and 1887: when the cattle were wild and when an occasional bear would make a sensation that shook the waves of sound to Longmont. We remember that we had to put four horses to our empty wagons to get them over the steep and rocky roads. Now the autos glide over better grades.

But Deer mountain hadn't changed any—the gorge above Horseshoe Park looks just as dark and sombre as it did in 1885. The Roaring Fork keeps up its racket, and the grand old mountains in all their majesty continue to tower as they have towered for ages.[34]

The friendship between F.O. Stanley and Enos Mills continued until Mills's sudden death in September 1922 at the age of 52. At his funeral, which took place four days later in the great lobby of Longs Peak Inn, one of the six pallbearers was F.O. Stanley. In accordance with the instructions found in a letter in his desk, the service, conducted by Judge Ben Lindsey of Denver, was a simple affair. No music, no prayers, no passages from the Bible. Lindsey spoke briefly to the 300 mourners standing in a semicircle around the casket, which rested on two logs at the foot of the stairway from which Mills had often spoken to his assembled guests. Lindsey read three of Enos Mills's favorite poems—one each by the "two Johnnies," John Muir and John Burroughs, and one by Alfred Lord Tennyson. Then the pallbearers, "Mr. Mills' oldest and staunchest friends stepped forward and silently lifted the heavy casket from its pedestal of logs, and bore it forth across the valley."[35] Accompanied by only the members of the immediate family, the small procession crossed the road to Mills's homestead cabin, next to which a grave had been "blasted out of solid granite." The other mourners stood outside the inn watching the burial from a distance of 300 yards.

F.O. Stanley left no record of what must have been a deeply moving experience. He did not have to, for all accounts agree that though the afternoon had been dark and lowering, "as if by miracle, just as the casket began its slow descent into the rocks, the pall of grim, darkening storm towering across the face of Long's Peak was torn aside, and the red gold rays of the setting sun poured brilliantly thru the giant 'notch' upon the mountain's summit."[36] A fitting *nunc dimittis*. Cards and letters of condolence poured in from across the nation. Among the most poignant was a brief note from novelist Edna Ferber, a regular summer visitor to Longs Peak Inn over many years. "I had always thought of him as somehow indestructible, enduring, like the mountains themselves," she wrote. "I can't imagine the Park without him. It will never be the same for me."[37] Many others, including F.O. Stanley, felt the same.

11

The Grand Years, 1909–1919

We have not yet recovered from our astonishment in finding so complete and elegantly appointed a hotel. . . . What a veritable palace in the wilds it is, and what a blessing to those who seek rest in this sanitarium of the gods!
—Clifford F. Hall, August 31, 1912[1]

Newton and the Mountain Wagon

By February 1908, F.O. Stanley once again listed his permanent residence as Newton, Massachusetts. Affairs in Estes Park, including hotel construction, were in competent hands, and the Denver office of the Stanley Motor Carriage Company at Cleveland Place operated quite independently under the management of auto racer George Herring, and later H. I. Spinney. Thanks to the Colorado climate, Stanley's health had dramatically improved, and New England winters no longer posed a particularly serious threat. There was, in short, no reason to prevent F.O. and Flora from returning to a business and social world that they had left five years before.

"Your Western Man." From the collection of the Stanley Museum.

There was one other reason as well. F.O. now had in mind the design for a new and different kind of Stanley Steamer. The soon-to-be-celebrated Stanley Mountain Wagon required access to the resources of the factory at Watertown. Having observed the Osborn's success on the Big Thompson Canyon road the previous summer with the 20-h.p. five-passenger Model F, Stanley had an idea. Why not take the 30-h.p. racer engine with which F. E had achieved such amazing results at Ormond Beach, put it in a delivery wagon body, and create a larger vehicle—one capable of hauling more passengers, including his own future hotel customers and their baggage, on the North St. Vrain and Big Thompson roads? Such vehicles could be used not only by Stanley's own automobile stage line and hotel business, but sold to the Osborns, other emerging stage line operators, and individual resort owners as well.

The steam car business was generally good, at least through 1908. Though the first carriages were built in the factory of the Stanley Dry Plate Company and in the small machine shop erected in the spring of 1898, the Stanley's reentry into the car business in 1902 required enlarged facilities. This was partially achieved by purchasing the three-story 40 x 100–foot factory building that the Locomobile Company vacated when it moved to Bridgeport in May 1901. Several additional neighboring buildings were also purchased, while others were built, including an 80 x 150–foot machine and assembly shop constructed of reinforced concrete, erected in 1904, which greatly increased capacity and allowed the Stanleys to keep up with demand.

Production figures reached a record of some 775 units in 1907, followed by 734 in 1908, and remained above 500 through 1914. From 1908 to 1914 these sales were helped by the popularity of the Mountain Wagon, which proved as useful at a number of the grand resorts in New England as it did in the mountain towns of Colorado.

The social routine in Newton, long since familiar and comfortable, was one that both F.O. and Flora Stanley thoroughly enjoyed. Flora had the Katahdin Club, the Social Science Club, the West Newton Woman's and Educational Clubs, and the Sarah Hull Chapter of the D.A.R., to name just a few of the organizations she mentions in her diaries. To most of these organizations her sister-in-law, Augusta, belonged as well.

That fact made little or no difference to the relationship between the two women, which was never a particularly warm one. Though various members of the family were aware of the tension that existed between Flora and Augusta, they remained ignorant of its causes. As late as December 12, 1940, just months after F.O.'s death, Raymond Stanley wrote his mother's sister, Emma Walker:

> I have one more question I would like to know the answer to.
> What was the cause of the feud between my mother and Aunt
> Flora? It started just before they were married and I guess it
> never ended? Did my mother and father try to discourage
> Uncle Freel from marrying Aunt Flora? There was not a great
> deal of love lost between them I know and I can't find any rea-
> son for the feeling.[2]

Unfortunately, Emma Walker's response, if there was one, apparently has not survived.

But life went on. There were plays, concerts, art exhibits, and lec-
tures in Boston, preceded by lunch at the Touraine Hotel; lady's
whist at the Hunnewell Club; and periodic, and almost always successful, forays in search of art and other treasures in the shops of
Boston. Both Flora and Augusta were trained students, critics, and
buyers of art (though their tastes differed), and both took full advantage of Boston's wealth of fine arts museums, exhibits, and galleries.
The involvement of their artist sister-in-law, Chansonetta, with the
Boston Arts and Crafts movement put them in frequent contact with
some of the important artists of the day, like German- and French-
trained John Joseph Enneking, who was not only one of
Chansonetta's daughter's instructors, but one of the best known and
most prolific American impressionists and landscape painters.

Evenings were usually spent with F.O. at home, dining with
Netta, Dorothy, and other family members. Until 1913, F.O. and
Flora would continue to occupy the house on Hunnewell Street that
they had built in 1894. That year, which climaxed the period which
saw the Stanley Motor Carriage Company achieve its greatest financial success, Freelan and Flora built a spacious Georgian Colonial
Revival mansion with tapestry brick exterior and pillars at the front
at 337 Waverly Avenue.[3]

The new house, with its curving driveway, beautiful trees and
shrubs, and spacious lawns, made it possible to entertain on a larger
scale. Like many well-to-do people, the Stanleys enjoyed opening
their home to others, where they could plan and control the evening's
agenda. In the case of the Stanleys, being "at home" invariably included some form of music. Weekends, by contrast, meant automobile drives in F.O.'s newest car about the city or into the nearby countryside,

or other, more formal, social events. Flora Stanley seldom had time on her hands.

F.O.'s life was similarly full. Until 1916 or so, there were the daily affairs of the Stanley Motor Carriage Company and other details of business. He also enjoyed the Hunnewell Club for bowling or billiards, as well as the weekly meetings of the Tuesday Club that were held there. To these lively discussion groups, made up of local teachers and professional men, Stanley contributed over the years papers on such topics as "The Arithmetic of the Labor Problem," "The Tobacco Habit, Its Evils," "A Lesson in Science," "After the Depression What?," "Laissez Faire," and "The Labor Problem," several of which he then saw into print. The club's annual "Ladies' Night" was often held at the Stanley home. "For over ten years the Club enjoyed Mr. Stanley's generous hospitality on Ladies' Night," one of his fellow members wrote the month of F.O.'s death, "and none can forget the music which brought each evening to a close."[4]

Chansonetta and Dorothy

Being back in Newton meant having the opportunity to frequently see F.O.'s younger sister, the talented Chansonetta (1858–1937), and her daughter, Dorothy (1891–1960), of whom both Flora and Freelan were especially fond. Like her older twin brothers, Chansonetta (her name was a Kingfield version of the French for "little song") had attended the one-room schoolhouse on the North New Portland Road in Kingfield, and then in 1876 had gone off to the Western State Normal School at Farmington.

"Netta," as she was called by the family, was endowed like her brothers with a great deal of natural talent, and with much the same confidence and determination. Unlike F.E., who came to drawing and photography after having been a teacher, Chansonetta set out from the beginning to be an artist, supporting herself by teaching drawing and sketching in the New Portland and Kingfield schools, as well as by giving private lessons. Her card of 1882 reads, in part,

MISS NETTA STANLEY
ARTIST

LESSONS GIVEN IN PAINTING & CRAYON DRAWING, BEGINNING
MARCH 28, 1882
STUDIO AT MR. WILLIAM BROWNS'S COTTAGE,
No. Anson.
TERMS 50 CENTS, PER LESSON."[5]

Then, in the late 1890s, when she was in her late 30s, Chansonetta discovered photography, the medium at which she would excel. Her brothers, F.E. and F.O., were still heavily involved with the Stanley Dry Plate Company, and their success provided her with financial support and a limitless supply of glass plate negatives for her work.[6]

In 1886, four years before her brothers shifted the dry plate company from Lewiston to Watertown, Netta had moved to Boston, where she taught and studied painting. There she met and fell in love with James Nathaniel Whitman Emmons, who ran a retail boot and shoe business on Washington Street in Roxbury. They were married in February 1887, and in June 1891 their first and only child, Dorothy, was born. Two years later, in 1895, the Emmons family moved into a big Victorian house in New Dorchester, which F.O. purchased for them.[7]

By 1897, Chansonetta had become thoroughly fascinated with the camera. It became her artistic passion. Chansonetta's background as a painter served her well, as she demonstrated in the well-composed scenes she took during a visit to North and South Carolina with Dorothy in the spring of 1897, a trip financed by F.O. Stanley. From that time on, Chansonetta created an impressive body of photographic work, most of it taken with her 1904 Century 5x8 view camera.

These were, however, years of tragedy as well. In August 1898, James Emmons, who had struggled financially throughout their marriage, died of blood poisoning at the age of 41, leaving Netta with a seven-year-old daughter, a large house, and no money. To conserve funds, mother and daughter moved to a small Queen Anne double house on Bennington Street in Newton. Again F.O. Stanley financially intervened: he paid the annual rent on the Bennington Street house for the rest of his sister's life. Later he financed Dorothy's education at Wellesley College as well.

Though Netta and Dorothy spent most of their summers in Kingfield, on several occasions during the late 1920s and early 1930s,

Chansonetta Stanley Emmons—self-portrait. From the collection of the Stanley Museum

they accepted the invitation of F.O. and Flora to join them in Colorado. From those visits came a number of remarkable photographs, the most memorable of which is a picture of Dream Lake in Glacier Gorge with a partially cloud-obscured Hallett Peak rising beyond. Netta found the beauty of Estes Park as compelling as did F.O. and Flora. Her other brother, F.E. Stanley, did not. He visited only once and, according to family tradition, did not find the place particularly to his liking. This was not surprising. The F.E. Stanleys had long-since found contentment in their own summer retreat, "Sunny Haven" cottage, on exclusive Squirrel Island, three miles off Maine's Boothbay Harbor.[8]

In the years after 1914 and Dorothy's graduation from Wellesley, mother and daughter were almost inseparable. This dependency deepened during the 1920s when Netta's hearing problems degener-

Chansonetta's photograph of Dream Lake. From the collection of the Stanley Museum.

ated into total deafness. Throughout these difficult years F.O. and Flora provided emotional as well as financial support, further anchoring their own ties to Newton and the East.

School Ties: Hebron Academy

There was also F.O. Stanley's devotion to Hebron Academy. He was elected to its board in 1911, and then made board president in 1914, a position he would occupy for 26 years. Stanley played a critical role in shaping the school's history for the better part of three decades. He regularly made the trip of several hundred miles from Newton to and from the small rural Maine town where Hebron was located, despite the weather and the press of other concerns. On more than one occasion he and Flora opened their home in Newton to Hebron alumni.

F.O. took his responsibilities to the school seriously. When principal William E. Sargent was incapacitated by an apoplectic stroke in January 1921, Stanley installed himself on the Hebron campus to manage the fiscal operations of the academy and to arrange the search for a new principal. He was president of the Hebron board during times of change and turmoil: he presided over the meeting of March 17, 1922, which ended 117 years of coeducation at Hebron, and twice over meetings that unhappily cut faculty salaries, in 1928 and again in 1934.

F.O. Stanley's gifts to Hebron were many, beginning in 1912 when he donated tools to put the newly constructed football field in order. In 1914, perhaps as a way of acknowledging his gratitude in being elected president of the board, F.O., together with his brother, F.E. Stanley, and John F. Moody, the principal under whom F.O. both taught and studied, gave the school a powerful 6.1-inch telescope, later mounted in the school's observatory. In 1923, Stanley renovated a room in Sturdevant Hall to provide a new private office for the principal and lent Hebron $7,000 to liquidate bills for food supplies and fuel. Two years later, in 1925, employing his own unique design, he paid for the building of Stanley Arena, the first covered ice hockey facility in an American preparatory school.

Stanley's major gift, however, came in 1926, when he announced that he would donate $200,000 to help fund a new and badly needed gymnasium.[9] When completed in 1929 it was clear that the design of the Sargent Memorial Gymnasium, with its two-story Doric porch, was very much Stanley's own. The same thing could be said of the school's Stanley Infirmary, a brick replica of his home on Waverly Avenue, as well as the pillars that framed Hebron's main entry gate.[10]

Whether it was hockey, football, or other sports, Stanley also cared strongly about Hebron's success on the athletic field. According to his nephew, Raymond Stanley, F.O. became so tired of seeing Hebron beaten by its rivals that he set up a series of scholarships in football, basketball, baseball, and hockey for young men from Massachusetts, including "tough kids" off the streets of Boston, who were invited to come to rural Maine and play for a year before matriculating as regular students at Bowdoin, Colby, Dartmouth, Harvard, or some other collegiate institution. The story may be apocryphal, but the fortunes of Hebron Academy, at least on the football field, did take a dramatic turn. From 1923 to 1929 Hebron teams won three state championships.[11]

The Heyday of the Stanley Hotel

Stanley managed his responsibilities at Hebron, at the Stanley Motor Carriage Company in Watertown, and at the Stanley Hotel in Estes Park with apparent ease. The pull of the West remained strong, however, particularly in the decade that followed the opening of the hotel in June 1909, unquestionably the Stanley Hotel's best.

The years from 1909 to 1917 also saw a rapid general expansion of the hotel and tourist industry throughout the Estes Park valley. New hotels and lodges seemingly appeared everywhere, initially spurred by the developments of 1905, which turned the old John Cleave property into a busy village, and then by the excitement and air of expectancy created by Enos Mills's campaign for a national park. The following list of the new establishments graphically illustrates the level of activity:

1908 Manford Hotel, Elkhorn Avenue Estes Park
(across from the Hupp Hotel)
Horseshoe Inn, Horseshoe Park—west of town
Columbine Lodge, Tahosa Valley—south of town

1909   The Stanley Hotel—Estes Park

1910   Stanley Manor House—Estes Park
        Sprague's Lodge, Glacier Creek—southwest of town
        The Brinwood, Moraine Park—southwest of town
        Moraine Lodge, Moraine Park—southwest of town

1911   Fern Lake Lodge—southwest of town

1913   Rockdale Hotel, Marys Lake—south of town

1914   Copeland Lake Lodge, Wild Basin—south of town
        Crags Hotel, Prospect Mountain—Estes Park
        Hewes-Kirkwood Inn, Tahosa Valley—south of town
        Lewiston Hotel—Estes Park

1915   Fall River Lodge, Horseshoe Park—west of town
        The Josephine—Estes Park

1917   Big Thompson Hotel, Beaver Point—south of town
        Baldpate Inn, Tahosa Valley—south of town

The years after 1908 also saw the rapid expansion of the facilities of the Western Conference of the YMCA in the picturesque valley above Wind River. By 1919 some 24 different establishments were offering food and accommodations to visitors in Estes Park.

With these hostelries came new shops, restaurants, liveries, and various kinds of entertainments, including the town's first motion picture house. Things became so busy as the 1917 summer season approached that carpenters of any kind were at a premium. That summer alone, 379 new hotel rooms were added. Moreover, as a Fort Collins paper reported, "These additions . . . are but a small fraction of the total of new accommodations which will be made available for the tourist trade, as countless hotels expect to erect tents and summer quarters of a temporary nature only."[12] Quoted weekly rates in 1919 ranged from $28 to $84. At $84 a week, the Stanley Hotel, as might be expected, was by far the most expensive.[13]

F.O. Stanley, a man energized by change, participated in the growth as well. In 1917, to take advantage of the growing interest in auto camping, he established a well-patronized overnight facility in Tuxedo

Vacationing in Estes Park, 1911. Courtesy City of Greeley Museums, Permanent Collection.

Park on the Bear Lake road just south of Moraine Park, where as many as 50 cars a night paid 50 cents apiece for the privilege of parking.[14] Stanley knew what he was doing. In 1908 there had been fewer than 200,000 cars on the nation's roads. By 1917 there were 3.5 million, and auto camping had become something of a national passion. Had Stanley needed a precedent he had only to look to Denver's 160-acre Overland Park, already one of the largest auto campgrounds in the nation, complete with a three-story clubhouse, ballroom, and restaurant. "It is an inspiring sight to go into a park like the beautiful City Park in Denver," Horace Albright, assistant director of the National Park Service, remarked that same year, "and see several hundred cars neatly parked in their allotted spaces and their happy owners, many of them with large families, enjoying the camp life."[15] By all accounts F.O. Stanley's new facility for automobiles in Estes Park received the same kind of testimonials.

The new hotel and guest ranch accommodations in Estes Park were built primarily in the traditional western style that one expected to find in the mountains. The Stanley and its outlying buildings were, of

F. O. Stanley at the Elkhorn Lodge. Courtesy Frank Hix.

course, the exception, and this was precisely the point. In a resort where roughing it in style was about all that visitors once could hope for, Mr. Stanley's hotel exuded "class"—meaning that it was not for everyone. Except for Dunraven's aging Estes Park Hotel across the valley, none of the other resort establishments offered anything much above the rustic. Stanley's new hotel appealed to a previously underserved group of summer visitors, and as such immediately and dramatically expanded Estes Park's tourist potential.

A summer routine at the Stanley was quickly established. Guests could enjoy a Saturday dance ("high-class balls") at the Casino to the music of the Stanley Hotel orchestra and a Sunday evening concert in the Music Room. On Sundays the music was provided by visiting chamber groups or the regular orchestra—both of which made use of the 7½-foot Steinway grand piano that F.O. brought up from the valley and presented to Flora to celebrate the hotel's opening. The Stanley also offered the activities expected at Estes Park's more traditional rustic resorts: weeknight fish fries, steak fries, and other forms of impromptu recreation and entertainment. In addition there were "special events." Particularly memorable in those first years was a minstrel-vaudeville show staged in August 1913 by members of the hotel staff.

In the tradition of the grand hotels of the day (and not unlike today's cruise ships), there was little excuse for idle time at the Stanley Hotel. There were facilities for almost every sporting taste: billiards, two bowling alleys, card playing, croquet, tennis, and golf. Guests returning for the 1919 season even found a new trapshooting range, said to be among the best in the West, and laid out so that the targets were protected from the sun at all hours of the day.[16] For those wishing to adventure farther afield to explore lakes and mountains, the liveries in the village brought strings of horses each morning directly to the hitching post below the hotel's front porch.

One of the Stanley Hotel's early guests was Clifford F. Hall of Kansas City. "Of course, I am charmed by the majestic beauty of this Park," he told the *Estes Park Trail* in August 1912,

but if I possessed the vocabulary of a John J. Ingalls [the U.S. senator from Kansas, a well-known lecturer and journalist] I would not waste it on the scenery, but would endeavor adequately to express my admiration for your splendid Stanley hotel and its superb management. It is not only on a par with the finest summer and winter resort hotels in America as to equipment and service, but it has a refined and delightful home atmosphere which few such places possess. We have not yet recovered from our astonishment in finding so complete and elegantly appointed a hotel in such a remote spot. We were prepared to put up with most any kind of accommodations in the Park, but a day's experience at the Stanley chained us to its comforts. Mr. Lamborn's table is perpetually satisfying and immaculate cleanliness pervades the entire place from basement to roof—and particularly the kitchen, which we had the privilege of inspecting, as all guests have. What a veritable palace in the wilds it is, and what a blessing to those who seek health and rest in this sanitarium of the gods! I should think that not only those who view the glories of Estes Park, but all who own property here, would feel under everlasting obligations to Mr. F.O. Stanley for the grand result of his costly expenditures toward making it a permanently popular pleasure and health resort, and in making it so easily accessible by the introduction of his wonderful Stanley steam automobiles.[17]

Good publicity was important. During the hotel's first years, management saw to it that the Stanley was well advertised in brochures, most of which were distributed, as well as paid for, by the railroads. Most important, of course, were the word-of-mouth endorsements from satisfied customers.

As Mr. Hall's quotation suggests, a large part of the success that the Stanley enjoyed during its first decade was due to the quiet competence of its first manager, Alfred Lamborn (1852–1941). Handpicked by F.O. Stanley, Lamborn at the age of 61 brought with him precisely the kind of experience with high-class entertaining that the hotel needed—his resume included Atlantic City, the Pullman Company, and the exclusive Denver Club, which he managed for nine years. Put simply, Alfred Lamborn knew just how to deal with well-to-do patrons.

Of equal importance, Stanley and Lamborn, who were about the same age, knew how to deal with one another. Good hotel managers, especially in summer resorts, are often as legendary as they are rare. Frequently they come and go with the season, a fact that did much eventually to undermine the reputation for service and quality of the Earl of Dunraven's Estes Park Hotel. Lamborn, who presided over the Stanley through the 1922 season, was an exception. F.O. Stanley was so appreciative of what Lamborn and his wife brought to his hotel that when he and Flora returned from Boston in July 1913 for the summer season, he presented his manager with "a beautiful five-passenger Stanley automobile."[18] When Lamborn retired at the age of 70, everyone in Estes Park believed they had lost a friend.[19]

Over the years the Stanley had its share of famous guests. Among them was Charles Evans Hughes, who spent six days at the Manor House in 1916 while running for the presidency. Hughes's visit quickly turned into a photo opportunity for the Denver press. One of the best, taken by Stuart Mace, staff photographer for the *Denver Times*, captures Evans in conversation with Enos Mills and F.O. Stanley on the front porch of the Stanley Hotel.

There were also famous guests who didn't come. So proud was Stanley of his hotel and its amenities that in April 1920 he instructed

Lamborn to telegram the White House and offer the 32-room Manor House to President Woodrow Wilson for the summer. It was not an altogether unrealistic invitation, for Wilson had lectured at Colorado College near Pikes Peak during the summer of 1894 and had family ties to the state.

As guests like Mr. Hall and those who followed him appreciated, events at the Stanley were always celebrated with style and class, in true grand hotel fashion. In August 1912 the 450 men of Batteries A, B, and C of the Fourth Field Artillery from Fort Russell, Wyoming, came through Estes Park with full equipment, including horses, on their well-publicized "thousand mile hike through the mountains of Colorado," and went into camp east of the barn at the Dunraven ranchhouse, creating a local sensation. F. O Stanley rose immediately to the occasion, unwilling to let such a colorful moment pass unrecognized and uncelebrated. He threw the hotel open to the artillery's staff of officers for a festive dinner, followed by a military ball in the Casino. "The dance was a big success," the *Estes Park Trail* reported, "testing the capacity of the Stanley Casino, beautiful gowns being in evidence." The hostess of the evening was, of course, Flora Stanley, resplendent in "beaded chiffon and diamonds."[20]

As her appearance at the military ball and at other hotel and community events suggests, Flora Stanley was almost as active a participant in the civic and social life of Estes Park as her famous husband. Flora's involvement came easily and naturally, and would continue until her eyesight grew so poor that getting about became difficult, and finally impossible. Flora Stanley's diary of 1910, her only diary after 1903 to survive, provides an ongoing account of her investment.

That April, F.O. made a quick 10-day trip to Colorado in connection with the completion of the Manor House, the new "year-round" part of the Stanley facility, scheduled to open in late summer or early fall.[21] The Stanleys' annual pilgrimage began six weeks later, on May 31. After a day in Denver, where Flora lunched with Nancy Bonney, she and F.O. came on to Estes Park, bringing with them hotel manager Alfred Lamborn. For much of that summer F.O. was occupied with hotel matters, including the important three-day meeting of the Colorado Hotel Men's Association in June, followed the very next day by the return of the Colorado Pharmacal Association, to whom he once again delivered a hearty welcoming address.

Flora, meanwhile, turned her attention to community activities, particularly those of the Woman's Auxiliary of the Estes Park Protective and Improvement Association, which she helped organize that summer and of which she became its "acknowledged leader."[22] She donated considerable time to the auxiliary's first-ever bazaar and vaudeville show, a continuous performance event that included lunch, supper, and a dance—"from noon to midnight"—under a big circular tent brought up from Denver,[23] put on by the Estes Park women to raise funds for such worthy projects as trail building and the fish hatchery. Planning for the bazaar began on July 10, with a meeting at the Elkhorn, and went on for several weeks. When the event itself took place on Thursday, August 4, Flora and Carrie Sanborn, the wife of F.O.'s real estate partner, Burton Sanborn, dressed themselves as gypsies and ran a fortune-telling booth, telling fortunes by using playing cards and reading palms. Though the rain that day "interfered with our business," Flora recorded in her diary, "We each made exactly the same $8.10—or $16.20 in all."[24] It was a role she would repeat by popular demand as long as the summer bazaars continued.[25]

Of the vaudeville show, Flora has less to say. It took place at the Casino three weeks later, on the evening of August 27, followed by dancing. Flora does make clear, however, that her dance of choice that summer was the Virginia reel, which necessitated a frequent change of partners. She reports dancing not only with her husband and Alfred Lamborn, among others, but "twice with a young man from Denver whose name I don't remember." Flora continued her involvement with the auxiliary (which later became the Woman's Club of Estes Park). In future years this group would help campaign for the new Rocky Mountain National Park, an activity in which Flora Stanley was again asked to take a leadership role.[26]

F.O. Stanley's interest in innovative technologies mixed well with his concern to find new and modern ways to serve his guests. Perhaps the most famous example was F.O. Stanley's brief flirtation with the airplane. It began in May 1919, with the announcement by Alfred Lamborn, Stanley's spokesman in such matters, that the hotel planned to open an airfield on a nearby site already selected with the help of "an expert in aeronautics." A two-passenger Curtis airplane was ordered to provide daily service to Denver and to take tourists on daily trips circling Longs Peak, and the reliable Byron Hall was set to work putting in foundations for the hangar.

The maiden flight took place at the very height of the tourist season, on Friday, August 8, 1919. On that morning a "huge crowd" gathered at the new 200-acre, mile-long field below the hotel to greet the arrival of a yellow Oriole Curtis biplane flown in over Mount Olympus from Denver by Ira B. Humphreys, Jr., and A. M. "Red" Lendrum. Copies of a special preprinted "extra" edition of the *Denver Post* ("AIRPLANE SETS NEW RECORD, TAKES DENVER POST TO ESTES PARK, HEART OF THE ROCKIES") were distributed to the crowd. "250 papers comprised the edition," the *Lyons Recorder* told its readers, "and it is reported that some copies changed hands at fancy prices since that event."[27] At exactly 12:01 the plane began its return flight, circling above the town three times to gain an altitude of 12,000 feet, while *Post* city editor Al Birch, a longtime summer resident of Estes Park, called the details back to Denver. Yet another Stanley first, this time with a disappointing sequel.

Regular flights began the following summer, in 1920, and shortly thereafter Estes Park's summer paper, *Estes Park Trail Talk*, was effusively praising Lamborn (and Stanley) for providing "the greatest attraction of the season. . . . There seems to be something intoxicating about flying above the Park in view of the snow-capped peaks," the paper continued, "because everyone that has had a flight seems to want another." It then listed the names of 44 people, including a significant number of park residents, who had had "the necessary nerve and the equally necessary dollar-a-minute fare" for the "trip in the blue ethereal." To encourage business, leaflets were several times dropped from the sky containing lucky numbers. Winners were entitled to a free ride.

Unfortunately, not all of the passengers that summer fared as well. On August 16, 1920, Alberta Yore, wife of Clem Yore, owner of the Big Thompson Hotel, ended up in the Longmont hospital with a broken jaw, cuts, and other bruises when the plane on which she was flying to Denver nosedived shortly after takeoff and fell 50 feet into the hill below the hotel. Though the "machine was smashed to pieces when it struck the ground," the pilot, an army air corps veteran ironically named A. D. Swift, escaped unharmed, suffering nothing more than "a severe shaking up."[28]

The first airplane arrives in Estes Park, July 8, 1919. Courtesy Estes Park Area Historical Museum.

The near catastrophe, as might be expected, put a damper on Alfred Lamborn's "intoxicating" attraction, and no further flight reports were issued from the hotel as the 1920 summer season came to its close. Though Estes Park's flirtation with the airplane would continue for a number of years, interest and excitement never again approached the level of that summer of 1920.

The fastidiousness of the habitually well-dressed F.O. Stanley established the tone that Lamborn and his staff reflected. Having set high standards during construction—down to the nine coats of hand-rubbed paint he insisted be applied to the Music Room—Stanley was committed to the best in amenities and service, and demanded exactness from others.[29]

Alfred Lamborn took his cue from Stanley. Norman Dunham long remembered the summer of 1913 and his first job, when he was hired at the Stanley as a messenger boy. Movies at the Park Theatre on Moraine Avenue were a new thing that year, and one night Dunham attended with a group of fellow employees. The next day he overslept, missed the mail truck up to the hotel, and was late for work. "I did meet Alfred Lamborn, the manager at the wrong time," Dunham recalled. "Result—I was fired, sent home, crying all the way." Norman Dunham had the opportunity to put the lesson to good use and to redeem himself. Some 30 years later, in 1942, Roe Emery, who by then owned the Stanley Hotel, invited Dunham to return as manager.[30]

During the first decade there were also changes and renovations. In 1912, to meet the needs of younger guests, a refreshment room and soda fountain, "equipped with the finest of fixtures and furniture," were installed in the parlor off the lobby (in what is today called the Piñon Room). An even more significant change occurred in the spring of 1916. During the hotel's first seven years, popularity and demand often outstripped available facilities. When Stanley discovered that it had been necessary to turn away some 800 prospective guests, he had two large wings added onto the rear of the original hotel, to make available additional guestrooms.[31] In 1921, again reflecting patron needs, part of the back veranda was enclosed and electric heat was added to convert it to a card room. That same year the Music Room was given a dance floor,[32] and some time later the original porte cochere was removed from the front of the hotel, both increasing the general utility and attractiveness of the front porch and considerably brightening the lobby.

The "New Stanley"

The largest of F.O. Stanley's new projects during these years was one that he launched only to abandon. Completed, it would have architecturally transformed the ragged hodgepodge of buildings that had become downtown Estes Park, setting a standard of style and tone for the village that others would sooner or later have sought (or been forced) to emulate. Public awareness of just what Stanley had in mind began in the early fall of 1916, when F.O. approached L. Claude Way, the National Park's newly appointed chief ranger in charge (a title later changed to superintendent). He told Way about his plan to build a new Colonial-style hotel just to the east of what was then the town's business section. He then offered a proposition.

Stanley asked whether Way would be interested in constructing a new administration building and residence. Way's Park Service headquarters, located in space that the government leased in the village, were clearly inadequate. The site Stanley had in mind, he told Way, was next to the post office (in what is now Bond Park), on a lot to be donated by the Estes Park Business Men's Association, the forerunner of the Chamber of Commerce. It was also, Stanley further explained, in the immediate vicinity of where he proposed to erect his own new hotel.

Way consulted his superiors in Washington. On October 16, Robert B. Marshall, interim director of the new National Park Service on loan from the Geological Survey, wrote Way about how best to "develop the lot for the proposed administrative building." Marshall was no stranger to Estes Park. It had been his visit of September 1912 and report early the next year that had recommended the establishment of Rocky Mountain National Park and given the park its name.

Marshall's response to Way was to make sure that the proposed buildings blended with "the general scenery" and with one another. "Now if you are too busy to do much of this," Marshall continued, "I think if you would turn the matter over to Mr. Stanley, giving him an idea of what is wanted, his architect could plan the building so as to blend with the new Stanley Hotel." Marshall expressed a concern about cost, and also suggested that Way obtain from Cornelius Bond a written commitment stating that the Business Men's Association "will donate this lot provided we can get the funds from Congress for the administrative buildings."[33] Ten days later, on October 26, 1916, John "Ed" Macdonald, Sam Service, and Pieter Hondius, in their capacities as association trustees, provided Way with the asked-for assurance.[34]

On October 30, L. C. Way again wrote Marshall, informing him that the lot in question was worth $10,000 and that "I had a conference with Mr. Stanley and his architect regarding building plans and they promised to submit sketches the latter part of the week."[35] The architect, it turned out, was none other than T. Robert Wieger of Denver, the man who had helped Stanley with his hotel complex a decade before and who was now, presumably, involved with Stanley's new hotel. Both Way and Stanley continued to pursue their separate plans.

On November 11, F.O. Stanley's plans became even more public. The *Fort Collins Morning Express* announced that he had paid the unheard-of price of $15,000 for two lots "on the outskirts of Estes Park" on which there were no buildings "and not even a fence." The *Lyons Recorder* and the *Longmont Call* soon had additional details to share: "Mr. Stanley will erect this winter a 140-room hotel that will cater to summer tourists who can afford only moderate priced accommodations." "The present Stanley hotels," one paper elaborated, "are exceedingly palatial in appointments, and cater only to the higher priced trade."[36]

During the next months, newspapers in Fort Collins, Denver, and elsewhere expanded upon Stanley's intentions. According to the *Fort Collins Express*, Stanley not only planned to build a third hotel in the village but was also intent on buying "the greater part of the town" so he might "put up a picturesque, model town."[37] "If he is successful in purchasing the land he desires," the *Denver Post* went on to explain,

> he will raze every house, every stick of timber, every fence of the property and build new from the ground up. The best municipal architects in the United States will be taken there and they will be given a free hand to lay out a truly model town. On one part of the plot he will erect a 140-room hotel, which will have a bath in every sleeping room. Stables and other business places will be moved away from the sight of tourists. The highways are to be places of beauty. . . . if Mr. Stanley succeeds in getting the land for which he is offering fabulous prices he will start work at once and by spring the model town will be a fact.[38]

Such plans and the activity that would accompany them naturally sparked a great deal of local interest and excitement. It also alerted residents that, technically speaking, Estes Park was not yet an incorporated town. On January 17, 1917, local realtor Albert Hayden and 42 others filed a petition to permit Estes Park to become Larimer County's fifth incorporated town. One of the reasons offered was: "impending plans for the beautification of the village and its transformation into one of the most sightly resort villages of the nation make its incorporation almost imperative."[39]

Discussions about the park's new administrative complex continued on into late November and December. On November 30, 1916, Way reported to Marshall that he was sending to Washington a drawing of Wieger's plan, together with a map of Estes Park showing the site. He also discussed "the Colonial style of architecture" that Wieger was recommending "to blend with the new Stanley." Though Way worried that the style Wieger was suggesting for the Park Service buildings might be too similar to the hotel's (rather than too "governmental"), he liked what he saw:

> The floor plan of the building I think very good, and we like the idea of the second floor bed rooms. The room over the office is especially desirable since it will give privacy either from a sleeping apartment standpoint or a living room. It will also afford a magnificent view of the surrounding country. This is equally true of the other bed rooms with exceptions of living room features. The administrative rooms in my opinion are well planned, with the exception of the entrance to filing room, which is a minor detail and can be changed so that it will not be necessary to pass thru private office to reach the files.
>
> As a preliminary plan I think this a good one and with a few minor changes, made to meet our needs.[40]

Way appended to his letter a brief postscript: "Reference enclosed letter from Mr. Wieger also cost sheet which is enclosed. Building was not to exceed $10,000.00. Enclosures recived todays [sic] mail."[41]

The document Way referred to is evidently Wieger's five-page one titled

ADMINISTRATION BUILDING AND RESIDENCE

IN THE

ROCKY MOUNTAIN NATIONAL PARK

FOR THE

DEPARTMENT OF THE INTERIOR

DESCRIBING THE DRAWINGS

SUBMITTED BY T. ROBERT WIEGER, ARCHITECT

DENVER, COLORADO[42]

The description of Wieger's buildings fully explains and justifies Way's enthusiasm. They were to include a "wide semi-circular gravel driveway" providing direct access from Elkhorn Avenue, a main office with exhibition space, a graveled promenade between office building and residence, and hedge-surrounded grounds with "suitable illuminated archways . . . grass, flowers and native shrubs and trees," and three concrete seats "placed at convenient intervals." The problem was that, as Way's closing postscript to Marshall broadly hinted, the "Schedule of Costs" amounted to $17,300, for the construction of the buildings only. Grounds, walks, driveways, hedges, and plantings were extra. A brief undated handwritten letter from Wieger accompanying this document offered the explanation: "I sent you yesterday the drawings & blue prints & enclose the description relative to cost. It runs higher than thought due to the comparative inaccessibility of Estes Park, no doubt."[43]

The Wieger-designed Park Service headquarters building was never built. At the time of these negotiations the entire annual appropriation for Rocky Mountain National Park was only $10,000, and Way had other, more pressing, needs. The project was quickly put aside and so, too, unfortunately, were the plans for the new hotel and for Stanley's "truly model town."

The Park Service would continue to locate its administrative offices in leased space in the Boyd Building in the center of the village of Estes Park for another six years. In May 1921 the Estes Park Woman's Club, the organization that Flora Stanley had been so instrumental in founding, by a vote of 30 to 4 passed a resolution to donate Lot 5 in the Buena Vista Terrace Addition for a permanent administration building. The site was not downtown, but on what was then the outskirts of the village, the southern slope of Davis Hill, where Moraine Avenue swings to the southwest toward Beaver Point. Across the street was a livery. Begun in May 1923 and occupied that October, the new building turned out to be a drab, functional, and nondescript government structure—a far cry from what Stanley once had in mind.

We hear only once more about F.O. Stanley's "Colonial style" hotel, but with news that would seem to confirm his original seriousness of purpose. On February 7, 1917, the *Fort Collins Express* reported that Stanley had concluded arrangements with John W. Howard to erect a new $75,000, 250-room hotel in Estes Park.[44] Howard, the article explained, was a Cheyenne contractor and builder who had just completed work on the wings of the Wyoming state capitol. From that time on, however, there is only silence.

To add to the irony, the 1917 summer season turned out to be a record one. "Estes Park has had more visitors than in any previous year, all hotels being filled," the *Loveland Daily Herald* told its readers that September, "notwithstanding this season's accommodations were 40 percent greater than last year."[45] Those new accommodations did not include Mr. Stanley's hotel for "people of moderate circumstances."

As for the fate of the site proposed for the "new Stanley"—the two lots for which F.O. Stanley had paid the unheard-of sum of $15,000—Stanley donated one of them to the Town of Estes Park in September 1925 for use in building a new and badly needed school. At the time, its valuation was set at $8,000.[46] Twelve years later, on March 31, 1937, Stanley entered into an agreement with Larimer County School District No. 30 to sell it the other lot. This contiguous 2.49 acres, bordered by Elkhorn Avenue and directly across from Bond Park, is the site of today's Municipal Building. It was purchased, at a reported price of $8,000, to provide the school with a new wing.[47]

One can only surmise why F.O. Stanley changed his mind about his new hotel and "model town." Perhaps he was upset with the Park Service's apparent lack of cooperation. Perhaps his decision had to do with the financial situation of the Stanley Motor Carriage Company and the plans being made in Newton that winter for both twins to retire from the steam car business. Perhaps it was the fact that on April 6, 1917, about the time he might have been expected to break ground for the new hotel, President Woodrow Wilson signed a declaration of war on Germany, convincing Stanley that the coming tourist season, despite confident predictions, was likely to be problematic.

With the hindsight of history, it is interesting to speculate about what Estes Park village might have looked like, and how it might have architecturally evolved, had Wieger and Stanley been allowed to bring their Georgian Revival architecture (for this was certainly what Way refers as the "Colonial style") into the very center of Estes Park. It is tempting to argue, in fact, that what Stanley sought to accomplish by way of architectural renewal had to wait a full 65 years, until August 1982, when the waters of Fall River, sweeping down from the breached dam at Lawn Lake, put the Stanley power plant out of commission, devastated the buildings and shops of Elkhorn Avenue, and forced the town fathers of Estes Park to ponder new beginnings. But history is filled with such hindsights.

The Other "Mrs. Stanley"

Frank and I went over to Freels [sic] this morning to see a new picture they have bought. I dont care much for the subject—Colorado mountains.
> —Diary of Augusta Stanley, February 19, 1911

The summer of 1917 marked the first and only visit of F.E. and Augusta—Mrs. Francis Edgar Stanley—to Estes Park. That trip had long been deferred because of the need for one of the brothers to remain in the East, in close proximity to Newton and the nearby Stanley Motor Carriage Company. But that spring, with the company being transferred to other hands, it was time for F.E. and Augusta to come west to see something of Flora and F.O.'s other world. The highlights of their two-week visit to Estes Park were carefully recorded by Augusta Stanley in her diary, as well as in the letter that she wrote back to the *Lewiston Sun* for the benefit of friends in Maine.

The F.E. Stanleys reached Chicago on the morning of Thursday, August 23. Frank Jay, manager of the company's Chicago offices, who was negotiating ownership in the Stanley Motor Carriage Company, sent a car to Union Station to take them "in hand." Most of the day was spent in Jay's car, visiting the University of Chicago, lunching at the Blackstone Hotel ("the best in Chicago"), and riding along Lake Michigan as far north as the Edgewater Beach Hotel and then back through Lincoln Park to the railroad station. By 5:30 P.M. they were again on their way to Denver.

The next day was long and hot. Most of it was spent in the train's observation car, where they watched the country west of Omaha slowly change from "wonderful corn fields acres & acres in extent" to the "very dry" and far less hospitable plains of eastern Colorado. They spent that night in "princely" quarters at the Brown Palace. After a "hot and dusty" and "bumpy" ride in F.O. Stanley's car, driven by the company's Denver agent, H. I. Spinney, they were met in Longmont by F.O. Stanley himself, who brought them to the park by way of the North St. Vrain. "I was frightened half to death on the narrow roads so near the edge of precipitous chasms," Augusta wrote that night. "But we finally reached the Hotel in time for luncheon."[48]

Whatever preconceptions Augusta brought with her about her in-laws' life in the mountains, she was impressed, at least to an extent. F.O. immediately took over, shepherding them "in his auto . . . up by the Power House and the Fish Hatchery and around to see the view of the mts." That night there was "a good concert" by six musicians in the Music Room of the hotel, presented "in honor of Mr & Mrs F.E. Stanley."[49] The following day it rained, forcing F.O. and Frank, who had tried to play golf, inside.

The change of weather was echoed by Augusta's mood. Other than to note that "they gave us fine quarters facing the mountains," she remained out of sorts all day and had little that was pleasant to record. She did not like the hotel's clientele, and its "table is not very good—nothing to Eastern hotels." Moreover, her in-laws were unresponsive. "Freels [sic] folks [referring to the staff of the Stanley Hotel] seem to want us to be comfortable—but it is not in Flora's nature to be really hospitable. She is a pitiful sight not able to see hardly a bit."[50]

The weather improved, Augusta's mood rallying with it as their sightseeing continued. Like so many visitors to Estes Park, she was immediately struck by the contrast between the Stanley Hotel and the other hotels and ranches that made up the mountain resort community. She was also struck by the transient nature of at least a portion of the park's summer population. "This morning we rode to Steads in Moraine Park," she wrote on the 29th.

> They like everybody else have a hotel, but everybodys except this one, are of the rustic order—made mostly of logs, and all brown, except Freels which are all Colonial in type and yellow with white trimmings. We called on Mrs. Stead at her home. The interior of their houses are usually a combination of City & rustic furnishing—nothing I have seen here is very artistic. There was a big excursion of people who came Sat. and left today. They seem coming and going all the time.[51]

Other visits followed, including one to the Crocker ranch, where Augusta met and talked with Frank Crocker and his wife, whom she found "very interesting." There was also a trip with Mrs. Lamborn and Flora to the park studio of Charles Partridge Adams, which they found "all packed up" for the season, followed by another to the studio of well-known local artist Richard Tallant, who had a home with attached studio on Elkhorn Avenue. Augusta, who prided herself on collecting good art, pronounced Tallant's work "pretty bad!"[52]

Before her rather short stay was over, Augusta had also been taken to The Wigwam, a tea room and "sort of gift shop" run by Anna Wolfrom on the way up the Wind River trail, and to a party at the summer home of Thomas B. Stearns of Denver. Though Augusta noted that the Stearns's home, two miles from the hotel, is "called . . . the most attractive in the Park," she pronounced her evening "not very pleasant." When F.E. was not accompanying his wife, he used the interlude to do business with F.O. and with Frank Jay, who had joined the twins in Estes Park to discuss the sale of the company's Denver branch office. One morning the Stanley brothers did find time to go up Deer Mountain on horseback, where the only known photograph of them together in Estes Park was taken.

As far as Augusta Stanley was concerned, the highlights of her short vacation were two: a visit with Enos Mills at Longs Peak Inn, and a 13- or 14-mile round-trip car ride up Fall River. Augusta was anxious to see Enos Mills, whose books she had read, and who, like many of her contemporaries, she tended to regard as a kind of western John Burroughs. Burroughs had visited Squirrel Island.

Augusta was also interested in meeting Mills because of his connection with Mary Belle King Sherman, wife of Chicago editor and writer John Dickinson Sherman, who spent a great deal of time at the inn. Mary Sherman, called "National Park Lady" because of her work as chair of the conservation committee and later as president of the General Federation of Women's Clubs, was a celebrity in the circles in which Augusta Stanley moved. She had heard both Enos Mills and Mrs. Sherman speak, the latter "at every Federation Biennial I have ever attended." "They have a hotel with several cottages—as seems to be the fashion here in the mountains," Augusta wrote of the Longs Peak Inn. "Mr. Mills gave us a beautiful picture that he had made. He is a very versatile man—and can seem to turn his hand to almost anything."[53]

Her trip up Fall River Road, by contrast, proved something of an ordeal. Though still incomplete, the new road, which was to link Estes Park and Grand Lake by way of the Continental Divide, was one of the places you took visitors by car. Work had begun four years

The Stanley brothers on Deer Mountain, 1917, F.O. left, F.E. on right. From the Collection of the Stanley Museum.

earlier, with much of the initial labor being done by convicts from the Colorado State Penitentiary at Cañon City (Warden "Tom Tynan's Boys"). They had been quartered in cabins in upper Horseshoe Park that were still very much in evidence. Progress on the road, which followed Fall River and the old Forest Service trail as far as Chapin Pass, had nonetheless been agonizingly slow. It was so slow, in fact, that by the end of the second season of work, the road had advanced only about a mile, as far as Horseshoe Falls. By the time of Augusta's visit, the road still reached no farther than Chapin Pass, and a decision had yet to be made whether to complete it by bringing it over Chapin Pass or by allowing it to climb to the Divide by way of the far more scenic Fall River Pass.

Though later travelers might argue that some of the more difficult going actually lay above Chapin Pass, the lower road, with its switchbacks and dizzying precipices, was more than enough for Augusta Stanley. It was, she wrote, "the most interesting and fearful trip we have made." The

> altitude did not affect me in the slightest, but I was frightened almost to death as the road wound up & up along the sides of the mountain. I wanted to stop until they came back, but they didn't want me to. So Frank got in by the side of me & we went to the end of the finished part of the road. We could look just across the chasm and see the snow, in fact in places look down on it—not over a quarter of a mile away.[54]

Far happier was her ride down the Big Thompson Canyon on the way back to Denver, which Augusta pronounced "the finest we have had yet—the scenery beyond description." Augusta reserved her ultimate judgment on Estes Park, however, to the closing paragraphs of her letter back to Lewiston:

> While I am enjoying all the grandeur and majesty of these Colorado mountains, and, the more quiet beauty of the valleys in the parks, when I think of a place in which to spend the summer months, nothing I have seen here could woo me from my dear old State of Maine and our much-loved Squirrel Island, the gem of the coast.[55]

Augusta Stanley made one more trip to Colorado. During the summer of 1922, now a widow of four years, Augusta came back to Estes Park, accompanied by her 22-year-old granddaughter, Frances Augusta Warren. This time her stay was considerably longer. She arrived on July 20, 1922, and remained until September 2. Augusta was 74 and suffered greatly from a chronically bad knee. As a result, much of her time was passed in the hotel, playing bridge with other guests, or quietly reading to Flora at the Stanleys' nearby summer home. Flora's eyesight, bad enough to elicit Augusta's comment in 1917, was now even worse. There were periodic trips about the park, and a special excursion to a garden party in Greeley where she met the famous Chicago lawyer Clarence Darrow. There was also another visit to Longs Peak Inn, where she again spoke to Enos Mills. Two months later Mills would be dead.

As in 1917, the highlight of Augusta's summer was a much-anticipated trip over the now-completed Fall River Road to Grand Lake. Augusta clearly wanted to take this trip, for it rated high on the list of most visitors. But given her experience five years before, she approached it with a measure of anxiety. "I got everything ready for my trip tomorrow to Grand Lake!" she confided in her diary on August 15.

> Some think we are almost fool hearty to take it but I am sure if every car that goes over that trip goes in safety, why cant I do the same? So I am going and I have decided not to be afraid, and as I have fully made up my mind to that effect I am sure I shall go through with it all right.[56]

The next morning was beautiful. Taking a small "red bus or car" driven by a chauffeur from Fort Collins, Augusta and three other women set out on their journey. Her fears were quickly dissipated, and that night she was ecstatic. "The ride is beyond description!" she wrote.

> It was the most remarkable of any of my whole life! We went 11789 feet to the top of the Continental Divide. Here the waters from one side flow into the Atlantic and the other into the Pacific. The cars all stop at the top and snow balled each other

as there was quite a considerable lot of snow there still. But the ride on down the mountain was the most thrilling of all. That side is steeper and the roads narrower, with no protection on the sides, where if one went over they must go to the bottom, thousands of feet below.[57]

The next day found Augusta still enthusiastic, to the point of gloating:

The day yesterday was one never to be forgotten, and an experience I wouldnt have missed for a hundred dollars. I can afford to sit around and hem napkins today, and live on the remembrances of yesterday. I think I stood it better than the other three ladies, of which I am very proud. . . . The driver said to the clerk at this hotel that he never took a party of ladies over that course before that was as calm as we were as they are usually very nervous.[58]

Augusta's only regret was Grand Lake itself, where they lunched. "But I must confess," she concluded, "I was greatly disappointed in Grand Lake. It was nothing like what I had expected."[59] Her response, perhaps, was to be expected. For "the other Mrs. Stanley," who spoke so glowingly of Squirrel Island as the "gem of the coast," there was, come summer, but one "gem." And it was not the "gem of the Rockies."

12

Disengagement

The Stanley-Sanborn Dissolution

On February 13, 1917, F.O. Stanley and Carl Sanborn, the son of Burton D. Sanborn, who had died three years before, signed a warranty deed bringing the decade-old Stanley-Sanborn real estate partnership formally to a close. The consideration was $10 and the cancellation of stock in the Estes Park Development Company, the original corporate vehicle that had been used to acquire the Earl of Dunraven's holdings.

Under the terms of their agreement, F.O. Stanley took title to some 14 pieces of property still being held by the company—the dissolution probably involved no cash. These lands, totalling almost 1,400 acres, were located across the northern part of the Estes Park valley, more than half in the area northeast of the village known as Dry Gulch.[1] Their southern boundary lay roughly in a line running east-west over Little Prospect Mountain, including the land occupied today by Stanley Park and the Estes Park schools. Carl Sanborn's share of the division lay to the south along Fish Creek, including the site of the English Hotel, and in and around Marys Lake, which he would subsequently turn into a private fishing preserve.

Map of Estes Park in 1927, by Richardson Rome. Courtesy National Park Service.

The Stanley Motor Carriage Company factory at Watertown, Massachusetts. From the collection of the Stanley Museum.

The Stanley Motor Carriage Company

The younger Sanborn's interest in ending his inherited relationship with Stanley is not known. There are several factors, however, that may have contributed to Stanley's decision to terminate his relationship with the Sanborn family. One may have to do with F.O. Stanley's plans in Estes Park. In February 1917, discussions of a new downtown hotel and "model village" were still very much alive, and if the newspaper reports are correct, this required some of the very property that had now come into his sole possession.

But of equal, if not greater, significance was another decision being made that winter in Newton. F.O. and F.E. Stanley at age 68 had decided that come May 1917, they would retire from the Stanley Motor Carriage Company. In a refinancing arrangement concluded with Chicago interests led by their Chicago dealer, Frank Jay, the Stanley twins had agreed to turn operations over to new management, a group that included F.E.'s sons-in-law, Edward Merrihew Hallett and Prescott Warren, who had been brought into the firm more than a decade before.[2]

The Stanleys had not given up on steam transportation. To the contrary, F.E. Stanley, his son, Raymond, and F.O. had quietly been turning their creative attentions to a new project, the Unit Railway Company of Boston. This new Stanley collaboration hoped to make use of Stanley patents to build self-propelled, steam-powered railway cars for interurban and branchline service.[3]

The decision to leave the automobile business was past due. If Prescott Warren is correct, the company's profits after 1908 were never large. Even in 1910, when 700 cars were sold, net earnings amounted to only $32,000, on gross receipts of $883,099.[4] The years after 1914 had been even less kind, and it was time to go. Thirteen years earlier, in 1904, the twins had come to understand that the changing dynamics of the photographic industry made the long-term outlook for their dry plate business, despite the quality of product, decidedly uncertain. Such was now the case with the Stanley Steamer.

For all its legendary features—simplicity and relative cheapness of operation, lack of a worrisome clutch and gearshift, smooth acceleration, and superiority in hill climbing—the Stanley had rapidly lost ground to the gas car. With the improvement of the internal combustion engine, once denounced as "noisy, unreliable, and elephantine,"[5] gasoline cars had gained ascendancy. Steam automobiles could no longer compete with the technically superior and less expensive machines that came rolling off the assembly lines of Henry Ford's factories in Detroit. The Stanleys measured their success car by single car; Ford measured his by the thousand. The famous Model T had been introduced in 1908; by 1915, Ford production had reached 300,000 units. The company had a million cars in operation and a network of 8,000 agents in place.

The figures said it all.[6] In 1907 there were more Stanleys than gas cars registered in Massachusetts. In 1916, by contrast, as F.E. himself was shocked to learn, there were only 799 Stanley automobiles registered in the state, as compared to 30,871 Fords. Even worse, 26 makers of gasoline automobiles had more registrations in Massachusetts than the Stanley.[7] On an average day, Henry Ford was turning out—and before noon—more automobiles than the Stanleys, the largest remaining major steam car manufacturer, were able to produce in an entire model year.[8]

As with the dry plate business, the Stanley brothers stayed a bit too long. Though innovative in a crisis, the Stanleys had stubbornly resisted pressures to improve the efficiency of their automobiles, even in the face of clear signs that they were falling behind the competition. The final blow was the electric self-starter, invented by Charles F. Kettering and introduced in the 1912 Cadillac, which eliminated the onerous task of hand cranking, previously touted as one of the biggest advantages of the steam car. It was now the steam car, not its gas-powered rival, that was the more difficult to operate.

Though one of the few remaining manufacturers of steam cars after 1910, the Stanleys made few concessions to those who purchased and drove their machines. The dashboard of a Stanley Steamer was literally filled with gauges measuring the water level of the boiler, steam pressure, fuel pressure, pilot tank pressure, water tank level, and cylinder oil feed to the steam line. Two valve handles were even located horizontally under the driver's seat. As one automobile historian has noted, "Just to start the car required the manipulation of thirteen valves, levers, handles, and pumps." In the early days, he continues, when "nobody bought a car to commute or run errands . . . [such] a high degree of operator involvement could actually be an enjoyable challenge."[9] Now it was just bothersome. Even such steam enthusiasts as Abner Doble, who continued to build luxurious and high-performance steam cars into the 1920s, admitted that such automobiles were "too complicated to operate, requiring intelligent and unfailing attention."[10]

It was not that the Stanleys refused to change, though they did so reluctantly, but rather that in their attempt to modernize and solve problems, they created others. In 1915, following Doble's example, they finally gave in to the need for a closed water system, radically redesigning the car, except for the Mountain Wagon. They got rid of the familiar coffin-nose and installed a radiator/condenser on the front of the car. Though this modification cut down on the aggravating need to stop for water, it was accompanied by other alterations. "In one design change, the car went from wood-frame to steel, from right-hand drive to left-hand, from Stanley-version rack-and-pinion to state-of-the-art Warner steering and Timken front axles, from large water tanks to small, enabled by the condenser-radiator."[11]

While all these changes were improvements, the problems they created were significant. Oil from the recycled water fouled the boiler, and the added weight of the heavier metal-bodied car, with its new and heavy condenser, was not accompanied by any additional boiler or engine power. The result was poor performance. Customers, even loyalists of long standing, began to complain.

Crisis came as the nation moved toward World War I. Having cut production dramatically to only 126 cars to accommodate the design change of 1915, the Stanleys were never able to recover. 1916 production was limited to 353 units, fewer cars than the Stanleys had produced in any normal year since 1903.

Surplus capacity was used to manufacture compact burner and boiler units for the British War Office, which put them to work pumping water from battlefield trenches. Doctors in frontline hospitals quickly discovered they could also use these compact steam plants to sterilize instruments, heat buildings, and "de-coot" soldiers' clothing. Not to be outdone, American medical men used trucks equipped with 23-inch Stanley boilers and 1,500-gallon water tanks to provide showers for troops subjected to mustard gas. On all of this, the company put a patriotic spin: "We Do Our Bit."[12]

What was left of the steam car business effectively died with the war, though the company itself, without the twins, would struggle on for almost a decade. In June 1917, with the help of financial interests from Chicago, the Stanley Motor Carriage Company's capitalization was increased to $2,500,000 of preferred stock and 100,000 shares of common stock of no par value. Prescott Warren, who had been serving as vice president, succeeded F.E. Stanley as president; Edward Hallett, formerly secretary, succeeded F.O. Stanley as treasurer. Carlton Stanley, the twins' nephew, continued as vice president of manufacturing. Frank Jay, who was clearly involved with the new financial backers, was brought in from Chicago, where he had been western manager, to become vice president of sales.

The steadily worsening state of the company's affairs is reflected in Augusta's diaries. "Frank is very much upset over business," she wrote on September 14, 1916. "It appears that they have been losing money all summer—in fact they will have to go out of business or lose all they have."[13] By February 1917 the Chicago interests had surfaced, and by the end of March the decision had been made, though it took until June to complete the transaction. Though F.E. agreed to remain on in some sort of advisory position, by the end of November he had been effectively shoved aside and frozen out. "Frank left the factory today for good," she wrote on November 28, 1917. "He is heart broken." Augusta blamed "the boys," sons-in-law Ed Hallett and Prescott Warren.[14]

The new Stanley Motor Carriage Company struggled from the beginning, and six years later, in March 1923, was placed in the hands of a receiver, though it continued to operate. In February 1924 the plant was sold to the Steam Vehicle Corporation of America, Stanley Division, which manufactured at least some cars at Newton into the 1925 model year, and then discontinued production. The Steam Vehicle Corporation of America ended its corporate life in Allentown, Pennsylvania, in 1926. Though the Stanley name reappeared briefly in 1934 amidst talk about patents obtained, recapitalization, and the imminent production of a new Stanley Steamer, talk that lasted for some two years, not a single vehicle was ever built.

The recapitalized company became a source of embarrassment to F.O. Stanley. "The management of the Stanley Motor Carriage Company since my brother and I sold out has been very unsatisfactory," he wrote to his Estes Park friend, Frank Woodward, in May 1923.[15] Woodward had attempted to purchase a car, which was never delivered, and 15 months later had asked Stanley to intercede on his behalf. In another letter, written the following day to one of the company's suppliers, F.O. Stanley expressed his regrets about "the failure of the Stanley Motor Carriage Company to pay its bills."[16]

Ever the realist, F.O. Stanley understood full well what had happened to the steam car industry. As was the case in his tribute to George Eastman, he was willing to give credit where credit was due. "I regard the invention of the internal combustion engine one of the most valuable inventions made by man," he wrote Byron Spence, a steam car hobbyist, in April 1939.

> It has not only revolutionized land transportation, but it has made the flying machine a most useful agent. And all that time, and all the money spent in trying to make a steam car as good, or better, than a gas car, is time and money wasted. This is the opinion of a man that has had more experience in making steam cars than any other man living in the world today.[17]

Pondering his future in Newton during the winter of 1917, F.O. Stanley saw little reason to continue making automobiles. But there was every reason to gain clear title to increasingly valuable real estate in Estes Park that Stanley could turn into cash or exchange as collateral as needed.

From the beginning of their automobile business, the Stanley twins apparently drew no salary. They simply withdrew funds from the company as they were needed against the time of a "grand settlement," as it is referred to in family correspondence. When that settlement came in the spring of 1917, it was found that F.E. had withdrawn several thousand dollars more than F.O., a debt that he made up by giving his brother Massachusetts state bonds.[18] Just what F.O. Stanley came away with in terms of cash is unclear, particularly given Raymond Stanley's insistence that his father had pumped a great deal of his own money into the Company over a number of years just "to keep the business going."[19] Whatever the case, as the result of these two decisions, made 2,000 miles apart in Newton and in Estes Park, by May 1917, F.O. Stanley had once again become captain of his own destiny—for the first time in more than 30 years.

Having left the steam car business and dropped plans for a "new Stanley hotel," F.O. Stanley was well on his way toward disengaging, both financially and psychologically. These feelings must have intensified the next summer when news reached him in Estes Park that F.E. had been killed in an automobile accident.

F.E. Stanley had a long history of speeding, accidents, and near-misses.[20] Returning to Boston from Squirrel Island in Maine on the afternoon of July 31, 1918, by way of the Newburyport Turnpike, to meet with engineers from the Unit Railway Company, he had reached a hill two-and-a-half miles east of Topsfield, Massachusetts. As he crested the hill, traveling at a high rate of speed, Stanley's car suddenly swerved to the left to avoid two vehicles parked on the road, climbed an embankment, and turned over, pinning F.E. Stanley underneath. He died on the way to Beverly Hospital, without regaining consciousness.[21] F.O. and Flora returned at once to Newton for the funeral and burial. The impact of Frank's death was profound. It was an event, F.O. would later admit, from which he never fully recovered.[22]

★ ★ ★ ★ ★

F.O. and Flora Stanley returned to Estes Park for the rest of the summer. Unquestionably F.O. brought back with him an altered view of things. Most of the F.O. Stanleys' wealth was tied up in real estate, the Waverly Avenue house in Newton, the hotel, power plant, house, and other properties in Estes Park, including the acreage that F.O. had received in the division with Carl Sanborn. At age 68 the prudent

F. O. Stanley on Oldman Mountain. From the collection of the Stanley Museum.

Stanley increased his efforts to convert these assets into cash. The surviving record of the next two decades documents those efforts.

Between April 1917 and March 1926 the County Clerk's office in Fort Collins recorded some 36 warranty deeds involving the sale of property in F.O. Stanley's name (with several more involving both F.O. and Flora). Such sales, together with other property transactions, continued throughout the 1930s and until the eve of Stanley's death in October 1940. In a letter to his aunt, Raymond Stanley would claim in December 1940 that an appraisal by Ernst and Ernst made during the 1920s set a value of $1 million on his uncle's Estes Park properties.[23] Much of this wealth, of course, disappeared with the Great Depression. Yet even with allowances for deflation, F.O. Stanley's disengagement was so complete that when his Colorado estate was settled in July 1942, the remaining assets were valued at a relatively modest $51,352.85, and they included his summer home on Wonderview Avenue.[24]

Real Estate Sales in Estes Park

In 1907–1908, fresh with enthusiasm, F.O. Stanley had made his investment in Estes Park in a matter of little more than two years. What he bought and built in those two years, together with the properties received from Carl Sanborn in 1917, would, by contrast, take more than a decade to divest. Even then he had to content himself for the most part with deferred payment in the form of mortgages and promissory notes. George Storer, A. A. Hyde, Joe Mills, and the others offered cash, which explains why Stanley found the direct sale of land, even in small parcels, so attractive.

Many of the parcels that Stanley sold were lots smaller than an acre, purchased by individuals intent on building summer cottages or starting a business. But some were considerably larger tracts. On September 20, 1917, Stanley sold Alberta Yore 12.4 acres along the Big Thompson River at Beaver Point, where she and her husband, the colorful journalist Clem Yore, would build their Big Thompson Hotel that same year.[25] The price was $1,830. Estes Park realtor-developers Albert and Julian Hayden purchased 57.9 acres in the same general vicinity for $2,000 on May 28, 1919, on which they would establish a series of rental cottages;[26] while on October 2, George Butler Storer, the founding president and general manager of the Standard Steel Company of Toledo, Ohio, paid Stanley $2,500 for 109.6 acres north and east of the village and the Stanley Hotel.[27]

On October 4, 1921, for $3,500 Stanley sold another tract totalling 19.09 acres to Joe Mills, Enos Mills's younger brother. Located on the northern shoulder of Prospect Mountain, the purchase allowed Mills to add materially to his resort hotel, the Crags, which he had built and opened in 1914 on land also acquired from F.O. Stanley.[28] During this period Stanley sold other small parcels to such well-known Estes Park residents as photographer Fred Payne Clatworthy,[29] newspaperman Al Birch,[30] and gift and tea shop owner Anna K. Wolfrom.[31]

Perhaps the most significant of Stanley's land transactions, however, was the one made with A. A. Hyde, founder of the Mentholatum Company of Wichita, Kansas, and an early and major supporter of the Western Conference of the YMCA. For a number of years the Y had hoped to acquire the 78-acre tract to the north of its Wind River property, bordered by the Big Thompson River, Wind River, and Glacier Creek. On December 21, 1921, Hyde purchased the acreage from Stanley for $5,000 and then promptly deeded it over to the Western Conference.[32] The next year, Hyde personally supervised the development of the site for what had long been his dream: a wooded retreat where people of Christian principles might gather to achieve "fellowship and understanding by living together in mutual helpfulness and cooperation."

Known as Fellowship Park, Hyde's gift would eventually consist of a central Fellowship Community House surrounded by six three-room sleeping cabins.[33] During its first summer alone, Fellowship Park was used by over 300 people. Unfortunately, Hyde's dream fell victim to the belt tightening of the Depression. Fellowship Park was closed after the 1934 season. Thereafter its facilities were rented to various conference groups, all traces of community soon disappearing "except for the buildings and the memories."[34]

Another of those who sought out F.O. Stanley to purchase land to build a summer cottage was 31-year-old Alpharetta Lemmon Somerville, a native of Evans, Colorado. She had been promised a mountain home by her husband of four years, Frank Somerville, if she could find property that was close to town, on level ground, and with a fine view of high peaks, and could obtain utilities. The land Alpha located was on the Big Thompson River near Joe Mills's Prospect Mountain Hotel. When she discovered who owned the land, Alpha refused to be intimidated. According to family tradition she promptly marched up to the Stanley Hotel, asked to see its owner, and told him what she wanted. Stanley was evidently impressed. He accompanied the plucky Alpha back down to the river and then helped her pace off three acres, which she purchased on September 14, 1917, for $900.[35] Frank and Alpha built their cottage, and although Frank Somerville died in 1922, "Somervilla" remained Alpha's summer home until her own death in 1976.

Property sales continued through the late 1920s and into the 1930s. In May 1932, Stanley sold Gordon Hutchings and Edward Krogh property on lower Elkhorn Avenue adjacent to the Big Thompson River. There Hutchings and Krogh constructed two retaining ponds and a filling station and opened the tourist fishing attraction they called "Trouthaven," which operated on the site until 1967. Somewhat later they built an amusement ride around the ponds, the popular Silver Streak Railroad, a miniature train run for many summers by engineer-conductor Phil "Casey" Martin, a local teacher.[36]

Not all of these transactions were outright sales. When Oscar Peter Low, F.O. Stanley's former partner in the Estes Park Transportation Company, decided to give up the campground and filling station he had been operating after his return to Estes Park on land owned by Stanley east of the village, Stanley had little difficulty finding a successor. Frank R. C. Rollins, at one time Estes Park's humane officer, wanted to go into business for himself, and Stanley agreed to help. Whether Rollins lacked the cash needed for an outright purchase, or whether Stanley was reluctant to let go of a piece of prime real estate so close to the center of things, is unclear. But in October 1924, when Rollins took over Low's operations, it was with the help of a five-year lease running from November 1, 1924, to November 1, 1929, at a rate of $500 per year. As part of this arrangement, Stanley received "fuel and oil for his personal automobile free of charge."[37]

Rollins proved to be a good tenant. He proceeded to paint the surrounding fences to match the colonial yellow, white, and red of the Stanley Hotel, and installed a playground and a number of fireplaces and picnic tables. He also built a comfort station with hot and cold running water where tourists could shower, do their laundry, use a room for reading, and purchase automotive and camping supplies. Equipped with electricity and featuring uniformed attendants, Rollins's campground was later praised as "one of the best equipped of such in the West."[38]

Letting Go of the Stanley

F.O. Stanley's decision to disengage from the responsibilities of day-to-day business extended to the power plant, the Stanley Hotel, and the Estes Park Water Company as well. Here, however, as he soon discovered, the challenge was far more difficult. Whatever the book value of these assets, Estes Park in 1917 remained a newly incorporated, relatively isolated mountain community, its economy tied to tourists, the resort business, and a short, three-month summer season. It was not the kind of economy that easily attracted major investors.

Though it had been rumored as early as September 1916 that Stanley was considering an offer to sell the power plant, nothing came of it.[39] Six years later, in the fall of 1922, rumors of an impending deal involving 45-year-old hotel- and businessman Roy K. Starkweather, and both the hotel and Manor House, were reported in the press.[40] The timing of these new rumors coincided almost exactly with the retirement of the capable Alfred Lamborn, which undoubtedly forced Stanley to ponder the hotel's future and the wisdom of his own continuing involvement. Fortunately, he found a suitable replacement, Frank J. Haberl. The 39-year-old, Viennese-born Haberl brought with him impressive credentials. Like Lamborn, he had managed the Denver Club, and before that had gained valuable experience at both the Antlers Hotel in Colorado Springs and Denver's Brown Palace.

The plain fact of the matter was that for all its commitment to high quality and impeccable service, and probably because of it, the Stanley Hotel never made money. Though F.O. Stanley was always reticent about such matters, he once told Henry Dannels, "Henry, I come out here in the spring and bring thirty thousand dollars . . . to operate, and I go back in the fall with ten or fifteen thousand." And, Dannels observed, "He was happy!"[41] This was all well and good, of course, providing there was a steady stream of incoming revenue to offset, or at least cushion, the losses, as there was, more or less, during the first decade of the Stanley Motor Carriage Company. But without such income, it was another matter. Undoubtedly there was at least some substance to the rumors regarding negotiations with Starkweather, just as there would be to subsequent ones.

Though it took another four years, F.O. Stanley did find a buyer for his major Estes Park properties. Roger Toll, superintendent of Rocky Mountain National Park, recorded the event in his monthly report for February 1926:

> On Wednesday, February 3, newspapers published an account of the sale of all the interests and holdings of Mr. F.O. Stanley in Estes Park and vicinity, the reported consideration of this sale being $650,000. There seems to be no true information available as to who the purchasers are, the only facts obtainable being that they are Chicago and Milwaukee capitalists. The sale includes all hotel buildings, power plant, and all land holdings of Mr. Stanley in this vicinity.[42]

Except for the price, which was actually $800,000, Toll was right in most respects, including the paucity of available details surrounding what was a most complex and complicated transaction. The newspapers of the day, as Toll suggests, made little attempt to explain Stanley's motives, other than to offer the suggestion that while bedridden with a broken leg the previous year, he had "conceived the notion of manufacturing violins on a large scale."[43] What did become clear in the following four years, however, was that the deal that Cornelius Bond brokered on his behalf was one that F.O. Stanley would come to regret.

Roger Toll was only partially correct in identifying the purchasers, for all were from Milwaukee rather than Chicago. They included George Frederick Bond, his wife, Erna Bond, and E. T. McCarthy, president, vice president, and secretary-treasurer respectively, of Bond Incorporated, a Milwaukee real estate and investment company; and 47-year-old Milwaukee lawyer James Deyo Shaw, who enjoyed an extensive background in tax and utility law.[44] An odd and seemingly unlikely collection of purchasers, surely, except for one thing: they had through one of their principals, George Frederick Bond, an immediate and long-standing connection with Estes Park.

Though Toll and the contemporary press, even in Estes Park, made no mention of the fact, George Frederick Bond, usually referred to as Fred, was the youngest son of Cornelius H. Bond, the man who had been so instrumental in the development of the village over more than two decades. C. H. Bond had recently completed five years of service representing Larimer County in the Colorado legislature. Though it seems incredible, given the prominence of the father, next to nothing is known about the younger Bond. What is known is that Fred Bond graduated from Loveland High School in May 1916 and then, a decade later, still not yet 30, suddenly returned to Estes Park as the pivotal figure of the syndicate that purchased F.O. Stanley's holdings.[45]

Lack of information about Fred Bond, particularly in a small town that from the very beginning boosted and celebrated its own, and where his father was a most prominent figure, is surprising. It is particularly so given the ambitiousness of the undertaking, and the fact that, for a time at least, the purchase that Bond seemed to have engineered so easily appeared to be a complete success, promising even greater things. Yet not once during the events that followed did the connection with C. H. Bond, surely known at the time, seem to matter. In the aftermath it was clear that there was every reason not to discuss it.

The Stanley Corporation, as Shaw and the two Bonds incorporated themselves on March 27, 1926, was headquartered in offices on Elkhorn Avenue—offices also occupied by Cornelius H. Bond & Company and the Estes Park Water Company.[46] On May 18, 1926, the negotiations complete, F.O. Stanley formally turned over to this new corporation most of his properties in Estes Park. In return he received three first mortgages totalling $800,000, an amount significantly larger than what Toll had reported to Washington, but one that tracks fairly closely the Ernst and Ernst appraisal.

When the directors of the new Stanley Corporation met in Estes Park on May 20, 1926, to conclude their transaction with Stanley, they also made public their future intentions. They would operate the Stanley properties through three separate departments, each with local management. Frank Haberl would stay on to oversee the hotel, and Byron Hall would continue to manage the Stanley power plant on Fall River. The only newcomer to the management team was Frank

Bond, the eldest son of Cornelius H. Bond and Fred Bond's older brother. The directors indicated that he would have charge of the land department, supervising all of Stanley's "acreage and leases." The *Estes Park Trail* reported on May 21 that, "Each of these departments from this date on will be distinctly separate from the others, and each manager will have sole and absolute control of the property and affairs of his particular department."[47]

James Shaw, at 47 the senior citizen of the new corporation and by far its most experienced member, initially served as secretary and spokesman. He announced that in the future the hotel would be asked to purchase its electricity from the power plant "at the usual rates." He also assured the community that it too would receive "the finest possible service." From an economic point of view, this made perfect sense. Shaw and the others clearly wanted to put the power plant on a firm operating basis for the first time, which meant establishing a full and accurate accounting of its actual costs.

Over the next two years, as promised, the Stanley Corporation made significant progress in improving and extending the plant's electrical service. With the help of a consulting engineer, transmission lines were extended almost three miles down the Big Thompson Canyon to the summer enclave known as Glen Comfort, east to Fish Creek Road, west into Horseshoe Park, as well as to the vicinity of the Y Camp, adding three hotels and 129 cottages to the plant's list of customers. The corporation also rebuilt the entire distribution system in the town of Estes Park, installed a new streetlighting system along Elkhorn Avenue, put in a new dam below the plant to accurately record the stream flow, and overhauled and improved the old generating equipment.[48]

The Milwaukee syndicate's plans were clearly ambitious. But at least initially, Bond and his associates appeared to have the money required for their implementation. As early as August 1926, at a time when the corporation had begun to construct a new gateway for the hotel, it hired Saco Rienk DeBoer, Colorado's premier landscape architect. His assignment was to redesign the four-block area on Elkhorn Avenue extending from the post office and library (in what is now Bond Park) as far east as the new Stanley Hotel gate in order to create "a model business district housed in structures of the Norman-Gothic type with arcade sidewalks."

"The buildings now comprising the business section of the town have long been considered an eyesore." the *Fort Collins Express-Courier* reminded its readers. "The new buildings," by contrast, "will be distinctive and in harmony with the scenery of the park, and will add much to the attractiveness of the town."[49] Though the article went on to say that Frank Bond, "representing the interests involved," had "approved" DeBoer's plan and that "the work will be begun in the immediate future," the plan languished—much the way F.O. Stanley's equally elaborate plan to revitalize the same area had done almost a decade before.

The Stanley Hotel and its grounds, now nearly 20 years old, on the other hand, did receive badly needed attention. In the spring of 1927 new carpeting and draperies were installed in the hotel, its interior was repainted, and furniture was refinished. At the same time the new owners rebuilt the hotel gateway, shifting it "back and a little east of the present entrance," and remodelled the manager's cottage into offices for use by the corporation.

The only other announcements by the new management team that year came on September 3, 1926. They were nearly as dramatic as the plans for the "Norman-Gothic" business district. The corporation let it be known that it intended not only to plat Little Prospect Mountain as a restricted residential area for 20 homes, but also to develop the site lying about halfway between the village and the old Dunraven Ranch property at the foot of Park Hill for an airfield and an elaborate recreational facility.

The plans for the recreation grounds were impressive. They included a polo field enclosed by a three-quarter-mile oblong track for horse and automobile racing, a grandstand, bleachers, and a baseball diamond. Immediately west of the track there were to be polo stables and corrals for rodeos, and to the north a polo practice field. That was not all. In order to catch the attention of arriving visitors, the road leading east to the old Dunraven ranch would be landscaped with drives and shrubbery, tennis courts, and an outdoor bowling field. Overflow parking from major events would be accommodated in space south of the polo stables. Not surprisingly, the *Estes Park Trail* found these plans "remarkable."[50]

Work on the park facilities went forward much as planned. By the first week of June 1927, with plans well under way for a parade, rodeo, historical pageant, and a July Fourth ceremony unveiling a boulder-and-bronze tablet to Joel Estes, "the discoverer of Estes Park," the promised racetrack, corrals, polo grounds, aviation field, and 1,500-spectator grandstand were being rushed to completion in order to take care of an expected 20,000 visitors.[51] The Estes Park Pioneer Day celebration three weeks later proved a grand success, the rodeo alone drawing 2,000 more than expected during two days of events.[52]

Evidently buoyed by that success, that same month the Stanley Corporation announced what was to be its most grandiose plan: its intention to lay out 17 100-acre estates in the north end of the park in the vicinity of Eagle Rock, to be "sold to eastern millionaires who want to make Colorado their playground." The asking price for each estate would be $50,000. To ensure their exclusivity, they would only "be sold to wealthy persons who can properly care for each estate and develop it along lines acceptable to the corporation." "Written understandings" would covenant and protect all parties.[53]

In November 1926 the Stanley Corporation went to court to gain clear title to nine parcels of land, most of them dating back to the days of the Earl of Dunraven,[54] an action that, though routine, only seemed to underscore the seriousness of their intentions. But except for the news about the rodeo grounds and Eagle Rock estates the following June, little more was heard about the corporation's activities or plans for the future. Whatever formal business there was took place behind the scenes in late December 1926 and early January 1927, as Shaw and his partners formalized their previously announced operating strategy by organizing the Stanley Hotel Company[55] and the Stanley Power Company[56] as separate corporate entities. They then transferred to each the first mortgages given to F.O. Stanley at the time of purchase. The third, or "Park Land Mortgage," remained with the Stanley Corporation.

Through the spring of 1927 the Stanley Corporation continued to exude confidence about the future and the ultimate success of its various plans. In early March one of its principals, probably Fred Bond himself, blithely wired the White House and President Calvin Coolidge to offer "one of its fine hotels in Estes Park for himself and his entire presidential party," promising to remodel and refurbish as needed. There would be no charge. A brief flurry of excitement followed. Even Estes Park's mayor, Sam Service, got into the act, and was quoted by the *Rocky Mountain News* as saying that

> the president and his party would be made the most comfortable in Estes Park and that the remarkable drinking water piped from the very edge of the huge glaciers of the Mummy Range, as well as the remarkable scenery, cool days, and invigorating atmosphere, should make a strong appeal to the nation's chief executive.[57]

The *News* put Service's invitation into word and picture, running a front-page "Welcome, Cal!" cartoon in which the great "glad" hand of Colorado is being extended to the president relaxing on a bank of snow. "Cool Cal" apparently had other plans for that summer, and nothing more was heard about the Corporation's generous offer.

Despite the outward appearance of stability, and the kind of periodic announcements of progress and plans noted above, the Stanley Corporation was in financial disarray. What precisely went wrong with the corporation's plans for financing its purchases is unknown, though its land development schemes on Little Prospect and below Eagle Rock openly hint at wealthy purchasers who failed to materialize. One can also surmise that the hotel and power plant, the corporation's only immediate sources of revenue, probably did little more than cover their own operating expenses, let alone provide the cash profit needed to pay taxes and service the debt on the mortgages given to Stanley.

Without a significant and sustained infusion of outside capital, of which there is no record, the situation soon became untenable. These were, of course, the "Roaring Twenties," whose boom times continued well into the summer of 1929, when America was on what F. Scott Fitzgerald called "the greatest, gaudiest spree in history." It was also a time in which many banks, bankers, and other investors were all too willing to ignore the accumulating weight of private, poorly secured debt. F.O. Stanley, as it would shortly turn out, was not one of them.

During the late winter or early spring of 1928, Fred Bond emerged as the major principal of the Stanley Corporation. There is much about Bond and his motives that remains unclear. What is quite clear, however, is that after less than two years, he wanted out of the hotel resort business. By April 1928 he thought he had a buyer: John Charles Shaffer, the wealthy president and publisher of the *Chicago Evening Post* and former owner of the *Rocky Mountain News, Denver News,* and *Denver Republican.* Shaffer had made a great deal of money in street railways and invested some of it in a 12,000-acre ranch, Ken Caryl, in the mountains 20 miles southwest of Denver. Shaffer was a plausible prospect. He had editorially supported the bill creating Rocky Mountain National Park and knew Estes Park well. Moreover, Shaffer and his wife had been vacation guests at the Stanley Hotel for many years and were well acquainted with both the Stanleys and the Sanborns.[58] Shaffer, it was reported, was so admiring of Estes Park that he was prepared to pay Fred Bond and the others some $300,000 to turn the Stanley Hotel "into a private club . . . supported largely by businessmen of Chicago looking for a pleasant place to take their vacations." Though Bond refused to "disclose details of the deal," he was confident enough of its outcome to declare, emphatically, that "in thirty days I will be out of it."[59]

The rumored April 1928 negotiations with Shaffer, if they ever existed, collapsed, leaving the Stanley Corporation without the funds it needed to meet its obligations to F.O. Stanley. Stanley, on his part, was prepared for a time to be patient. He probably had no choice. By May a mortgage payment of $19,750, due January 1, 1928, had still not been paid; and accrued payments from January to April 1928, totalling $9,875, were also outstanding. In addition there was the matter of a $65,000 cash advance made by F.O. Stanley to the Stanley Corporation, of which there was also no sign of repayment.

In late May 1928, Fred Bond and F.O. Stanley attempted to rescue the situation with a new agreement. Bond agreed to pay Stanley $75,000 in cash, and Stanley agreed to restructure $620,000 of outstanding debt. Stanley was also to receive two cash payments: the first of $40,000, to be made on or before August 1, 1928; the second for $55,000, to be made on or before November 1 of the same year. The remaining $450,000 was to be paid either in cash, on or before November 1, 1928, or over five years through two newly executed mortgages. The first of these mortgages, for $300,000, was secured by the hotel and its 140 acres; the second, for $150,000, was secured by other property, presumably including (though it was curiously not so stated) the Stanley power plant. The two mortgages, backdated to April 1, 1928, carried an annual interest rate of 5 percent.[60]

The terms of this new May 1928 agreement were, understandably, strict. Stanley was to receive a significant amount of cash up front, and a second payment within six months. Even if the option for new mortgages was exercised that November, Stanley was to have all his money returned within five years. Bond and his associates moved forward on their end. In mid-September 1928, they sold the Stanley Power Company and its distribution system to the Public Service Company of Colorado for a reported $200,000,[61] no doubt as a way of raising some of the cash required to meet the terms of the May agreement. The deal was not, however, without its complications. On November 17, 1928, Willard L. Warnock, a Loveland auctioneer, filed a complaint in district court charging that the corporation had not paid his 5 percent commission on the sale, amounting to $10,000.[62] Warnock's problem was a hint of trouble yet to come.

Stanley tried to be helpful. In December 1928 he made a special trip from Newton to Denver to meet with Fred Bond and famous Colorado financier Charles Boettcher, one of America's richest men. They met at the Brown Palace, which Boettcher owned and where he made his home in a private suite. There they reportedly discussed a "refinancing project."[63] Boettcher's financial and business empire was vast, far larger even than John Shaffer's. Only three years Stanley's junior, he had made much of his early money in the mines of Leadville and another fortune with the Great Western Sugar Company. Though Boettcher had become enormously successful and wealthy by taking calculated risks, and believed in economic diversification, facts that doubtless made him an attractive target, there is no evidence that his interest extended to the Stanley properties in Estes Park.[64]

In April 1929, Boettcher's name once again became linked with Fred Bond and the fate of the Stanley Hotel, when he was visited by Milwaukee businessman Daniel F. Breslauer,[65] another of Bond's reported backers. Boettcher, Breslauer had learned, was a director of Roe Emery's Rocky Mountain Parks Transportation Company (or Rocky Mountain Motor Company, as it had been renamed in 1927 when Emery consolidated his holdings). Breslauer wanted to know whether or not Boettcher would favor the merger of the Stanley Hotel and Emery's hotel interests, which included the Lewiston Hotel and the Chalets in Estes Park and the Grand Lake Lodge across the Continental Divide.

Though Breslauer left without "immediate prospects for consummation of the deal," news of that possibility was reported in the press. The prospects for such a merger were apparently bleak, for as the *Longmont Daily Call* told its readers, citing Fred Bond as its source, F.O. Stanley was opposed to such a deal and so was Boettcher. This fact, however, did not stop Bond, who now appeared like a desperate man. He mentioned the Elkhorn Lodge, Baldpate Inn, and Stead's Ranch as other likely merger candidates.[66] When the news of a prospective Stanley-Lewiston partnership reached Estes Park, however, it was reported very much as a done deal, the "forerunner of a hotel combination for Estes Park that may include other of the most prominent hotels in a strong chain of hotels that is now becoming the vogue throughout the east."[67]

By the summer of 1929 F.O. Stanley was thoroughly aware of the precariousness of the situation. Whether opposed or not, he had every right to be skeptical about the likelihood of such a merger, and when Bond could not meet his 1928 payment deadlines, Stanley took immediate steps to take back control of his Estes Park properties. At the time of the original sale in 1926, Stanley had asked the man who had arranged it, Cornelius H. Bond, to serve as a trustee. In that capacity it had been Bond's duty to look after Stanley's interests until such time as the terms of the contract were fulfilled.

This was clearly a mistake. With two sons intimately involved in the day-to-day operations of the Stanley Corporation, such an arrangement had always contained a potential conflict of interest. Stanley now understood just where such a conflict could lead. His first action was to have Cornelius Bond replaced as trustee by Samuel Black, the hotel's accountant.[68] Black had been in F.O. Stanley's employment since the opening of the hotel in 1909. He was someone whom Stanley clearly believed he could trust.

On June 29, 1929, F.O. Stanley took his second step. He had Samuel Black file suit in Larimer County district court against Fred Bond and the Stanley Corporation so that he could foreclose on the mortgage encumbering the hotel. In naming his defendants, Stanley cast a broad net, including not only G. Fred Bond but also Cornelius

H. Bond and Alfred D. Lewis of Estes Park, John A. Zimpelmann of Chicago, and the Public Service Company of Colorado.[69]

The Public Service Company may have been named because earlier that month, on May 9, 1929, it had won a judgment against the Stanley Hotel Company and the Stanley Corporation for nonpayment of bills in the amount of $4,466 plus $37.25 in costs.[70] There had been no immediate settlement, and nine days later, on May 18, with the tourist season about to begin, the Public Service Company cut off electric service to the hotel, forcing it to operate on portable generators for the next three weeks.[71]

The harsh and unqualified findings rendered by the district court in open session on August 16, 1929, fully justified F.O. Stanley's concern and the actions he had taken. The Stanley Corporation and the Stanley Hotel Company were both insolvent. Not only was the "property in the Stanley Hotel Group Mortgage . . . wholly insufficient to pay the principal and interest of the notes secured by the Stanley Hotel Group Mortgage," but

> the property is threatened with waste, and the improvements on the property are being wasted, deteriorated, and the security being lost through the acts of the defendants and their failure to keep the property in repair.[72]

The defendants, it turned out, had not met a single interest payment since January 1, 1928, and were now in default by $49,250. Moreover, they had not paid taxes for the years 1927 and 1928, a delinquency, with interest and penalties, that amounted to $12,144.39.[73] The court's judgment was definitive. It placed the hotel and its assets in receivership, appointed Samuel Black as receiver, and ordered him to take immediate possession of the property.

The final chapter of what had become a twisted and sorry spectacle began on September 24, 1929, when District Judge Robert Smith entered a judgment in favor of trustee-plaintiff Samuel Black for $511,394.39, the amount owed by the Stanley Corporation and the Stanley Hotel Company. In addition to ordering the defendants to pay the "costs of these proceedings," Judge Smith authorized a foreclosure sale.[74] That sale took place two months later, on November 24, 1929, only weeks after Black Friday and the crash of the stock market in New York.

Stanley, of course, had his original investment to protect, but there were few, if any, other bidders. F.O. Stanley's bid of $300,000 was accepted and the hotel was once again his.[75] Though the price Stanley paid was challenged in court the following July on grounds that the "properties are worth a million dollars," Judge Smith subsequently confirmed the purchase.[76] To this there was no appeal.

As these details of the litigation suggest, feelings on all sides ran deep and left scars. This was particularly true of F.O. Stanley, who had been badly bruised, if not used, by those he thought he could trust. Cornelius Bond had not performed well in his capacity as trustee, and Fred Bond had acted in ways that Stanley had become convinced were reprehensible and even dishonest. Gentleman that he was, however, F.O. Stanley kept his own counsel in the matter. His silence continued into the mid-1930s, even though by then the hotel was once again in other hands.

The reasons for Stanley's silence reflected his belief in forbearance and right conduct. But there were other reasons as well. Many of them surely had to do with the Bond family and the place they occupied in Estes Park. Fred Bond had disappeared once again from the Estes Park scene. His older brother, Frank, was successfully serving the town as mayor. Cornelius H. Bond, dead since 1931 after suffering through a painful amputation of his leg the year before, had long since been elevated to community icon.

The elder Bond had held almost every public office in Estes Park, and with good cause was almost universally regarded as having contributed more than any other individual to the founding and subsequent growth of the town. This esteem, which was as deep and sincere as the esteem in which F.O. Stanley himself was held, would find its greatest public expression in May 1944, when the Estes Park Board of Trustees, by resolution, named the parcel of land in the village occupied at that time by the post office and library "Bond Park" to perpetuate his memory.[77]

Stanley is known to have broken silence on the role of the Bond family in his affairs only once, and even then he chose to be discreet and polite and act in a way that still protected both confidentiality and reputation. But he was also firm. In the aftermath of the events of 1929, Cornelius Bond's wife of 35 years, Alma, had naturally felt the full force of Stanley's removal of her husband as trustee and the criticism of his integrity that such a public act seemed to imply. Those feelings were finally and fully expressed in the late winter of 1936, when she wrote F.O. Stanley a blistering and emotion-charged letter accusing him of dishonesty in dealing with her late husband and her second son.

That letter apparently has not survived. Fortunately we do have F.O. Stanley's response of April 10, 1936, a letter that sheds important light on Stanley's attempt to divest himself of his Estes Park properties, and on the sensibility and sensitivities of the man himself. Stanley wrote:

Dear Mrs. Bond,

I have delayed in answering your letter because I wanted to be sure I could answer it without passion or prejudice.

Now your letter hurt greatly. I am nearly 87 years old, and . . . you are the first person to accuse me of being dishonest or dishonorable. I am certain if you had known all the facts in the case you would never have written that letter.

The sale of my property to Fred Bond was what is called a Trustee sale. A trustee is appointed to protect the seller and to see that the terms of the contract are fulfilled. The seller appoints a trustee. Here is where I made a great mistake. I should never have appointed Mr. Bond Trustee. I should have realized it would be very natural, in case of difficulty, for him to decide in favor of his own son.

Now I do not accuse Mr. Bond of dishonesty, but he was very careless in protect[ing] me. I will mention one case. I could mention many. When we decided to sell the power plant to the Public Service Company, it was necessary to deliver the bonds to the Public Service Company on receipt of the cash. I sent the power bonds to Mr. Bond, and instead of turning them over and getting the cash from the Public Service Company, he gave them to Fred and he delivered the bonds to [the] Public Service Company, and did not turn the cash [over] to me but used it to pay his own debts. Do you wonder I decided to have a new Trustee? A little later, at a trial at Fort Collins, Judge Coffin discharged Mr. Bond, and appointed Mr. Black Trustee.

Now I found Fred thoroughly dishonest and untrustworthy. He called me from Denver one day, and asked me to meet him and Mr. Horace Bennett[78] at the Brown [Palace] Hotel at 9 a.m.

the next day. I went down to the Hotel, and was there on time. A clerk at the hotel handed me a letter from Fred, stating he was obliged to go to Colorado Springs and could not meet me. I learned later he was in his room at the Hotel all the time.

You speak, in your letter, of insurance. Now I am quite certain Mr. Bond never took out any insurance policies on the Stanley for me. While the hotel was being built and furnished, I kept it insured. Mr. Sherman of the Estes Park Bank wrote the policies for me. After that it was not insured.

Now I have no doubt you were honest and sincere when you wrote that letter, but you were entirely in error as to the facts. [If you are?] a woman that wishes to be just and fair, as I certainly think you are, you will inform yourself of what took place in that deal, and when you do and get the true story, you will be sorry you wrote that letter, and will feel it your duty to apologize.[79]

Given the clear depth of emotion in his response to Alma Bond, it is interesting to note that Stanley never felt it necessary to explain in public "the true story" of his relationship with the two Bonds. That fact alone speaks worlds about the equanimity and character of the man who was F.O. Stanley.

Roe Emery

Having regained legal title to his Estes Park properties on November 25, 1929, a transaction confirmed by the court in July 1930, Stanley was free to seek a new buyer. It cannot have been a happy period, particularly because he had promised to use some of the proceeds from the original sale to fund a new gymnasium at Hebron.[80] Though it apparently took only months to locate another purchaser, it took almost a year to conclude the sale.[81] Although Boettcher and Stanley had not been in favor of the purchase of the Stanley Hotel by the Rocky Mountain Motor Company while Bond and his Stanley Hotel Company and Stanley Corporation were involved, once the bankruptcy proceedings had wiped the slate clean, Roe Emery's transportation conglomerate became interested indeed. Serious negotiations followed.

On October 9, 1930, following a quick trip from Newton to Denver, Stanley assigned to Emery the certificate of purchase he had been granted by Judge Smith.[82] Emery, ownership in hand, immediately merged the Stanley Hotel and his own Estes Park Chalets[83] into a newly formed subsidiary corporation, the Estes Park Hotel Company, of which he himself was president and to whose board F.O. Stanley was named as a director.

Their final agreement was close to ideal. Emery brought with him what few other buyers in 1930 Colorado could: a steady cash flow generated by his transportation empire. Though the 1930s depressed Colorado's tourist industry as it depressed every industry of American life, Emery's transportation company had a built-in safety net that most others lacked. Without Emery, who managed to make money during the worst economic times the nation had seen, it is unlikely that the Stanley Hotel could have survived.

Years later Roe Emery would laugh with members of his family about F.O. Stanley's behavior the day he closed on the hotel. Their arrangement called for an up-front cash payment of $75,000, the rest of the undisclosed purchase price taking the form of 1,630 shares of preferred stock in the new Estes Park Hotel Company. F.O. Stanley politely received Emery's check, folded it, and carefully placed it in his inner breast pocket. The stock certificates, on the other hand, he simply crumpled up and crammed into the outer pocket of his pants.

When Emery chided him to be "careful with that stock," Stanley is reported to have responded, patting his breast pocket, "Here's the good I'll get out of this deal."[84] In time Emery's amusement was probably tempered a bit, particularly as he came to know more about the economics of the Stanley Hotel and, perhaps, something of the problems that Stanley had encountered from those who tendered him promises rather than hard cash. The important thing for F.O. Stanley, however, was that he was once again, and this time finally, out of the hotel business.

As for the value of the shares received, F.O. Stanley was, as usual, correct. Their value proved largely a sentimental one. The preferred shares held by Stanley, 1,630 out of a total of 4,500, never paid a dividend. They became part of F.O. Stanley's Colorado estate after his death on October 2, 1940, and though his heirs attempted for a number of years to establish their value, they were unsuccessful.

"Mr. Roe Emery, as President of the Hotel Company, told me," E. G. Knowles wrote to the Denver law firm of Bingham, Dane & Gould on March 11, 1941, as part of the settlement process, "that Mr. Stanley realized that there was no actual value in the preferred stock and rather looked upon the holdings as an interest in a concern which was in a sense a monument to him rather than an investment."[85]

Roe Emery was as good a steward as circumstances would permit, given the difficult times. Though he would subsequently maintain that when he took over the Stanley Hotel "it was outmoded and . . . required a considerable sum to bring it up to date,"[86] there were no major attempts at remodelling until the 1935 season. That year Emery put together and set to work a crew of 30 men—carpenters, plumbers, plasterers, paperhangers, and electricians. Each bedroom was provided with its own private bath and with hot and cold running water, hundreds of new light fixtures were installed, and the old hydraulic brass elevator was replaced with a new Otis electric one. The fact that the Otis tower was placed behind the cupola had the unfortunate effect of disturbing the hotel roofline, but greatly improved the usefulness of the elevator. Its hydraulic predecessor had been known to descend rather than ascend when the load was too heavy.

Emery also erected and furnished a new steam laundry building, redecorated many of the bedrooms, and repainted the hotel's exterior. It was at this time, or shortly thereafter, that the hotel's original mustard-yellow color was exchanged for white. Three years later, in 1938, in order to gain more room for employees, Emery had the former five-room gatehouse moved from the foot of Elkhorn Avenue to a new site just west of the hotel, where it was placed on a concrete slab and remodelled to contain 10 rooms and five baths. At the same time, the adjacent building, originally built to house the hotel's manager, received "a complete overhauling," giving each of its nine original rooms its own bath.[87]

Of equal significance, Emery indulged the hotel's former owner, treating him with patience and deference. Throughout the 1930s, F.O. Stanley continued to be a familiar presence at the hotel. Though during the early years of the decade he appeared with Flora, more and more he began to come alone, taking his lunch in the dining room, attending concerts and other events, and sitting, sometimes for hours, in a favorite rocker on the hotel veranda. For Emery, and for others, it was still Mr. Stanley's hotel.

Even with the resources and expertise that Emery brought to its operations, the hotel continued to be a financially losing proposition. As Arthur K. Underwood, general agent for the Lincoln National Life Insurance Company of Denver, explained in November 1940, the month after F.O. Stanley's death:

> The Stanley Hotel has lost money every year and the Rocky Mountain Motor Company [Emery's parent corporation] has had to advance the funds necessary for the upkeep of the hotel, which they have done by building up a nice fat mortgage on the hotel property. The mortgage now amounts to about $250,000. The nearest that the Stanley Hotel has ever come to making enough money to even pay the depreciation charges was this year when they came within $10,000 of doing it. Some years the hotel has been in the red to the tune of $50,000 to $60,000. This deficiency has been made up by the Rocky Mountain Motor Company which merely accepted an increase in the mortgage each year it made this adjustment.[88]

Such facts were hardly surprising. F.O. Stanley, given what we know, never made money on his hotel, even in flush times. Emery's stewardship came during the Depression years when most Americans, even those who remained employed, cut back on discretionary spending.

The highlight of the first decade of Emery's ownership was no doubt the 1936 season, the summer that saw the attention of the entire state and nation focused briefly on Estes Park, when Republican presidential candidate Alf Landon and his family arrived to vacation both before and after his nomination.[89] They did not stay at the Stanley Hotel, where the glare of publicity would have been almost constant. With two small children, four-year-old Nancy Jo and two-and-a half-year-old John Cobb, to consider, the Landons wisely retreated to the seclusion of the McGraw ranch on Cow Creek, off the Dry Gulch road north of town, a spot sufficiently removed from the village to offer at least the prospect of privacy. There, where before the turn of the century, cattle had roamed freely, the Kansas governor was photographed "wearing hip boots and wading into the rushing stream clear up to his ankles" and holding a 12-inch trout.[90]

Alf Landon's entrance into Estes Park was a spectacular one. Escorted by police from Longmont, the cavalcade was met at the outskirts of the village by Mayor Casey Rockwell and a party of 200 mounted horsemen gaily dressed in "brightly colored shirts" and "super gallon" hats. "A stupendous sight" was the governor's comment.[91]

The Stanley Hotel, with Emery in the role of host, played a prominent role throughout the governor's visit as the campaign communication center where the large press entourage received its daily briefings. With Emery's blessing, its members, preferring less rustic quarters than the candidate, took over the third floor of the hotel. What followed was not the press corps' finest hour. With much too much time on their hands between well-orchestrated appearances of "the candidate" and other public events, the journalists' behavior became so raucous that other guests asked to be removed to the Manor House where they could enjoy peace and quiet.[92]

F.O. Stanley apparently kept out of the way. Though he considered himself a good Republican, Stanley did not yield to the temptation to have his photograph taken with the man who many in Estes Park hoped that fall would become the next President of the United States.

As his letter of 1936 to Alma Bond suggests, the years of F.O. Stanley's disengagement from Estes Park included experiences as difficult, distasteful, and disappointing as any that he ever faced. The fact that he kept this to himself, rather than sharing it with others in Estes Park, however, pointed to where Stanley's values finally lay. For F.O. Stanley success was not measured in dollars or current business success—it was measured in the good he could do with money he was not born with and with recaptured health that made every day a gift.

13

The Rocky Mountain National Park Transportation Controversy

See America first? Sure! But remember this: If you do not know Colorado, you do not know America.
—Gilbert McClurg, November 19, 1915[1]

F.O. Stanley knew how to use the courts and the legal system to protect his financial interests. During the celebrated transportation controversy that spanned more than a decade, from 1919 to 1929, Stanley showed himself willing to fight for principle as well. Like so many causes célèbres, this one began with an administrative decision.

On May 13, 1919, park superintendent Lewis Claude Way, with whom Stanley had cooperated over the possible construction of a new headquarters building, awarded an exclusive long-term franchise to Roe Emery's Rocky Mountain Parks Transportation Company to transport tourists into and through Rocky Mountain National Park. He did so without a public hearing or competitive bids. The franchise agreement also banned from the park private rent-cars (or "jitneys"), which operated either on their own or on behalf of local resort owners. The trouble developed over the restrictions placed on these private vehicles.

Way's action was the result of a new policy initiative from Washington. The motives of Stephen Mather, the National Park Service's first director and Way's immediate superior, were largely benign. Most agreed on the need to control the negative impact of rival concessions within the nation's national parks, where competition often meant hucksterism, poor service, and high prices. Such a policy, it was argued, was long overdue and constituted a step forward for the newly created Park Service and its efforts to give order and direction to the parks under its jurisdiction.

Regulating automobile traffic in Rocky Mountain National Park, Mather also knew, had an additional appeal. The park's existing road system was clearly inadequate. Given its accessibility from the valley towns, traffic congestion during summer months was a matter of growing concern. The new policy most immediately affected independent drivers. It also had an impact on F.O. Stanley, for whom introducing tourists to scenic attractions of Rocky Mountain National Park by automobile had long been a distinctive feature of his hotel operation.

The first to take opposition to Way and the new policy was Stanley's friend, Enos Mills, the man widely praised as "father of Rocky Mountain National Park." Having fought to create a park for all the people, Mills objected strenuously to what he considered an illegal, undemocratic, and bureaucratic monopoly that restricted the access of some.

Stanley and Mills were men of strong belief and principle. Mills was unwilling to compromise on matters he considered unjust. What this meant in practice was that, for all the friendliness and public high-mindedness that he projected from the lecture platform and in the pages of his books, Enos Mills could be a difficult man to get along with and, if and when aroused, a formidable opponent. Like many self-made men, he tended to be suspicious of authority and those who wielded it. Such was the case in his collision with L. Claude Way and the new transportation policy.

Initially, as Way told his superiors at the end of May, there seemed to be little or no opposition, even from among the jitney drivers. The written complaints received came mostly from Mills, who protested

The Longs Peak Inn Mountain Wagon at Lily Lake. Courtesy Fort Collins Public Library.

that Way's policy was discriminating against his guests at Longs Peak Inn. Way did, however, raise an important concern with Washington: whether or not he actually had the authority to exercise police jurisdiction over roads that had never been formally ceded by state or county to the United States. It was precisely this issue of jurisdiction that soon became the center of contention.[2]

Had it not been for Enos Mills, Way's authority and the authority of the United States government might well have gone untested. But Mills had, once again, become a man with a cause. On August 16, 1919, he telephoned Way and matter-of-factly notified him that he was sending a car, driven by Edward Catlett and carrying three passengers, from Longs Peak Inn over the High Drive and into the park. Way had no choice. A former army captain and veteran of the Spanish-American War, he, too, could be tough when occasion demanded. Way personally intercepted Catlett on Fall River Road near Chasm Falls, and ordered car and driver from the park.

Mills had his test case. He promptly filed suit in the U.S. District Court of Colorado, charging that the Park Service had interfered with his "common rights as a citizen of Colorado in traveling over the Park roads." Despite the fact that Judge Robert Lewis turned down his petition for a temporary injunction against the Park Service, Mills persisted, turning his considerable literary abilities against this new form of "Prussian" tyranny. At the same time he openly encouraged other like-minded individuals to join him in challenging the government's authority.

What had at first been mainly a war of words soon turned ugly. A group of local residents who operated for-hire cars during the summer months joined in the agitation. With increasing aggressiveness they circulated petitions, erected a large billboard advertising their services on Stanley's land at the approach to Estes Park, and encouraged tourists and residents alike to make their protests heard. Local civic and commercial clubs along the Front Range, mixing principle with fear that the transportation monopoly would impact their tourist business, joined their voices to the public debate.

The issue would not go away. The embattled Way and his successor, the popular Roger Toll, found themselves caught up in the so-called Cede Jurisdiction controversy, in which the State of Colorado sued the federal government over its right to regulate traffic over roads built with state and county funds. Enos Mills unfortunately did not live to see the issue through. He died unexpectedly in the early hours of September 22, 1922, leaving others to carry on the fight. One of those was F.O. Stanley.

Stanley, like Mills, was his own man. Siding with Mills meant breaking ranks with Estes Park's other hotel owners, the vast majority of whom supported the concessions policy. It also meant taking a position against the very same men who had publicly praised him a decade earlier for his cooperation—for never having "done a solitary thing which . . . interfered with any other hotelkeeper in the Park." Though Stanley and Mills differed on the approaches they chose to take, they were in perfect agreement on the basic principles defining the issue.

Stephen Mather knew how important good public relations were to the future of the Park Service. In September 1919, with the transportation policy and the controversy surrounding it only months old, he personally came to Estes Park and, in an effort to calm the waters, asked to meet with those concerned. Enos Mills, with whom he had stood side by side at the park dedication four years before, was one of those whom Mather particularly wanted to engage. As Way later told Washington, "A special car was sent to convey him to the meeting in order that his opinions might be heard and considered,"[3] but Mills refused to attend. Instead Mills said he "would have Mr. F.O. Stanley speak for him."[4]

Stanley did precisely that. Mather presided over an open meeting of Estes Park businessmen held on the afternoon of September 6 at Way's office in the village. Undaunted by Mather's presence or the presence of those who he knew disagreed with him, Stanley directly raised the subject. In Way's retelling, Stanley

> stated that 90 to 98 percent of the people of Estes Park, also 90 percent of the visitors, to the Rocky Mountain National Park, were opposed to the concession; that the principle was wrong; that he was not criticising the concessioner or myself, but was criticising the policy.

About seven people applauded Stanley's speech, Way said, while the rest remained silent. Stanley concluded by stating

> that the people of Estes Park did not want the park administered by officials in Washington, who did not know anything about the needs of the Park, etc., insisting as has always been done, that the Estes Park people should take over the management of this park and run it for themselves.[5]

In the aftermath of that visit, Stanley and Mills became irrevocably linked, at least for Way. "It is singular," he told Mather,

> that of the 28 hotels served by the concessioner's machines, Mr. Mills and Mr. F.O. Stanley are the only ones, so far as I can learn, who claimed that the concessioner gave poor service, was indifferent to the desires of the public, and that the drivers were mostly poor. . . . It is also singular that neither Mr. Mills nor Mr. Stanley has yet reported one specific case to me for investigation.[6]

In his dealings with his various opponents Captain Way proved to be a superb tactician. What he failed to understand was that a man like F.O. Stanley had motives that transcended narrow self-interest. Stanley meant what he said; he had no desire to achieve private advantage by displacing Roe Emery and his company. Way decided that Stanley was jealous. He reminded his superiors at the Park Service that three years earlier, shortly after he purchased the Estes Park Transportation Company, Emery had junked Mr. Stanley's steamers in favor of White gasoline-propelled automobiles.

Stanley did not, however, have any quarrel with Emery. Roger Toll, Way's successor, reported to Park Service Director Mather that at a meeting of the Estes Park Chamber of Commerce on October 26, 1921, Stanley had made it clear that "he was not in favor of an exclusive franchise, but did not wish to criticize the Transportation Company, since he felt that they have furnished good service during the past year."[7]

Though Stanley, like Enos Mills, was capable of employing words like "autocratic," "unreasonable," and "unjust" in describing the transportation concession, he tried to be fair and balanced in his opposition. To the extent that he felt others were not, he was willing to challenge them in public. When, for example, the *Denver Post* ran an article in November 1921 headlined "Estes Business Men Condemn Fight Waged on Automobile Transportation Plan in Park," Stanley found it "so misleading and likely to cause so much harm, not only to Estes Park, but indirectly to the entire state of Colorado," that he responded with a letter occupying nearly half a page. "Take my own case as an example," he wrote.

> In my nineteen years in Estes Park, I have paid in taxes approximately $40,000 and in addition I have contributed towards building roads in the park and the approaches to the park, over $15,000—and yet I am denied the full use of the roads and what is true in my case is true in the case of every taxpayer in the state.
>
> Of all the social problems man has to consider, none has been more thoroly [sic] solved than the road problem. Public roads are public property and can be used alike by all.
>
> The head of the richest corporation has no privilege on a public highway that is not shared by the humblest individual. Whatever restriction is placed on the liberty of one in the use of the roads is placed on the liberty of all. If the poor man has to

pay a tax on his low priced automobile the rich man has to pay like tax, and in proportion to the value of his machine.

Stanley then went on to explain that the park bill of 1915 had deliberately exempted private property within park boundaries from "the provisions of this act," and that this exemption covered the use of roads. "Yet," he continued, "in spite of the fact that the common law and custom in the use of the roads would prevent it, the park management makes the transportation of passengers in the park an absolute monopoly."

Stanley also took great pains to underscore for his audience just where his objections were being directed:

> Now I hope that the reader will not infer from what I have written that I am criticizing the transportation company in their legitimate work of transporting passengers to and from Estes Park and the railroad stations. This work is well done. And so long as it is well done the company will have no more loyal supporter than I am.
>
> What I am criticizing is the granting, by a department of our government, [of] an exclusive franchise to one party to carry passengers into the Rocky Mountain National Park over roads built by the people for public use, and in many cases roads built decades before anyone had dreamed of such a thing as a national park. The personality of the agent that receives this concession is not of the slightest importance. It is the concession we criticize and not the agent, and this we shall continue to criticize until this concession is abolished and the roads given back to the people.

The Denver Post, famous for its flamboyant and one-sided reporting, treated Stanley's letter with deference. In fact the paper's subheading managed to capture with succinctness and accuracy the entire thrust of Stanley's argument: "F.O. Stanley Has No Criticism for Firm Operating Line, but He Declares Principle of Giving Exclusive Franchise over Public Property Is Wrong."[8]

With the death of Enos Mills in 1922, the battle over the transportation franchise lost its most active and dedicated participant. But others, including F.O. Stanley, kept the issue alive. On September 2, 1923, Mills' widow, Esther, hosted a mid-day dinner at Longs Peak Inn. The occasion was the first anniversary of Mills' death, to be commemorated by forming the Colorado chapter of a new organization, "Friends of Our National Parks." That afternoon, as its first order of business, it passed a resolution supporting "the stand taken by the world famed naturalist and author [against the Transportation Company monopoly] and pledging the support of the organization to the cause for which he stood."[9] Among the 75 in attendance was 72-year-old F.O. Stanley. One of the strategies adopted was an attempt to influence the shareholders of Emery's company. "I find we can get the entire list of stock holders of the R.M.P.T. Co. at the State House, Denver," Stanley wrote Mrs. Mills three weeks later, on September 21. "Mr. Bond is going to Denver in a few days and will attend to the matter."[10]

As the transportation controversy dragged on, F.O. Stanley was one of the last to reconcile himself to an outcome that most observers regarded as inevitable. As late as September 12, 1928, Stanley spoke out once more. The occasion was a well-attended first meeting of the Estes Park Welfare Association, an organization formed by Estes Park landowners, 32 of whom signed a declaration not only to renew opposition to the transportation monopoly but also to protest the rates being charged by the Rocky Mountain Motor Company.[11]

Stanley's eloquence was roundly applauded. After a slate of officers was elected, he was asked to summarize his remarks in writing for the organization's new president, Colorado's former governor, William E. Sweet, who was absent. Stanley's letter, dated October 1, 1928, provided the opportunity to restate his position and to address the issue in terms of what he believed was best for the future of Estes Park. "Unfortunately," he told Sweet,

> the interests of the railroads and the transportation company, and the interests of Estes Park are not identical. It is for the interest of the railroads and the transportation company to take as many people to Estes Park, and have them stop only the shortest time, for they make their money in transportation.
>
> On the other hand, the hotels, the stores, the cottage owners, and all places of amusement want the people to sojourn in the Park, as the revenue to these places comes only when the people are there.

*Estes Park in 1925 looking east along Elkhorn Avenue. Courtesy
Estes Park Area Historical Museum.*

Also, at all times the transportation company has tried to
monopolize transportation to Estes Park, and it has largely succeeded in doing so. As a result of the favoritism it has obtained,
the taxi owners in Denver are so offended they are doing their
best to boycott Estes Park.

I asked a taxi owner in Denver what he would charge me to
take me to Estes Park, and he replied "Ten Dollars". I then asked
how long I could stay in the park, and he said "Two Hours".
When I suggested that two hours seemed a short time to see all
of Estes Park, he assured me it was ample time to see all of interest in Estes Park. Then he said, "Why do you go to Estes Park?
For Two dollars I will take you to Colorado Springs, through the
Garden of the Gods, to the top of Pikes Peak and back to
Denver". I learned that the taxi franchise did not allow a stop in
Estes Park of more than two hours, and the party must be taken
up and back the same way.

If Estes Park is to become a summer resort of the greatest possible value to the State of Colorado, adding millions to its taxable property, and hundreds of thousands of dollars to its annual income, it can be done only by having the greatest possible freedom in transportation. Any kind of monopoly in Estes Park would be suicidal. The moment one party is given a monopoly, immediately all others are antagonized, and will do all they can to injure the park, just as they are doing now.

The Rocky Mountain Parks Transportation Company has a certain monopoly that is perfectly legitimate and necessary. In their co-operation with the railroads they have a great advantage. All through tickets to Estes Park are of necessity honored by them. This is a perfectly legitimate protection; it is ample and all they are entitled to. Any further monopoly than this would be unjust, and in the end injurious to the party that secured it. Injustice is always a dangerous commodity to go to market with.

A vigorous attempt will be made this coming winter to induce the legislature to cede complete police jurisdiction in Rocky Mountain National Park to the U.S. Government, and no one will be more active to bring this about than the transportation company, because it will make transportation in the park a monopoly in their favor.

It would be a great mistake to allow this to take place. It would be ruinous to that absolute freedom in transportation necessary to the future development of Estes Park.

But it is argued that the Government would not appropriate money for roads in the park unless this franchise is granted. Very well; does Colorado want to sell its birthright for a mess of pottage? The injury to Estes Park by such a grant would greatly outweigh any money the Government would give for roads. Colorado is amply able to police its own territory, and I certainly hope the legislature will not be influenced by the selfish propaganda that will be offered in support of this bill.[12]

His letter, detailed and persuasive though it might be, was too late. With a decisiveness that surprised even its staunchest supporters, the legislation ceding jurisdiction over the roads in Rocky Mountain National Park passed both houses of the Colorado legislature, and was signed into law by Governor Teller Ammons on February 19, 1929. Stanley was then, of course, in Newton. Hopeful to the last, he had telegraphed Esther Mills on February 2, "YOU CAN USE LETTER SWEEP [to Sweet] AS YOU SEE FIT."[13]

The concessions fight was over. But watching events unfold, it is unlikely that F.O. Stanley failed to miss the announcement made by the director of the National Park Service just three days before the final vote. The sum of $650,000 would soon be made available to construct a new "wonder road" along Trail Ridge and across the Continental Divide.[14] It was the sort of offer that the dollar-short legislature of a tourist-conscious state could ill afford not to take advantage of.

When it came to fostering business and protecting the independent entrepreneur from government intervention and regulation, F.O. Stanley remained adamant. "Expediency in government," he would later write, "is a departure from justice and is always dangerous."[15] Artificial combinations, whether in the form of organized labor or business monopolies, were simply wrong in Stanley's mind.[16]

Invited in 1934 to join the National Recovery Administration's (NRA) new Consumers Advisory Board, Stanley declined. To join the Board meant implicit endorsement of the NRA's code of fair business competition. "I am wholly opposed to the NRA, the Code and about everything the present administration is doing," he wrote in declining the honor. "In my long life of eighty-five years, nothing, in my opinion, has happened that is so destructive to personal liberty, initiative and the sound principles upon which permanent industrial progress must rest, as is happening today."[17] Stanley, like many other good Republicans, took great satisfaction when a year later, after the Supreme Court declared the New Deal agency unconstitutional, Roosevelt abolished it.

Goodwill and principle dominated F.O. Stanley's approach to life. In the Cede Jurisdiction controversy over transportation in Rocky Mountain National Park these two collided. Here, F.O. Stanley chose to risk goodwill and stand on principle.

14

"The Grand Old Man
of Estes Park"

F.O. Stanley ripened gracefully into old age, increasingly aware of the changes that had taken place during his own lifetime. No "one who ever visited Estes Park," he wrote in 1928,

> has had a more varied experience than I have had. For twenty six consecutive years I have been a summer visitor to Estes Park. This has given me an opportunity to watch its growth . . . ; to see the village grow from one having only two cottages, to one having several hundred cottages; to see the hotels increase from four to some twenty-five; and the time required to go from Denver to Estes Park reduced from an all-day's hard journey, to a comfortable ride in an automobile in two and one half hours.[1]

With the hotel at last in the hands of others and the transportation controversy over, Stanley largely retired from the public arena, his reputation secure. To the press of Colorado he was "the man who is largely responsible for the development of Estes Park into the nationally popular summer vacation spot that it is today."[2] To those in Estes Park—those who knew him best—he was simply "the grand old man."[3]

To the extent that Stanley had a developed credo to explain his longevity and success, it is contained in a letter written to Herbert and Alilia Wing of Kingfield in 1932:

My very dear friends.

Now most old people have some kind of a complaint to fall back on as an excuse for not doing things. But I seem to be unfortunate in not having any. I have a good appetite and good digestion. I sleep well nights and can drive my car 250 miles in a day and not get tired.

To what extent my unusually good health is due to my personal habits is difficult to say. The following are the facts: I am a total abstainer from alcoholics. I have never tasted tobacco in any form, and I never drank a cup of coffee. My daily routine consists of work, temperance and fun, all very important. My religion is based on the theory that true happiness comes from contributing to the happiness of others. Hope of heaven and dread of hell form no part of my daily life. I know no more about those things than I did the day I was born.[4]

Wealthy men of the day were often portrayed by cartoonists as portly men, grown soft by too much good living. Such dissipation, either real or imagined, was not for him. Though Stanley was usually reluctant to preach his own habits of abstemious living to anyone (the Stanley Hotel would continue to sell alcohol until the state of Colorado went dry on January 1, 1916), he willingly made an exception when it came to the use of tobacco. Though smoking, too, was permitted at the hotel, it was his personal anathema, as his nephew, Raymond, could testify from riveting firsthand experience. Caught by his uncle smoking a pipe in the lobby of the Newton Trust Company, where he had gone to cash a check (a pipe that he tried to conceal by stuffing it in his pocket), Raymond Stanley was icily told, "Young man, as long as you smoke you'll never fill your father's shoes."[5]

F.O. was even more emphatic in print. In a 1931 essay, *The Tobacco Habit, Its Evils*, he wrote, "I believe that the tobacco habit as practiced today is the most dangerous drug habit confronting the American people, even more dangerous, owing to its universality, than the alcoholic or drug habit." F.O. Stanley considered the eradication of smoking nothing short of a sacred obligation. "I should be a moral coward," he continued, "if I did not use every means in my power to prevent the young from acquiring the habit."[6] Stanley firmly supported Hebron Academy's no-smoking policy as president of the board, even when it led to the expulsion of his niece's son, Stanley Hallett, who had been caught smoking.

As the force of these opinions suggests, F.O. entered the final decade of his life as a man of strong views about most subjects. These views were courted by others, both in Newton and in Estes Park, where he continued to be much in demand as a speaker. Despite advancing age, Stanley's memory and intellectual dexterity, and his droll understated Yankee sense of humor, remained largely unimpaired. Moreover, as his audiences discovered, Stanley took their invitations seriously. Where some older men might be content to share personal reminiscence or simply rehash old themes, Stanley relished the opportunity to educate his listeners.[7] Appearing before the Longmont Rotary on his way back to Boston in September 1936, Stanley chose to present an illustrated lecture addressing the question "Why the earth continues to revolve on its same axis year after year?"[8]

Always charming and sociable in public situations, Stanley was ever politic, even disingenuous, particularly, as he said, when it meant "contributing to the happiness of others." Making a stop in Lyons in July 1927, he told the editor of the *Recorder*, with apparently the greatest sincerity, that he had originally come to the "gateway town" in 1903 with the intention of "putting up a big hotel." But "owing to the fact that the price of the property he was negotiating for was boosted to a point he considered out of all reason, he dropped the proposition here and went up to Estes Park where he purchased property from the English syndicate operating the old Dunraven ranch, and built his hotel there."[9] The *Lyons Recorder* reported Stanley's words without comment.

F.O. Stanley liked people. Stories of his kindness and acts of charity, large and small, are legion. The majority of these involve children, of which both Stanleys were extremely fond. Without children of their own, F.O. and Flora frequently took the children of relatives and others into their home and into their lives. While much of the surviving evidence is anecdotal, the anecdotes themselves are so pervasive and persuasive that there is every reason to trust them.

These stories begin as early as 1895, when one of F.O. Stanley's horses killed a man in Newton named Herbert J. Johnson, leaving his small daughter, Pearl, orphaned. Touched by Pearl's situation, Stanley made formal legal arrangements with the girl's guardian to raise her

F. O. Stanley in the Billiard Room of the Stanley Hotel. Photograph by Fred Payne Clatworthy. From the collection of the Stanley Museum.

and provide financial support until she reached the age of 21. In this case, however, the Stanleys' generosity was not accepted. Some 14 months later, F.O. relinquished all claims to the child because Pearl's grandmother, unwilling to part with the child, caused them so much trouble.[10]

Estes Park residents of the 1920s and 1930s noticed this fondness for children, many recalling at least one story about F.O. Stanley and the young, surprisingly often a story that involved themselves. The Stanley they remembered, usually looking back over a considerable period of years, was an imposing, somewhat austere old man who seemed willing to spend hours patiently testing children on their spelling, making up mathematical problems to solve, explaining how things worked, doing tricks with swallowed pennies that suddenly reappeared and pieces of string magically made whole, or giving away the wooden puzzles and crossbows he had carefully put together in his workshops in Newton and Estes Park. At times their tone is one approaching awe. Walter Baldridge speaks of

a box 8″ x 4″ x 3″ filled with every shape of wood ever turned out—cones, balls, squares, etc. all made of hard maple. . . . He [F.O. Stanley] would pour all the pieces in his lap, and then put them back in the box and close the lid. He would then pour the pieces in your lap and tell you to put the pieces back, but the pieces had to fit just right and nobody else could ever get all the pieces in the box.[11]

There were also stories of stray children brought home by steamer;[12] of small presents, usually dimes, produced surreptitiously from pockets and given away; and of a standing arrangement at Elijah "Lige" Rivers's Stanley Livery on Elkhorn (so named because of its proximity to the hotel) to take care of any child who could not afford to ride, periodically paid for with a $50 bill. (F.O. himself also loaned Rivers money, which the Stanley estate later had to write off as uncollectible.)

While some of these stories are probably apocryphal, or at least exaggerated, all of them fit the persona that Stanley projected to those who knew him, especially to those under the age of 10. You cannot fool children, at least not for long. F.O. Stanley did not have to try, for his interest was real. The spirit of childish playfulness, delight, and love of surprise that he radiated was an essential and deeply rooted part of a man who was himself ever young.

F.O. Stanley's sincerity and sensitivity in dealing with children are well illustrated by a series of surviving letters he wrote over a period of years to Jean and Jane McNab, twin girls from Omaha, who were frequent summer visitors to Estes Park. "My dear Jane and Jean," Stanley wrote from Newton on May 3, 1929, at the very moment when his troubles with the hotel might easily have distracted him:

Your very nice letters came a long time ago. I have read them many times, and our friends have read them and they enjoy them and think they are very nice.

I wish you would write me again and tell me about having your tonsils out, and whether it hurt very much, and if they gave you some good ice cream.

It will not be long now when we will all, I hope, be out in Estes Park again. You must come over often and take dinner with us and we will have lots of fun playing hide and seek again.

I felt much pleased to know you wanted my picture to hang up in your room, so I am going to send you one as soon as I can get it framed.

Mrs. Stanley and I are both very well, and with kindest regards to your father and mother, and to Dorothy and Robert. And very much love to my dear Jane and Jean, I remain,

Your sincere friend[13]

His correspondence with the McNab twins continued. "I had a number of presents and nice cards on my birthday," he wrote on June 3, 1930, "but yours was by far the best."[14] As late as 1938, at a time well after both girls had begun teaching school and were adults, Stanley continued to address them with the same tone of affection. "The horses will be all ready for you when you get there," he wrote on June 5, 1938, noting that he and Flora planned to arrive in Denver on June 22.

Mrs. Stanley and I are well and Minnie is to be with us again this year. She was with us every year since 1903. She goes up from Denver before we get there, and gets the house in fine shape, so we simply walk in and feel at home at once.[15]

Stories about F.O. Stanley's relationship with children extend to Newton as well. Frank and Robert Hopewell, whose family lived next door to the Stanleys at 315 Waverly Avenue, both remembered Stanley as someone who well into his 80s took keen delight in the young, and when the situation arose found small ways to instill what became life-long lessons. The foot-operated wooden turntable in the Stanley garage, which stood behind the house at the end of a long curved driveway, particularly fascinated the boys of the neighborhood, who received Mr. Stanley's permission to use it as a merry-go-round. One day they got the turntable going so fast that it came off its track. Chagrined, young Frank Hopewell went home and told his father, Henry C. Hopewell, who promptly marched his son back to the Stanley house to announce that he would hire someone to fix the turntable. F.O. Stanley was undisturbed. He politely told Mr. Hopewell (in effect) to

*The McNab twins with their friend F. O. Stanley. From the collection
of the Stanley Museum.*

mind his own business—that he and the boys would fix the turntable.
And they did.[16] The Hopewell boys also recalled being allowed to sled
down a hill into Mr. Stanley's lawn with impunity, even though their
runs often ended among Mr. Stanley's rhododendrons.

F.O. Stanley's wooden crossbows were particularly coveted by the
youngsters of Estes Park and Newton. Easy to cock because of a device
that he had designed, they were powerful enough (because the bows
themselves were made of steel) to be used for target practice at the
range he erected beside his garage. Pieter Hondius, whose father had
married into the James family of the Elkhorn Lodge, recalled being
"dragged" by his mother up the hill to the Stanleys for a visit. "The one
thing you don't want to do when you're eight or nine years old," he
recalled with honesty, "is to spend the afternoon visiting old folks." On
one of those occasions, F.O. took young Hondius over to his wood-
working shop:

> Then I heard he was pleased with me and was making me a sur-
> prise. I thought, "Hot-darn, he's making me a crossbow!" I dis-

covered instead that he was making me a toy violin. I really blew it when I told him what he could do with his violin. It was a bad mistake. I could have been the proud possessor of a genuine Stanley violin.[17]

Stanley was very proud of his crossbows, and on occasion he invited adults to take target practice with him. One of the fortunate was Forrest Williamson, owner of Williamson's Toggery, opened in 1923 on the southeast corner of Elkhorn Avenue and Moraine Drive, adjacent to the Transportation Company offices. "At one time," Williamson recalled in 1979, "he tried to interest me in putting these crossbows downtown to make a target range, kind of like a rifle shoot, but I thought it was too dangerous."[18] Instead Williamson settled for "Target Golf," a popular amusement game he established during the early 1930s next to his store, the object of which was to hit a golf ball into a set of concentric circles placed against a slope 100 feet away.

The stories about Stanley's relationships with children seem a good deal more authentic, it must be noted, than some of those concerning his supposedly curmudgeonly-like behavior toward adults. One of these tells of his alleged habit of sitting in the lobby of the Stanley Hotel during the 1930s, personally passing on the acceptability of guests seeking accommodations. When he objected to anyone, so the story goes, he simply nodded his head in the direction of the clerk at the front desk. Those so identified were told that the house was full.[19] (Stanley is supposed to have wielded such dictatorial power, it should be noted, at a time when the hotel itself was no longer his, and when the Depression made any kind of tourist with money welcome almost anywhere.)

Another often-repeated story concerns his passion for pool. The fact that Stanley was an avid pool player, and so competitive that he was suspected of sometimes missing shots to fool opponents, was true enough. But that those who misunderstood and laughed were promptly asked to leave the hotel[20] is a story that can probably be dismissed. It is simply not in keeping with what we know about the character and personality of the man.

Some of the most poignant stories of Stanley's charity and kindness do, however, involve adults, and rest on the authority of those in a position to know. The story of Stanley's involvement with Walter

The Stanley Crossbow. From the collection of the Stanley Museum.

Baldridge and the members of his family is perhaps the best-known case in point. A native of Missouri, Baldridge had come to Estes Park in March 1915 to help bring electricity to James Stead's ranch resort in Moraine Park. Stanley was apparently so impressed with Baldridge's expertise that he hired him to handle the electrical work at both the hotel and the power plant.

Stanley treated his employees well, and Walter Baldridge was no exception. When he was struck by lightning and seriously injured in 1918 while servicing a transformer behind the Stanley home, F.O. Stanley not only kept Baldridge on the payroll, but allowed his family to occupy the hotel gatehouse, then located at the eastern end of Elkhorn Avenue. Later, when Baldridge decided to become a partner in a hardware and electrical shop, Stanley loaned him the money and later still, in 1928, helped him buy the business outright. F.O. Stanley's concern for the welfare of his former employee extended to the three Baldridge daughters, two of whom, it is said, he sent to college. When the youngest, Doris, elected to attend Simmons College in Boston and then stay on to work at Massachusetts General Hospital, she was frequently invited as a guest into the Stanley home in Newton.[21]

Stanley is also known to have befriended Estes Park's most eccentric resident, William Currence, known as "Miner Bill." Born in 1868 or 1869, Currence arrived in Colorado from Nebraska shortly after the turn of the century. Before coming to Estes Park he had prospected the area around Ute Mountain in Montezuma County. By June 1908, Currence and his partner, Julius Bussman, had moved to Estes Park and were living in a rough 14 x 16–foot, lean-to cabin ("Hackmandy") on the side of Mount Chapin above Chasm Falls near where they had filed on four mining claims.[22] Two months later the *Estes Park Mountaineer* reported that the two men had located a promising ore-bearing ledge.[23] The next July, there was news of a "remarkable" find: "a large ore chamber about 50 by 100 feet, with small veins running into it from various directions."[24]

In 1909, Currence began to have trouble with the authorities. His problems intensified with the coming of Rocky Mountain National Park, culminating on June 7, 1919, when he was forcibly ejected by park superintendent Claude Way for erecting buildings and other improvements on federal lands without a permit. That same month Way wrote to M. B. Tomblin, secretary of the Colorado Metal Mining Association, who had attempted to intervene in Currence's behalf: "the records show that Currance [sic] is subject to spells of insanity. He is considered a dangerous person, by residents of this section, who have known him for several years."[25] Way's information was correct. Currence had experienced episodes of strange and erratic behavior at least as far back as December 1904, when he spent 10 months in the Colorado State Insane Asylum. The record spoke of fits of wild incoherence, "most of his conversation being on astrology, and about Divine things."[26] That he was "considered a dangerous person" by the residents of Estes Park seems less certain.

Unstable or not, Currence was sane enough to invent a large, crank-and-gear-operated machine for sawing wood and ice, using a large, 6-foot crosscut blade. He was also sane enough to file an affidavit about his invention with Larimer County in January 1925, and then corresponded with the U.S. Patent Office. It was this machine that apparently first brought Currence to the attention of F.O. Stanley. From that time on, Stanley took an active interest in Currence and his hermitlike existence. He began by purchasing firewood sawed on Currence's machine and later allowed him to build a crude half-cave, half-shack on land he owned off Big Horn Lane. Like a number of others, Stanley also helped Currence out from time to time by offering odd jobs.

Their relationship was cordial, if formal. Found among Currence's effects following his death is a letter from Newton, written on March 15, 1930, in which Stanley thanks Currence for the "amusing" clipping, sending in return his "kind personal regards."[27] Another memento, a postcard written from Estes Park on July 11, 1931, reads, "Dear Mr. Currence: Kindly call and see me. F.O. Stanley."[28] Whatever other residents may have thought about Currence's danger to the community apparently did not much matter to Stanley. He continued to allow Currence to squat on his property until the time of his own death, after which the people of Estes Park had Miner Bill taken down to the Colorado General Hospital in Denver for psychological evaluation. In January 1943, William Currence was committed to the Colorado State Hospital, where he died on March 1, 1951.

Whether apocryphal or fact, these stories and others are hard to ignore because they have long since become part of the written and oral history of Estes Park. Their value lies in the decidedly human dimension they give to the Stanley legacy, suggesting how a very public man quietly intervened in the lives of those who needed help. They also explain, in a way the mere facts of history never can, the respect and affection in which Stanley was held by an entire community.

Violin Making

No glimpse into the final decades of F.O. Stanley's life would be complete without reference to his decision of 1924 to seriously pursue the art of violin making. The interest was not new. It dated as far back as 1859 when, inspired no doubt by his grandfather Liberty's interest and experience, Stanley not only constructed a serviceable instrument using available tools and native wood but also taught himself how to play it.

In 1866, F.O. Stanley made another violin, which was kept in the family, and again three years later, when he used the income from the manufacture of several more instruments to supplement his salary as a high school principal. He then turned his attention to other matters. Violins and violin music remained, however, lifelong enthusiasms. "If . . . I were asked to name the most perfect musical instrument," F.O. Stanley told the members of Newton's Tuesday Club in 1922, "I should answer, unhesitatingly, the violin. All through the centuries . . . the violin has held the undisputed title 'The King of Instruments.'"[29]

F.E. Stanley shared his brother's passion. During the early years of the Stanley Motor Carriage Company, the twins used the long narrow office they shared at the rear of the Watertown plant overlooking the Charles River as a workshop for violin making. Turning their drafting table into a workbench, they spent much of their time trying to produce Stradivarius-quality violins, bringing to the task much the same focused creativity and ingenuity they had applied earlier to dry plates and steam cars.

Each made as many as 25 violins. There were periods both before and after the turn of the century, however, when their hobby became all-absorbing, leading to stories about exasperated salesmen and employees made to wait outside the office while important (but unspecified) work went on within.[30]

At times the violin and violin making cut into home life as well. Augusta Stanley noted in her diary on Christmas Day 1908, almost as if it was to be expected, that "Frank staid [sic] at the factory all day and evening, working on violins."[31] The brothers also spent considerable time playing their violins ("fiddling," as Augusta puts it), both together and alone. "Frank kept the violin going all day," she wrote with evident consternation in March 1908, "and I wonder if there could be a worse combination than a gramophone and a violin off the key."[32]

Many of the instruments they made were copied from originals borrowed and then minutely studied and measured. The Stanleys were so proud of their replicas that they sometimes invited experts into their homes, including professors from nearby M.I.T., whom they asked to distinguish in appearance and tone the difference between a Stradivarius and a Stanley. The verdict, on at least some occasions, was that the two instruments were virtually indistinguishable.[33]

Then came the late spring of 1924. At an age when most men have long since put aside thoughts of new ventures, F.O. Stanley suddenly announced his intention (using, somewhat ironically, the language of Henry Ford) "to apply the principles of quantity production and by the use of machinery, new processes and standardization, to manufacture a violin that will equal the Stradivarius." These, he estimated, could be sold for $100, a full $70 over cost.[34]

Stanley attacked the problems of turning out violins in quantity with his customary dedication and thoroughness. He had already painstakingly acquired the skills and tools of the craftsman, including as much firsthand knowledge as possible about the techniques of the master violin makers of Europe, particularly their use of woods and varnishes. He even visited Cremona in Italy (the home of Stradivarius and Amati), where he obtained pieces of rare spruce wood to study

Mr. Stanley in his workshop. Photograph by Chansonetta Stanley Emmons (F.O.'s sister). From the collection of the Stanley Museum.

and test. Later he added to the art by inventing a new type of bridge for which he sought a patent shortly before his death.

Stanley's "factory" was the well-equipped and well-lighted workshop in the garage behind his home on Waverly Avenue in Newton. There, in January and February 1924, he turned out eight violins, four made from green wood taken "fresh from the forest" and then kiln dried. The other four were made of old wood, some of which came from furniture. The challenge, he noted that June, was to see if old wood was absolutely necessary, for his initial experiments suggested that violins made with green wood were "just as good if not better" than those made with wood 100 years old.[35]

Stanley subsequently found wood for his new instruments in a most unlikely place, an abandoned mining tunnel above timberline near the town of Silverton, Colorado, where someone had stumbled across a large cache of blue spruce originally cut to timber the mine in 1884. For over 40 years, he told a summer visitor to Estes Park, those "logs had lain in the dry well-ventilated tunnel . . . perfectly seasoned, knot free, ideal tone wood," enough wood, in fact, to make violins for the rest of his life.[36]

In typical Stanley style, F.O. also used his violin making to give his nephew, Carlton Fairfield Stanley (1872–1956), a living after the Stanley Motor Carriage Company finally closed its doors in 1924. Carlton Stanley, the second son of the twins' older brother, Isaac, was a well-tested veteran of Stanley family enterprises. He had been intimately involved in the twins' ventures since the 1890s, when they installed him as manager of their new dry plate manufacturing plant in Montreal. In 1905 he had become general superintendent of the Stanley Motor Carriage Company, where he remained past the time of the twins' departure and until the company was finally sold.

F.O. Stanley set high standards of performance for everyone, including members of his own family, and Carlton fully met the challenge. "He is a man of perfect habits," F.O. wrote of his nephew in 1923, "a total abstainer from alcoholics and has never used tobacco in any form. He is honest, pleasant to meet, and generally liked by his associates and operatives in the factory."[37]

The collaboration between the two men lasted for the rest of F.O. Stanley's life. Credit for the success they enjoyed, however, clearly belonged to Carlton, who handled the actual manufacturing. By 1954, working under his uncle's supervision and then on his own, Carlton Stanley completed just over 500 violins, violas, and cellos, using a varnish of his own making. Carlton actually had to buy the tools of the workshop at F.O.'s estate sale in 1941, explaining to Raymond Stanley, the family-appointed estate executor, that those tools were his livelihood and entreating Raymond not to bid against him.[38]

Though self-taught, Carlton produced instruments that were highly enough regarded to be included in John H. Fairfield's authoritative list of "American Makers" (1942). Carlton Stanley's "instruments are exceptionally well made," Fairfield informed his readers, "show beautiful workmanship and have fine tone. His better violins sell for $150.00 to $200.00, violas $150.00 and cellos $600.00."[39]

As with their dry plates and steam cars, the Stanleys kept advertising to a minimum, using only a modest brochure featuring several well-known Boston-area violinists who were willing to lend their photographs and endorsements to the Stanley product. Their reputation spread. Much to F.O.'s delight, following a two-day trip to Dearborn, Michigan, in 1933, where Stanley "visited Mr. Ford, and his marvelous factory,"[40] Henry Ford bought several Stanley violins for his own private collection.

Toward the close of what would be his last summer in Estes Park, F.O. Stanley attended one of the regular Sunday night concerts at the Stanley Hotel, thrown open as usual to the people of Estes Park. The evening of August 18 was, however, a special occasion. It was "Stanley Night," and the program played by the Stanley Ensemble consisted of music that was F.O.'s favorite.

By way of additional tribute the small orchestra played some of F.O.'s own compositions, after which "Mr. Stanley spoke of his violin shop and played on one of his own instruments two old-fashioned jigs to a delighted audience."[41] Inspired by that event, Stanley announced before departing for Newton that he intended to match Stradivarius's record by making two violins at the age of 94.[42] It was one of the very few occasions on which F.O. Stanley did not prove as good as his word.

As the years passed, there were the infirmities of old age to deal with. F.O.'s health, on the whole, remained surprisingly robust. He broke a leg in March 1924 at the age of 73, and 13 years later, in 1937, at age 88 sustained cuts, bruises, and three fractured ribs when he was thrown from a car in Estes Park. On both occasions, however, Stanley recovered quickly. A member of Newton's Tuesday Club recalled encountering the energetic Stanley one day in 1937 at his home on Waverly Avenue, just as he was completing, single-handedly, the installation of a new air-conditioning system of his own design. Stanley told his visitor that he'd done the job himself because "none of the systems on the market . . . were sufficiently good."[43]

The only serious illness of F.O. Stanley's later years occurred in early March 1938. Injured by a fall down a flight of stairs at home, he was hospitalized in Boston. His condition, though unspecified, was sufficiently serious to bring Byron Hall, by then Stanley's close friend and confidant, to his bedside. Hall reported back to the Estes Park community, in a letter dated March 21, 1938, subsequently published in the *Trail*, that though the situation had been pronounced by the doctors to be "very serious," Mr. Stanley, thanks to his "wonderful vitality," was now sitting up and cheerfully "talking and planning what he would do this summer when he comes to the Park."[44]

Stanley was back in Colorado by late June, well enough to pose for a photograph in front of a Stanley Steamer with Estes Park pioneer Abner Sprague. The occasion was a parade celebrating the reopening of the newly rebuilt road through the Big Thompson Canyon in which Stanley, using one of his now-legendary automobiles, had been asked to help depict the changes in transportation over the years. Sprague, on his part, had come to the Big Thompson Valley in an ox-drawn covered wagon after crossing the Great Plains from Illinois with his parents in 1864. It was not to be. As F.O. Stanley was preparing to join the procession, the boiler of the steamer sprung a leak and the transportation pioneer was forced to ride down the canyon in a modern automobile.[45]

Flora Stanley's health, by contrast, was far more tenuous. She had been plagued throughout her adult life with lingering and serious eye problems. These gradually worsened. In the spring or early summer of 1928, Flora underwent an operation in an attempt to obtain at least some relief. Though F.O. pronounced the operation "very successful," saying that he hoped it would allow her to "see quite well out of one eye,"[46] Flora's eyesight continued to deteriorate. By the early 1930s she had reached a point of near-blindness, barely able to distinguish between light and dark. Because of her eyesight, Flora elected to spend the summer of 1937 in Newton, and for the very first time F.O. Stanley came to Estes Park alone.

Flora was as plucky and determined as her husband. She was back in the park the following summer as usual, publicly expressing her "delight," but now confined to a routine that greatly limited her activity. F.O. sought to compensate for her handicap and in ways of which Flora herself was probably unaware. Though the hotel was no longer his, Stanley asked that the furniture in the great lobby not be moved about so that his wife might find her way around by memory and touch. Visitors reported the two of them slowly promenading the lobby hall and front veranda, Flora's hand resting lightly on F.O.'s elbow for guidance.

So well did they carry this off, one former employee recalled, "that the casual and uninformed observer would never have known that Mrs. Stanley could not see." When Estes Park artist Dave Stirling brought a new painting to the hotel for exhibition, he continued,

> Mr. Stanley would describe to his wife the form of the painting, and would continue to describe the exact textures and hues used in the execution of the painting. So well did Mr. Stanley describe the pictures that Dave Stirling used to listen attentively for any criticisms that Mrs. Stanley might have of his work. Mr. Stanley also used to describe the views of the mountains from the veranda of the hotel, going into great detail as to their appearance, the amount of snow on the mountains as compared to last year, and other details.[47]

There were other small subterfuges as well. F.O. would sometimes read off to Flora a list of expected guests who had visited the hotel frequently in the past and whose voices she was often able to recognize from memory. With this advanced preparation she was able to greet them in her own voice—a feat she performed with little apparent difficulty.

Flora Stanley bore her infirmity with dignity and grace, a task no doubt made more difficult by recollections of earlier summers when she had delighted in the beauty of the mountain scenery about her and had personally entertained hotel guests with picnic trips to Horseshoe Park, Gem Lake, and other places. By 1935, however, Flora seldom ventured beyond her home.

The fact that her husband continued to appear regularly at the hotel for lunch gave rise among the unknowing to stories about Flora's reclusiveness. The facts were otherwise. As F.O. Stanley wrote to his friend, Henry Lynch, on May 14, 1935, declining an invitation: "We are very sorry we cannot accept your very kind invitation. But Mrs. Stanley, owing to being blind, makes her very timid in going into new places, so we have to deny ourselves of many pleasures we might otherwise greatly enjoy."[48]

Stanley Park

Stanley continued to liquidate his assets in Estes Park through the mid- and late 1930s. The majority of these transactions were for platted lots in the Little Prospect Mountain Subdivision. The largest was with Muriel MacGregor, the only child of Donald MacGregor, who in January 1937 added to the family ranch in Black Canyon by purchasing 585 acres for $11,700 (or $20 an acre).[49]

F.O. Stanley was not yet through, however, with his generosity to Estes Park and its residents. On August 14, 1936, he signed a warranty deed conveying to the Town of Estes Park 54 acres of meadowland east of the village, bounded on the north by what was then Colorado State Highway 16 (now Highway 36), for use "solely as a public park and recreation grounds." Its value was $10,000.[50]

Stanley's desire to provide a place for sport and recreation for residents and visitors was not new. As early as July 1913, in fact, the *Estes Park Trail* reported that

> Mr. F.O. Stanley has offered to donate the use of eighty acres of land, lying just across the Thompson, south of the village, for an amusement park, if the citizens of the Park will lay off the grounds for polo and baseball, and organize clubs for their use.[51]

Editor John Munson, one of the men who had purchased and laid out the original Estes Park townsite, endorsed the idea and then concluded with a question: "Who will take up the matter? The ladies [a reference to the Estes Park Women's Auxiliary] have their hands full with the trails. Will the men be sports and play the game?"[52]

For some reason the men did not. Perhaps because local attention was then focused on securing the national park, the rather modest conditions that Stanley proposed were not met. The idea itself remained very much alive, however, for the area that Stanley selected had been used since before the turn of the century as a site for informal rodeo events and races. By the mid-1920s, what was sometimes referred to as "Aviation Field" because of its use as a landing field was being leased for town-sponsored events, including the 1927 Estes Park Stampede, which its promoters confidently predicted would "eventually . . . rival . . . the famous Pendleton, Ore., roundup and the Cheyenne, Wyo., frontier show."[53] This expansion of the summer rodeo into a major summer tourist attraction followed the announcement of the previous September that the Stanley Corporation planned to develop the property as an elaborate recreational complex. By this time the facility contained a half-mile track and grandstand.

Stanley's 1936 offer, coming as it did during the dark of the Depression when dollars for any kind of new civic project were in short supply, represented a significant opportunity for tourist-conscious Estes Park. Even then, progress was slow. In the fall of 1936 the Chamber of Commerce organized a Civic Improvement Committee and agreed to develop a plan for the park's development by securing the services of landscape architect J. Lloyd Fletcher.

By January 1938, Fletcher had completed a schematic proposal designed to bring the grounds into "correct harmony with the rugged mountains that surround the village of Estes Park."[54] Fletcher called for a park without commercial concessions, set off from the surrounding area by means of a well-landscaped bridle path and a natural rock main entrance located to the west. Within the park Fletcher proposed an improved half-mile racetrack for rodeo events enclosing a baseball diamond, with a large, adjacent, north-facing grandstand so that spectators would have "a perfect view of every race, rodeo event, or baseball play without any glare from the Colorado sun."

To make Stanley Park a place that everyone might enjoy, Fletcher included a number of other permanent facilities, including a picnic ground and a large rock shelter house equipped with a fireplace and running water. Nearby he laid out grounds for tennis, croquet, archery, shuffleboard, and horseshoes, and a well-equipped children's playground. His proposal also called for the construction of a historical museum, the town's first, "where one may see and study the historical features of the park."[55]

Before steps could be taken to implement Fletcher's design, however, the United States Bureau of Reclamation entered the picture. The long-anticipated Colorado–Big Thompson water diversion project had finally been approved by President Roosevelt on December 27, 1937, and the bureau was now ready to set in motion plans of its own. Just days before the scheduled release of Fletcher's report, the bureau formally asked to purchase 23.39 acres of the property that Stanley had given the town, substantially reducing the size of the proposed park.

Such a purchase, of course, violated the terms of Stanley's gift and required Stanley's approval as well as the approval of the citizens of Estes Park. Stanley was agreeable. On June 4, 1938, he signed a release and quitclaim agreement with the town.[56] A month later, on July 19, the residents of Estes Park ratified the transaction by a vote of 82 to 0. For $10,400 Stanley then sold to the government of the United States an additional 53.995 acres, providing the rest of the half section needed by the Reclamation Bureau as the site for both the administrative and residential complex known as Reclamation Village and the power plant to be located at the foot of Prospect Mountain.[57]

Nothing more was done about the park itself, however, until August 1941, nearly a year after F.O. Stanley's death, when a meeting was held at the high school auditorium and attended by representatives of every local civic, service, and social organization. Thanks to the generosity of Carl Sanborn, the son of F.O. Stanley's original partner, and early hotel owner John Manford, who had come forward to contribute 17 acres and 7.5 acres respectively, Stanley Park was more than restored to its original 54-acre size. That evening a budget of $15,000 was approved to complete the job, though on a much less elaborate scale than the one that Fletcher had proposed. To help with future maintenance and improvement, the town agreed to set aside most of the money it had received from the Bureau of Reclamation to establish a permanent Stanley Memorial Park Fund.[58]

Fund-raising began at once. On September 23, 1941, with subscriptions of over $4,500 in hand, William Allen White, the famous newspaper editor from Emporia, Kansas, and a longtime summer resident of Moraine Park, turned the first shovel of dirt for the new Stanley Memorial Park, with the expectation that it would be complete and ready for dedication on July 4, 1942. By November a new "construction plan" had been drawn up by S. S. Magoffin Company, the general contractor in charge of building the East Portal tunnel on the Colorado-Big Thompson reclamation project.

Magoffin's plan showed "Stanley Stadium," a large oval five-eigths-mile racing track designed by William Dupont, Jr., of Wilmington, Delaware, enclosing a football and polo field, as well as a 50 x 16–foot clubhouse building, with a social room at one end, rest rooms at the other, and an 18 x 16–foot covered porch in the middle.[59] With America's entrance into World War II that December, the project came to a halt. One of the two large log block houses designed to flank the entrance, an obvious compromise with the native stone entryway that Fletcher had proposed, was built by June 1943, using peeled logs donated by the Forest Service.

With the project yet unfinished the following spring, Dorothy Emmons, F.O. Stanley's niece, by then the widow of summer resident Harry Kremser-Stoddard, reported still another potential addition to the project. She had just heard that there had been talk among mem-

Dedication of Stanley Memorial Park, September 23, 1941. Courtesy Estes Park Area Historical Museum.

bers of the Summer Residents Association about honoring F.O. Stanley with some sort of special museum. As she told her cousin, Raymond Stanley:

> We discussed the possibility of building a room in the club house or a separate building altogether reproducing perhaps the old kitchen living room of the New England Kingfield Stanley house, and putting some mementos of Uncle Freel's therein for a kind of memorial-museum or whatever it might be called. . . . I have some pictures and things that would be interesting to keep in such a place. And Estes seems appropriate inasmuch as he (uncle) was so well known and so much loved there.[60]

Like so many of the nation's dreams, the completion of Stanley Park had to be set aside for the duration of the war. The rodeo grounds were not completed until the 1950s. The museum that Lloyd Fletcher had suggested for the site, and which the history-rich town had talked about since at least 1916, took much longer. It did not become a reality until 1966.[61] The proposed museum to honor F.O. Stanley had to wait another 30 years, until 1997.

In mid-July 1939, Flora Stanley suffered a stroke. She died 10 days later, at 1:25 A.M. on Monday, July 25, 1939, at her home at Estes Park of a cerebral hemorrhage. She was 92. At her side were F.O. Stanley and Dorothy Emmons. Dorothy had come out from Boston at the first news of Flora's illness and had arrived in the park just days before her death. Flora's remains were taken to Denver and placed in a vault until the fall, when they were taken back to Kingfield for burial in the Stanley family plot. The Stanleys had been married for 65 years.

The summer following Flora's death, F.O., accompanied by Dorothy, who after her mother's death in 1937 had moved in with the Stanleys and become their companion, returned for the 38th time to Estes Park and the yellow frame house on Wonderview. In spite of his own increasing feebleness, Stanley puttered around his workshop, entertained a few guests (including the Reverend Monsignor E. J. Flanagan, the founder of the famous "Father Flanagan's Boys

Town"[62]), and occasionally put in an appearance at the hotel and other places.

Those appearances included the ceremony attended by 2,500 spectators on June 23, when an electric switch touched off blasting on the Colorado–Big Thompson project, beginning construction on the world's longest transmountain irrigation tunnel,[63] the concert given in his honor at the Stanley Hotel, and a service club luncheon at Longmont.[64] As the summer waned and Stanley prepared to return to New England, these appearances became less frequent.

The mountains were there that summer, looking just as they had in 1903 when F.O. and Flora first cleared the top of Park Hill and gazed down on the beauty of Joel Estes's valley. But without Flora, F.O. Stanley's Estes Park, the world that had for so long defined his very sense of being, was now a changed and sadly diminished one.

If F.O. Stanley needed a reminder of that change, it was in the muffled sounds of blasting from the work going forward at the East Portal tunnel at the head of Wind River. Its completion meant the flooding of acres of native grass in Stanley Meadows and the creation of Lake Estes—human acts that would alter the face of Estes Park forever. But Stanley had left his mark, too: the Stanley Hotel, Stanley Park, the Stanley Power Plant on Fall River, and a mountain town much better prepared for the influx of visitors and new residents attracted by its beauty.

CHAPTER
15

Afterword

The Stanley Legacy in Estes Park

> . . . he will be known as a pioneer who blazed an upward trail.
> He planned always for tomorrow. He lived in the future tense.
> —*The Hebronian*, November 1940[1]

Freelan Oscar Stanley died at Newton on October 2, 1940, 10 days after returning from Estes Park. That morning he had walked out of the door of his home on Waverly Avenue to pick up the morning paper, only to collapse on the front lawn. Brought inside and treated, F.O. Stanley died shortly afterwards. With him were Dorothy Emmons, his faithful niece, and Byron Hall, his former employee, by then a friend for nearly four decades. F.O. Stanley was 91. He was buried beside Flora on a sloping hillside in Kingfield's Sunnyside Cemetery, not far from the banks of the Carrabassett River, where he and F.E. had played as boys.

Newspapers, east and west, used their obituaries to comment briefly on the major events of Stanley's public life, alluding always to the contributions made by "his twin brother, Francis."[2] Not surprisingly, the eastern press was uniformly silent on Colorado and Estes Park, and what Stanley had achieved there. Even the *Denver Post*, which noted that Colorado had lost a "staunch friend" and Estes Park the builder of "the resort it has become," saw little else to comment on and reported Stanley's death as fifth-page news.[3]

Estes Park, as might be expected, did better. W. G. Jackson, publisher of the *Estes Park Trail*, caught much of the essential spirit of the man, both his determination and playfulness, in his simple editorial tribute:

> Estes Park mourns the death of F.O. Stanley. More than any other summer visitor, Stanley identified himself with the region that he loved so much.
>
> Never one to do anything half-heartedly, Stanley contributed untold effort and cash to the development of the region. Had it not been for him, Estes-Rocky Mountain National Park would not have progressed to the point that it has, a world-famous resort to which hundreds of thousands of visitors come each year.
>
> F.O. Stanley, during the years to come, will continue to be an inspiration to those who are left to carry on the work that he began.
>
> Ninety-one years of age last June, Estes Park's number one summer visitor was interested in the affairs of the community, intensely aware of world problems and conditions, and yet never lost the ability to enjoy himself hugely. The Trail staff will always remember him as he would come into the office during the summer months inquiring if there was any work for a young man.
>
> Those of us who have had the privilege of knowing F.O. Stanley will continue to draw inspiration from the example he set—how to live happily, usefully and fully.[4]

F.O. Stanley, as Jackson suggests, always felt at home in Estes Park. Despite his down-east accent and the fact that Colorado was never more than a summer residence except during those first five years when he was recovering from tuberculosis, this man from Maine and Massachusetts had in many ways long since become a man of the West. He had become, as he had put it facetiously to Flora during his first visit to Denver a half-century before, "Your Western Man."

Stanley admired the rugged, tenacious individualism and entrepreneurial energy he found in Colorado and in westerners like Enos Mills.

He also admired his friend's willingness to invest himself in causes and to adopt, when necessary, a healthy populist stance against the ineptitude of bureaucracy—even when doing so meant taking a stand against government itself. He valued such qualities in Mills and others because they were also his own.

Unlike many westerners, however, F.O. Stanley was by no means an egalitarian. As his hotel and its clientele suggest, he showed little inclination to break down social barriers between classes, though he himself had little trouble negotiating his way among those who came from very different economic and social backgrounds. Stanley believed in human distinctions and distinctiveness much in the way that Jefferson did. His world was defined not by the artificialities of birth or antecedent but by talent, industry, the ability to get things done, and all those intangibles we lump together and call character.

There is nothing intangible, however, about Stanley's contributions to Estes Park, much of it now, finally, in the hands of those committed to its restoration and preservation. The centerpiece of that legacy is, of course, the Stanley Hotel, with its red roof and distinctive cupola and flag, since 1977 entered in the National Register of Historic Places.

Though its mustard-yellow paint has long since been exchanged for white, the Stanley is stately still, its back against the gray granite of the Twin Owls and Lumpy Ridge, its front facing the glories of Longs Peak, Halletts Peak, and the entire Front Range. Much as it was in Stanley's time, it has survived into our own. For all its struggles the Stanley remains one of America's truly great resort hotels, an imposing reminder of the dreams and accomplishments of its designer-builder and of affluence and summers now long past.

The Stanley legacy in Estes Park, however, is far larger and more enduring than any of the historic structures that bear his name. It is a legacy that extends to community and region and to the dreams of a remarkable man who through ingenuity, courage and persistence found ways to harness the emerging technological forces of the twentieth century to make those dreams a reality.

Enos Mills was certainly correct: the day of F.O. Stanley's arrival was indeed the "epoch-making event in the history of the Park." Equally correct was the Estes Park *Mountaineer*, which had insisted that the new hotel on the hill must bear the name of its builder because

Mr. Stanley's hotel. Lew Dakan photo. Courtesy Fort Collins Public Library.

"Mr. Stanley's name will always be associated with the upbuilding of the Park, making it a place delightful for all the people."

Notes

Abbreviations
Frequently cited collections of materials and public records, as well as the two journals published by the Stanley Museum, Kingfield, Maine, are identified in full the first time only; subsequent citations make use of the following abbreviations:

Collections

BCA	Bowdoin College Archives, Brunswick, Maine
CCEPPL	Colorado Collection, Estes Park Public Library, Estes Park, Colorado
EPAHM	Estes Park Area Historical Museum, Estes Park, Colorado
FNSHF	Frank Normali, Stanley Historic Foundation, Estes Park, Colorado
LRMNP	Library, Rocky Mountain National Park, Estes Park, Colorado
SMA	Stanley Museum Archives, Kingfield, Maine
SMR	Superintendent's Monthly Report (Rocky Mountain National Park)

Public Records

IRSC	Incorporation Records, State of Colorado, Denver, Colorado
LCRD	Larimer County, Registry of Deeds, Fort Collins, Colorado
MBTEP	Minutes of the Board of Trustees of the Town of Estes Park, Colorado

Stanley Museum Journals

SMN	Stanley Museum Newsletter 1981–1992
SMQ	Stanley Museum Quarterly 1993–present

Author's Preface
Pages i–xi

[1] F.O. Stanley, letter to William E. Sweet, October 1, 1928, SMA.

[2] Henry M. Lynch, Letter to Elizabeth M. Stover, May 16, 1949, SMA. The

book in question, whose preface is dated June 24, 1949, is Estes Park, Resort in the Rockies (Dallas: University Press in Dallas, Southern Methodist University, 1949), by Edwin J. Foscue and Louis O. Quam. The authors, somewhat ironically, thank Lynch in their preface for having "furnished us with additional material on F.O. Stanley."

Lynch might also have cited the lavishly illustrated 32-page brochure on the Stanley Hotel published in 1927 by the Stanley Hotel Corporation, the Milwaukee syndicate that had purchased the hotel from F.O. Stanley the previous year. It gives 1914 as the date of the completion of the Stanley Hotel. *The Stanley, Estes Park, Colorado* (Milwaukee: Meyer-Rotier-Tate Company, 1927), p. 3, copy, Rocky Mountain National Park Museum Storage Facility.

Chapter 1: Beginnings
Pages 1–16

1 Enos Mills, *The Story of Estes Park* (Longs Peak, Colo., 1914), pp. 91–93. Mills presented a signed copy to F.O. Stanley, "With best wishes," SMA.

2 The best single source of information on the Stanley family is the manuscript history written by F.E. Stanley's son, Raymond Walker Stanley (1894–1985), titled "Some Descendants of Matthew Stanley of Topsfield, Massachusetts," Vol. 1, dated December 1934. Portions of this history have been published serially in *SMN*, 7 (March 1988): 9–10; 7 (June 1988): 6–7, 9; 7 (September 1988): 12–13, 15; 8 (March 1989): 7–9; 8 (June 1989): 11. See also Chansonetta Stanley Emmons, "The Stanley Family," *SMN*, 11 (December 1992): 5–13. SMA.

3 See John Daggett, *Sketch of the History of Attleborough, From Its Settlement to the Present Time* (Dedham, Mass.: H. Mann, 1834), pp. 81–82, SMA.

4 Everett S. Stackpole, *History of Winthrop, Maine* (Auburn, Maine: Merrill & Webber Company, 1925), p. 117.

5 See Marion Jacques Smith, *General William King: Merchant, Shipbuilder, and Maine's First Governor* (Camden, Maine: Down East Books, 1980); Alan Taylor, *Liberty Men and Great Proprietors: The Revolutionary Settlement of the Maine Frontier, 1760–1820* (Chapel Hill: University of North Carolina Press, 1990).

6 Gwilym R. Roberts, "Some Thoughts on the Early History of Kingfield, *"Franklin Journal and Farmington Chronicle*," July 24, 1976. SMA.

7 Philip H. Stubbs, letter of February 26, 1902, quoted in Raymond W. Stanley, "Some Descendants of Matthew Stanley," p. 91. Stubbs, of Strong, Maine, was treasurer of the railroad.

8 The note attributing the source is in the hand of Raymond W. Stanley. The handwriting of the three-page document clearly belongs to F.O. Stanley. SMA.

9 Freelan O. Stanley, "Maple Sugar," incomplete typescript, SMA. Published, SMN, 10 (March 1991): 13–14. See also Raymond W. Stanley, *The Twins, Including the Mink Story and Others* (Boston: privately printed, December 1932). The Stanley Museum in Kingfield owns the copy of Greenleaf's

National Arithmetic that belonged to the twins (Boston: Robert S. Davis & Co., 1862).

[10] Freelan O. Stanley, letter, December 20, 1894, SMA.

[11] Quoted in Frank and Judith Normali, "Stanley," unpublished typescript, 1984, p. 6, SMA. The word "apple" has been changed to "stone" on the authority of Raymond Stanley, verbally to Susan S. Davis.

[12] The name "Freel" apparently suited F.O., for as he wrote in April 1923, "I never liked my own name, and then the unusual way of spelling it, by leaving off the 'D' has given me a great deal of trouble. Important papers would be made out and my name would be spelled 'Freeland,' and this would cause trouble." F.O. Stanley, letter to Agnes S. Huse, April 10, 1923, SMA. (Agnes Huse was F.O. Stanley's niece, the daughter of his youngest brother, Bayard Taylor Stanley.) The November 1908 *By-laws, House Rules and List of Officers and Members* of the Hunnewell Club of Newton, Massachusetts, the social organization that F.O. Stanley was instrumental in founding (see below), make exactly this mistake. So did the Locomobile Company in 1899, when F.O. and F.E. Stanley were listed as general managers.

[13] Susan S. Davis, *The Stanleys: Renaissance Yankees, Innovation in Industry and the Arts* (Exton, Pa: Princeton Academic Press, The Newcomen Society of the United States, 1997), p. 15. Richard P. Mallett, in his history of Farmington Normal, indicates that F.E.'s "later accomplishments were . . . recognized with an honorary diploma." Richard P. Mallett, *University of Maine at Farmington: A Study in Educational Change* (1864–1974) (Farmington: University of Maine at Farmington, 1974), p. 40.

[14] In 1935, Hebron Academy gave Stanley a diploma reading as follows: "Freelan Oscar Stanley, student, teacher, writer, internationally known industrialist, friend of little children and of mankind, patron of music, and great benefactor of Hebron Academy, on behalf of the Board of Trustees, I present you this diploma of graduation as of the class of 1873, together with the great love and esteem of the entire school." Raymond E. Stanley, "Notes RE: F.O. Stanley," undated typescript, SMA.

[15] Quoted in Charles C. Calhoun, *A Small College in Maine: Two Hundred Years of Bowdoin* (Brunswick, Maine: Bowdoin College, 1993), p. 191. See also Louis C. Hatch, *The History of Bowdoin College* (Portland, Maine: Loring, Short & Harmon, 1927), pp. 132–148.

[16] Quoted in Calhoun, p. 193.

[17] Joshua L. Chamberlain, letter to the fathers of Bowdoin students, May 28, 1874, BCA.

[18] F.O. Stanley, letter to Mr. Purington, November 19, 1918, ibid. Bowdoin continued to maintain a "Biographical Record" on F.O. Stanley as a nongraduating member of the Class of 1877, sending him on at least one occasion a form on which Stanley dutifully summarized the facts of his life and career. Bowdoin remained vitally interested in its onetime student. "Stanley left college at the time of the 'Drill Rebellion,'" Purington wrote in a memo dated June 20, 1916, "and was somewhat soured against the college in his early life. Possibly time has softened his resentment and possibly now he would

accept a degree from the college <u>if he were offered one</u>," BCA. This under-lining, it should be noted, appears in Purington's original.

19 Hebronian, 18 (November 1940): 1.

20 Freelan O. Stanley, "The Stanley Dry Plate," SMN, 6 (March 1987): 9.

21 Ibid.

22 Ibid., p. 14n.

23 F.O. Stanley also worked for a year as an assistant cashier for Boston safe manufacturer G. L. Damon, but whether this occurred before or after he attempted to revive the Practical Drawing Set is unclear.

Chapter 2: The Stanley Dry Plate
Pages 17–32

1 F.O. Stanley, letter to Flora Stanley, March 26, 1889, SMA.

2 Blanche Stanley Hallett, "Memoirs, 1870–1899," pp. 2–3, photocopy, SMA. The originals are owned by Blanche Hallett's daughter, Augusta Tapley of Needham, Massachusetts.

3 Ibid., p. 4.

4 F.E. Stanley's airbrush and career as a portrait artist are briefly discussed in Susan S. Davis, "The Artistic Side of the Stanley Family: F.E. Stanley, Drawing and the Airbrush," *SMN*, 11 (June 1992): 12–13, 20.

5 One of these books, bearing F.E. Stanley's signature, is Charles Hearn's well-illustrated *The Practical Printer, A Complete Manual of Photographic Printing*, published at Philadelphia by Benerman & Wilson in 1874. It is on display at the Stanley Museum in Kingfield.

6 The best single account of the history of the Stanley Dry Plate is F.O. Stanley's "The Stanley Dry Plate," dated May 15, 1936, written for deliv-ery to members of the Tuesday Club in Newton. The typescript manu-script has been reprinted in *SMN*, 6 (March 1987): 8–9, 14, 16; 6 (June 1987): 8–9; 6 (December 1987): 8–10. See also F.E. Stanley's brief account of the firm's history, which he delivered as part of his testimony during the 1914 Eastman Kodak antitrust hearings, as reprinted in *SMN*, 10 (September 1991): 12–13. The most authoritative study of the nineteenth- and early twentieth-century photography business in America is Reese V. Jenkins, *Images and Enterprise: Technology and the American Photography Industry 1839 to 1925* (Baltimore: Johns Hopkins University Press, 1975).

Emma Walker, Augusta Stanley's sister, who worked for the Stanley Dry Plate Company beginning in 1894, critiqued F.O. Stanley's paper in a letter to Raymond Stanley, written on May 24, 1936. "You ask me to com-ment on the accuracy," she wrote. "Perhaps the composer forgot some details; but even if he remembered them I do not think it would bother him at all to omit them, and I do not think the omission would bother the club members for whom he prepared the paper. So, as an interesting nar-rative I should say it is O.K. As for being historically accurate I should say it is far from it, in spots. That is—he leaves the wrong impression." Her major complaints are that F.O. overemphasized the company's reliance on direct sales to consumers and failed to mention that the Stanleys somewhat disingenuously stayed with the trade association formed at the time of the St. Louis convention long enough for them to replace the $50,000 worth of bad dry plates they then had on the market. This tactical decision cut their financial loss to $10,000, and kept their business integrity intact. Emma E. Walker, letter to Raymond W. Walker, May 24, 1936, SMA.

[7] Jenkins, p. 67.

[8] F.O. Stanley, The Stanley Dry Plate," *SMN*, 6 (March 1987): 9n.

[9] Davis, *The Stanleys*, p. 18.

[10] Interview with Augusta Stanley Tapley (1908–   ), January 14, 1999, Needham, Massachusetts.

[11] F.O. Stanley, letter to Flora Stanley, May 7, 1885, SMA.

[12] Ibid., May 14, 1885, SMA.

[13] Ibid., June 1, 1885, SMA.

[14] *Lewiston Daily Sun*, 48 (October 3, 1940): 6. Information on F.O. Stanley's horse breeding and horse racing efforts is found in Flora's diaries and in their letters of the period, as well as in occasional newspaper articles. During his travels on behalf of the Stanley Dry Plate Company, F.O. found time to visit stock farms in western New York, Ohio, and Kentucky. "Besides the races," he wrote to Flora from Lexington on October 15, 1887, "the exhibition of trotting stock has been far ahead of anything I ever saw." F.O. Stanley, letter to Flora Stanley, October 15, 1887, SMA.

The Stanleys' horses were pastured during the summer in Kingfield, helping to make the twins' native village for a time "one of the liveliest light-harness horse towns extant." As newspaper clippings in the Stanley Museum suggest, the pride of their stable was the stallion "La Mont," foaled in 1883 by Redwood, whose impressive lineage and credentials the Stanley brothers had printed up on a small wallet-sized card. Half interest in "La Mont" was later sold to one W. B. Horton for $1,000.

F.O.'s interest in horses followed him to Newton, where in 1895 one of his horses killed a man named Herbert J. Johnson (see below). F.O. had more trouble two years later, in 1897, when a roan colt that he was trying to train threw his trainer from a carriage and wildly took off on a madcap dash through the streets of the quiet town. The next day, according to Raymond Stanley, F.O., in disgust, gave the horse away to a man who "promised to keep him out of Newton." *SMN*, 2 (May 1983): 5.

[15] Leading Business Men of Lewiston, Augusta and Vicinity (Boston: Mercantile Publishing Company, 1889), pp. 50–51.

[16] Ibid.

[17] F.O. Stanley, "The Stanley Dry Plate," *SMN*, 6 (March 1987): 14.

[18] Charles Notman, notes from Notman Photographic Archives, McCord Museum of Canadian History, Montreal (Canada), 1955, SMA.

[19] F.O. Stanley, letter to Flora Stanley, February 10, 1889, SMA.

[20] Ibid., February 5, 1889, SMA.

[21] Ibid., February 20, 1889, SMA.

[22] Ibid., April 13, 1889, SMA. F.O.'s letter from St. Paul, written on March 1, is equally revealing: "The fact is we are on the highway to a big business.

The only thing I regret is that for the next six months I shall be on the warpath most of the time. The fact is I can do more business in six months than any man we can hire in as many years." Ibid., March 1, 1889, SMA.

23 Ibid., February 24, 1889, SMA.

24 Ibid., March 3, 1889, SMA.

25 Ibid., April 15, 1889, SMA.

26 Handwritten document, SMA.

27 Flora Stanley's Diary, May 31, 1890, SMA. The actual anniversary of F.O.'s move from Boston to Lewiston had occurred the day before.

28 Newspaper article attached to Flora Stanley's Diary and dated June 3, 1890, SMA.

29 Flora Stanley's Diary, June 26, 1890, SMA.

30 John Allen, letter to Dorothy Emmons Whitchurch, May 15, 1954, SMA.

31 Flora Stanley's Diary, November 8, 1890, SMA.

32 Quoted in John R. Prescott, *The Story of Newton, Massachusetts* (Newton, Mass.: Newtonville Library Association, 1936), p. 40.

33 J. C. Rochford, letter to F.O. Stanley, May 9, 189?, SMA.

34 Such turntables, it should be noted, were fairly common in Newton, where they are associated primarily with "the Stanleys." This fact has led more than one local home owner to believe they are living in a "Stanley family house" because they have a turntable in the garage. F.O., however, was the only one of the twins to install and use them, and he did so both in Newton and in Estes Park.

35 Blanche Stanley Hallett, "Memoirs, 1870–1899," p. 76, SMA.

36 By about 1905 the F.E. Stanleys and their daughters were owners of six separate lots; F.O. and Flora Stanley owned at least five, three of them in Flora's name. They are illustrated in a period map provided by Sid Marston of Newton and published by the Stanley Museum in 1997 in connection with its Stanley Steamer Centennial, SMA.

37 Mason H. Stone, Jr., *History of the Hunnewell Club of Newton*, April 13, 1980, typescript, SMA.

38 Ibid., p. 5.

39 Augusta Stanley's Diary, February 22, 1909, SMA.

40 Stone, p. 6. Well before World War II, as Stone explains, the Hunnewell Club had begun to decline. Its older, wealthier members, men like F.O. Stanley who had been responsible for the club's founding and initial success, were dead. Mobility made a local neighborhood club far less desirable and attractive. There was also the problem of rising costs and declining membership. The building now houses condominiums.

41 F.O. Stanley, *The Stanley Dry Plate, SMN*, 6 (December 1987): 9.

42 F.E. Stanley, letter to George Eastman, November 28, 1903, *SMQ*, 13 (June 1994): 17. The details of Eastman's negotiations with the Stanleys are found in a series of letters to and from George Eastman between June 1902 and December 28, 1903, reprinted in *SMQ*, 13 (June 1994): 12–20.

43 Ibid.

[44] Jenkins, p. 75.

[45] F.O. Stanley, "The Stanley Dry Plate," *SMN*, 6 (December 1987): 10.

[46] Raymond W. Stanley, *Stanley Family Reunion: A Transcription of Conversations During the Stanley Family Gathering, June 7, 1981 at Kingfield, Maine* (Kingfield, Maine: The Stanley Museum, 1981), p. 25.

Chapter 3: The Stanley Steamer
Pages 33–48

[1] Emma E, Walker, letter to Raymond W. Stanley, December 11, 1940, SMA. According to Emma Walker, F.E. "wanted to get his car completed so as to meet your mother and Blanche in New York and bring them to Newton in the car." F.E.'s daughter, Emily (Emma Frances, Mrs. Prescott Warren), recalled in 1968 that her father's interest in automobiles was motivated by his love of bicycling and by the fact that at 200 pounds, Augusta was unable to accompany him. A horseless carriage was his way of regaining her companionship. Arthur F. Joy, "My Father Built the Stanley Steamer," *Antique Automobile*, 32 (March–April 1968): 17.

For a history of the steam automobile and the role played by the Stanleys, see Robert B. Jackson, *The Steam Cars of the Stanley Twins* (New York: Henry Z. Walck, Inc., 1969); Anthony Bird, *The Stanley Steam Cars, 1897–1907, Classic Cars in Profile*, Vol. 3 (Garden City, N.Y.: Doubleday and Company, 1968); John H. Bacon, *American Steam-Car Pioneers, A Scrapbook* (Exton, Pa.: The Newcomen Society of the United States, 1984); Raymond W. Stanley, "The Stanley Steamer," *Floyd Clymer's Steam Motor Scrapbook* (Los Angeles: Clymer Motors, 1945), pp. 17–22; Carlton F. Stanley, Early History of the Stanley Company," ibid., pp. 23–26; John Bentley, *Oldtime Steam Cars* (New York: Arco Publishing Company, 1953). The many myths surrounding Stanley steam cars arc explored and exploded in Raymond W. Stanley, "Evaporating the Stanley Steamer Myth," *Automobile Quarterly*, (Summer 1963): 122–129.

[2] *Boston Daily Globe* (June 2, 1896): 1.

[3] F.E. Stanley, letter to Augusta Stanley, June 14, 1897, SMA.

[4] F.E. Stanley, letter to Augusta Stanley, July 11, 1897, SMA.

[5] In the memoir written for Thomas Derr's history of the Stanley automobile, F.O. Stanley describes the building of that first car as a joint endeavor. The problem is that he gives the date as "the fall of 1896," some nine months before the surviving record suggests the first Stanley machine was actually built. See Thomas S. Derr, *The Modern Steam Car and Its Background* (Los Angeles: Floyd Clymer Publications, 1944), pp. 45–59.

F.O.'s account is also contradicted by Augusta Stanley's sister, Emma Walker, who wrote her nephew in December 1940 that F.O. Stanley's interest was only piqued after the spectacular success enjoyed by F.E.'s car at the Charles River exhibition in 1898 (see below): "When your uncle found what a great hit your father had made (not having had any interest in the contraption up to this time) he devoted all his time to trying to learn all about it and he couldn't sceme [sic] to learn half fast enough. Your uncle was very busy that summer." Emma E. Walker, letter to

Raymond W. Stanley, December 11, 1940.

6 Shortly after joining his father's firm, A. R. Penney had built the machinery that allowed F.O. Stanley to manufacture his "Stanley's Practical Drawing Set."

7 The Stanleys, F.E. wrote in 1917, got the idea for wrapping their boiler in piano wire from a technique employed by Hiram Stevens Maxim, a native of Sangerville, Maine, to strengthen the barrel of the famous machine gun he invented in 1889. *Automobile*, 29 (March 1, 1917): 469.

8 *The Steam Car*, 1, No. 8 [1919?]: 1–2. The Steam Car was the publication that the Stanley Motor Carriage Company launched after the twins relinquished control in 1917.

9 F.O. Stanley in Derr, p. 46.

10 F.O. Stanley in Derr, p. 47.

11 F.O. Stanley in Derr.

12 F.O. Stanley, letter to Flora Stanley, July 9, 1898, SMA. A more serious accident had occurred earlier that year. As the *Newton Graphic* reported on March 4, 1898, F.E. Stanley's motor carriage had "exploded" while driving through Newtonville Square, engulfing the vehicle in flames and singeing the fur coat of its passenger, H. E. Hibbard, Newton's former mayor and a neighbor of the Stanleys on Hunnewell Avenue. Hibbard then leapt from Stanley's auto, injuring both legs. F.E. Stanley, in the same issue of the *Graphic*, denied that there was an explosion at all, and insisted there could not have been. Rather, the gasoline burner had flamed too high in the wind, singeing Hibbard's coat. The inference was that the ex-mayor had panicked in exiting from a vehicle not going more than six miles an hour. Both articles are in Raymond W. Stanley's hand, SMA.

13 Quoted in Raymond W. Stanley, "The Birth and Early Days of Newton's Stanley Steamer," *SMN*, 2 (Fall 1983): 6.

14 Quoted in Bacon, p. 73.

15 F.O. Stanley in Derr, p. 48.

16 *Horseless Age*, 3 (August 1898): 6. F.E. Stanley says the same thing in a letter published in the March 1, 1917, issue of *The Automobile*.

17 *Boston Herald* (November 10, 1898), typescript copy, SMA.

18 *The Automobile* 29 (March 1, 1917): 469.

19 Quoted in Derr, pp. 48–49.

20 Ibid.

21 *Horseless Age*, 4 (June 28, 1899): 4.

22 Rudy Volti, "Why Internal Combustion?" *Invention & Technology*, 6 (Fall 1990): 42.

23 Flora Stanley, *An Account of the First Ascent of Mt. Washington in an Automobile, August, 1899*, typescript, p. 9, SMA.

24 Harry Van Demark, "Our Motoring Presidents," *The Texaco Star*, 35 (Winter 1948): 22.

25 George Eastman, letter to Frank Seaman, August 6, 1901, reprinted in "Eastman Buys Steam Cars, 1899–1903," *SMQ*, 13 (September–December 1994): 22.

[26] George Eastman, letter to H. A. Strong, January 8, 1902, ibid., p. 26.

[27] These Stanley production figures, like those cited below, are from a table that appeared in *Antique Automobile*, 32 (March–April 1968): 14. Another and different set of figures, in Raymond W. Stanley's hand, is in the Stanley Museum Archives.

[28] Flora Stanley's Diary, January 1900, SMA. F.O. Stanley would later claim at age 82, in a "Longevity Inquiry" filled out in 1931 for Professor Irving Fisher of New Haven, that his physical condition was "robust" except between the ages of 50 and 58 (1899–1907). SMA.

[29] Isabella Lucy Bird, *A Lady's Life in the Rocky Mountains* (Norman: University of Oklahoma Press, 1960), pp. 42n, 41.

[30] Quoted in Robert G. Athearn, *The Coloradans* (Albuquerque: University of New Mexico Press, 1976), p. 93.

[31] Roscoe Fleming, quoted in Stephen J. Leonard and Thomas J. Noel, *Denver: Mining Camp to Metropolis* (Niwot: University Press of Colorado, 1990), p. 121.

Chapter 4: First Years in Colorado
Pages 49–78

[1] Charles Edwin Hewes, *Autobiography*, p. 174. Unpublished typescript, EPAHM. Hewes had come to Denver from Iowa in 1901.

[2] See Emma E. Walker, letter to Raymond W. Stanley, February 7, 1937, SMA. Bonney's wife, the former Nancy B. Little, was also a resident of Lewiston and the daughter of Horace Little, the town's postmaster. Sherman Bonney's father for many years had been a pathologist at Lewiston's Central Maine General Hospital. Two of Bonney's uncles were twins who at one time "were nationally known as the oldest twins in the United States." *Denver Post*, 39 (October 5, 1930): 11.

Flora Stanley's single-volume diary covering the years 1888–1890, the period when she and F.O. were living in Lewiston, mentions the name "Bonney" on several occasions.

[3] Flora Stanley's Diary, April 25, 1902. Flora had come West that spring with her sister-in-law Augusta Stanley on a tour, sponsored by Raymond & Whitcomb of Boston, which after the close of the Denver meetings took them to California by way of Colorado Springs, Manitou, and Salt Lake City. They returned home to Massachusetts after briefly seeing Yellowstone National Park. Augusta subsequently wrote a series of letters describing her trip, including the Denver visit, which were published in installments in at least one Maine newspaper. Though the copy of her printed letters in the Stanley Museum does not identify the place of publication, internal evidence suggests it was probably Lewiston.

F.O. had visited Denver even earlier, in March 1889 and possibly in 1890 as well, in connection with the dry plate business. "I cannot saw [sic] that I like Denver," he wrote to Flora from the Windsor Hotel on March 14, 1889. "The climate is beautiful so far as sunshine is concerned. There are not more than five days in a year that the sun does not shine some time during the day. There has been no rain since last Nov., and the ground is as dry as an ash heap. Vegetation will not grow here at all unless supplied with water by irrigation, and it flourishes in grand style." He signed his letter "Your Western Man." F.O. Stanley, letter to Flora Stanley, March 14, 1889, SMA.

4 *Denver Post*, 51 (November 20, 1942): 18.

5 *Denver Republican*, 25 (March 7, 1903): 12.

6 Thomas Crawford Galbreath, *Chasing the Colorado Cure* (Denver: self-published, 1908), p. 15.

7 Ibid., p. 31.

8 *Denver Times*, 33 (March 9, 1903): 3.

9 Ibid., 33 (March 31, 1903): 7.

10 The 1904 *Denver City Directory* lists Minnie Lundburg as a dressmaker residing at 53 Washington Avenue.

11 Flora Stanley's Diary, March 17, 1903, SMA.

12 Channing F. Sweet, *A Princeton Cowboy* (Colorado Springs: Dentan-Berkeland Printing Company, 1967), pp. 2–4. See also "An Interview with Channing Fullerton Sweet," Oral Interview Transcript, April 4, 1980, p. 8, CCEPPL.

13 *Longmont Times-Call*, 46 (May 28, 1938): 1.

14 *Longmont Call*, 5 (July 25, 1903): 1. Welch sold his resort for $12,000 in the spring of 1937, the year before his death.

15 *Denver Post* (December 25, 1938), Sec. 2: 8.

16 *Lyons Recorder*, 3 (May 14, 1903): 1.

17 See, for example, *Estes Park Trail*, 12 (April 7, 1933): 10.

18 Just exactly who drove the first car to Estes Park has been the matter of some debate. The earliest successful trip, however, was apparently made by Dr. Howell Pershing of Denver, who arrived from Lyons in a Locomobile on July 3, 1901, to spend the summer near the Rustic Hotel. Judge J. Mack Mills of Fort Collins would claim in 1920 when he drove his one-cylinder Oldsmobile to Estes Park during the summer of 1902, his was "the first motor vehicle ever to enter that scenic fairyland." From Flora Stanley's diary we know that there was a gasoline-powered Winton in the park during the summer of 1903, driven by a Mr. and Mrs. Woods of Denver. LeRoy R. Hafen, "The Coming of the Automobile and Improved Roads to Colorado," *The Colorado Magazine*, 8 (January 1931): 4–5; *Estes Park Trail*, 4 (September 5, 1924): 1; *Fort Collins Courier*, 28 (February 2, 1920): 3.

19 Flora Stanley, "A Tenderfoot's First Summer in the Rockies," SMQ, 16 (June 1997): 15. Original manuscript, FNSHF. Included in that collection are two other manuscripts in which Flora described her experiences with nature in Estes Park, "An Hour in My Back Yard, Estes Park" and "Little Chip." Flora also wrote several poems in praise of Estes Park now preserved in the archives of the Stanley Museum at Kingfield.

20 Milton Estes, "Memoirs of Estes Park," *Colorado Magazine*, 16 (July 1939): 121. For an account of the early history of Estes Park before the time of the

Stanleys' arrival, see James H. Pickering, *"This Blue Valley": Estes Park, The Early Years, 1859–1915* (Niwot: University Press of Colorado, 1999). This book is the source of much of the information and detail given below.

[21] William N. Byers, "Ascent of Long's Peak," *Rocky Mountain News*, 5 (September 23, 1864): 2.

[22] Mills, *Story of Estes Park* (1914 edition), p. 13.

[23] Bird, p. 110.

[24] *The Field, The Country Gentleman's Newspaper* (London), 42 (September 13, 1873): 279.

[25] The story that "Dunraven was so delighted with the abundance of game and the beauty and grandeur of the scenes that he determined to have Estes Park as a game preserve" was given wide circulation by Enos Mills in his *Story of Estes Park and a Guide Book* (Denver, 1905). It became so pervasive that, at the time of the Earl's death in 1926, papers like the *Larimer County Independent*, published in Fort Collins, included as part of its obituary the statement that "he purchased nearly 6,000 acres of land . . . for use as a game preserve." *Larimer County Independent*, 6 (June 18, 1926): 6.

The fact of the matter is that by late July 1874, within months of the fraudulent land claims, the Earl of Dunraven had announced his intention to make Estes Park into "a summer resort of the first magnitude" and build "a large hotel" together with "a sawmill, new roads through the park, a hotel at Longmont, and a half-way house on the road between that place and the park." Such plans, clearly designed to bring an increasing number of summer tourists to the park, are simply incompatible with a the idea of a private game preserve that would keep people out. See *Fort Collins Standard*, 1 (August 12, 1874): 3; *Rocky Mountain News*, 16 (July 29, 1874): 4.

[26] *Estes Park Trail*, 18 (April 22, 1938): 28.

[27] Abner Sprague, "An Historical Reminiscence," ibid., 2 (June 16, 1922): 3.

[28] "A Tenderfoot's First Summer in the Rockies," p. 16.

[29] These two cottages still stand off Wonderview Avenue to the west of the Stanley home.

[30] "A Tenderfoot's First Summer in the Rockies," p. 18.

[31] Charles Partridge Adams, "Go West Young Man." Typescript, Western History Department, Denver Public Library, pp. 11–12. In the fall of 1903, Adams secured a quitclaim deed from the Earl of Dunraven, hired an architect, and built a permanent studio and summer home named the "Sketch Box," completed in July 1905. See also Ann Condon Barbour, "Charles Partridge Adams, Painter of the West," *Denver Westerners Roundup*, 32 (January–February 1976): 4–17; Barbara Dell, "Charles Partridge Adams, 1856–1942," *Artists of the Rockies and the Golden West* (Winter 1985): 80–85; and Dorothy Dines, Stephen J. Leonard, and Stanley C. Cuba, *The Art of Charles Partridge Adams* (Golden, Colo.: Fulcrum Publishing, 1994).

[32] Edna Ferber, *A Peculiar Treasure* (New York: Garden City Publishing Co., Inc., 1940), p. 243.

[33] "Mr. Stanley used to come up here every Tuesday afternoon," Lou Livingston, a later owner of the Rustic, recalled in 1977. "He said he liked our view better than his! Somebody used to drive him up here. I was just a

kid then . . . but he'd come up here and sit on the porch in a rocking-chair to watch the mountains and the beaver go up Long's [sic] Peak." "A Museum Talk with Lou Livingston," July 10, 1977, typescript, CCEPPL, p. 6.

34 Flora Stanley's Diary, July 31, 1903, SMA.

35 *Longmont Ledger*, 29 (August 14, 1908): 8.

36 "A Tenderfoot's First Summer in the Rockies," p. 18.

37 Ibid., p. 19.

38 Flora's diary indicates that F.O. gave Frank Gove $100 for the property, apparently as earnest money. The warranty deed, notarized on September 23, 1903, was in Flora Stanley's name. Flora Stanley's Diary, September 23, 1903, SMA.

39 Flora Stanley's Diary, September 24, 1903, SMA.

40 "A Tenderfoot's First Summer in the Rockies, p. 19.

41 *Denver Post*, (November 17, 1903): 2.

42 Blanche Stanley Hallett, "Memoirs, 1899–1908," p. 173, SMA.

43 Flora Stanley, letter to Blanche Stanley, ibid.

44 *Denver Post*, (November 17, 1903): 2.

45 *Boston Globe*, 79 (February 18, 1911): 2. As the *Globe* explained, after Stanley had stopped his automobile, "he started again, and was not going more than 10 miles an hour . . . when the Black girl [Vivian Black] ran directly in front of the auto. Mr. Stanley ran on the opposite sidewalk to avoid striking her, but the machine skidded, and the rear mudguard struck the child on the side of the head and threw her several feet."

46 *Denver Post* (February 19, 1911): 11. The Lyons Recorder came to Stanley's defense in reporting the incident: "The accident is a very unfortunate one, as a more careful driver never handled a machine than Mr. Stanley. The papers stated that the accident was practically unavoidable." *Lyons Recorder*, 11 (February 23, 1911): 1. Others, including some of F.O.'s own relatives, were rather less certain about his carefulness behind the wheel.

47 Fort Collins *Weekly Courier*, 26 (January 13, 1904): 12.

48 Sherman G. Bonney, letter to Augusta Stanley, January 30, 1904, SMA. Bonney, it might be noted, had been treating patients in Estes Park since before the turn of the century.

49 Information on the Stanleys' Estes Park home on Wonderview Avenue can be found in Ann Widmer, "Stanley Mansion, A Rarity," *Estes Park Magazine* (Winter 1983), Pamphlet File, CCEPPL; Joanne Ditmer, "The House That Stanley Built," *Empire Magazine, Denver Post* (February 19, 1978): 26–32; "An Estes Park Historic Residence," Marden-Steffens, Realtors, Estes Park, Colorado, realty brochure, SMA.

50 Charles F. Hix to James R. Bissell, Jr., August 18, 1975, SMA.

51 Widmer, op. cit.

52 This parcel, like the first, was purchased from both Frank Gove and Fannie G. Baldwin, and is registered in the name Flora J. R. Stanley. LCRD, Book 187, p. 322.

53 Manuscript letter, May 21, 1907, EPAHM.

Chapter 5: Mr. Sanborn, Mr. Stanley, and the Earl of Dunraven
Pages 79–86

[1] *Loveland Reporter*, 24 (August 6, 1903): 2.

[2] *Longmont Ledger*, 26 (April 21, 1905): 4.

[3] Fort Collins *Weekly Courier*, 29 (January 23, 1907): 1; *Greeley Tribune*, 37 (January 24, 1907): 1; *Longmont Ledger*, 28 (January 25, 1907): 1.

[4] *Greeley Tribune*, 38 (July 1, 1908): 1; *Loveland Reporter*, 29 (July 2, 1908): 1; *Longmont Call*, 10 (July 4, 1908): 1.

[5] *Greeley Tribune*, 38 (July 1, 1908): 1.

[6] The original idea apparently belonged to Henry J. Heinricy of Longmont, who in 1902 interested Sanborn in the project. Sanborn, in turn, recruited 20 individuals willing to invest $100 each. Work was begun about July 15, 1902, and completed about September 20, 1902. The Eureka Ditch was later acquired by the City of Loveland. See Harold Dunning, *Over Hill and Vale: History of Larimer County* (Boulder: Johnson Publishing Company, 1956), I, 164–166.

[7] The barest hint of their relationship is conveyed by one of the few letters between Stanley and Sanborn to survive. Writing from Newton on September 25, 1911, Stanley indicated that he was returning to Sanborn two notes due August 5, 1912, marked "Paid in Full." The letter goes on to say that Sanborn still owed him something in excess of $4,000. SMA.

[8] *Longmont Ledger*, 28 (January 25, 1907): 1.

[9] *Loveland Reporter*, 27 (February 14, 1907): 1.

[10] *Longmont Ledger*, 28 (February 15, 1907): 6.

[11] *Loveland Reporter*, 27 (February 14, 1907): 1. Sanborn's letter was dated February 6, 1907.

[12] *Longmont Ledger*, 28 (February 15, 1907): 6.

[13] *Loveland Reporter*, 28 (September 19, 1907): 1. The Dunraven ranch was located at the base of Park Hill, near what is today the intersection of Route 36 and Fish Creek Road.

[14] B. D. Sanborn, letter to O. B. Willcox, September 26, 1907, SMA. Willcox (1867–?) was a graduate of the University of Michigan, who had come to Denver to practice law. He later practiced at Cripple Creek and then at Colorado Springs, where he represented mining companies and other large corporations. Soon after this letter was written, Willcox moved back to Denver.

[15] O. B. Willcox, letter to B. D. Sanborn, September 30, 1907, SMA.

[16] Loveland Reporter, 29 (March 12, 1908): 1.

Chapter 6: Racing Cars and Mountain Roads
Pages 87–106

[1] Unidentified newspaper clipping, SMA. The race in question is the 1904 race up Mt. Washington, the "Monarch of New England."

[2] For accounts of the Stanley racing cars see Dick Punnett, *Racing on the Rim, A History of the Annual Automobile Racing Tournaments Held on the Sands of the Ormond-Daytona Beach, Florida, 1903–1910* (Ormond Beach, Fla.: Tomoka Press, 1997); Thomas C. Marshall, "Interviews with the Late Fred Marriott," SMQ, 15 (September–December 1996): 20–23; Susan S. Davis, "Fred Marriott, King of Speed and a Tradition's Link," *SMN*, 11 (June 1992): 3–7, 16; Raymond W. Stanley, "Evaporating the Stanley Steamer Myths," *Automobile Quarterly* (Summer 1963): 122–129.

[3] Brent Campbell, "Models H & K—High Performance, 1905–1908," SMQ, 13 (September–December 1994): 31.

[4] Unidentified newspaper clipping, SMA.

[5] Stanley had been asked by the *Boston Herald* "to describe the sensations which I experience in running an automobile at high speed." 1903 clipping, SMA.

[6] *Automobile Week* (July 16, 1904), reprinted in *SMQ*, 13 (March 1994): 11, 13. Augusta Stanley wrote about her husband's experience "from my point of view" for the *Lewiston Journal*, and later had it reprinted in a small pamphlet titled *The Climb to the Clouds, and How It Impressed Me*. Clipping and pamphlet, SMA. The 1905 race was reported in the July 27, 1905, issue of *The Automobile*.

[7] Punnett, op cit, p. 1.

[8] The first story is attributed to Raymond Stanley. See John F. Katz, "F.E. & F.O. Stanley: The Challenge from Steam," *Automobile Quarterly*, 25 (1st Quarter 1987): 23. The second comes from Frank Gardner of Newton, an early steam car owner of some repute, who visited with Fred Marriott regularly and on occasion interviewed him. Note from Susan S. Davis to James H. Pickering, December 1999.

[9] Raymond W. Stanley, "Fred Marriott, 1873–1956," typescript, p. 3, SMA.

[10] Augusta Stanley's Diary, January 26, 1906, SMA.

[11] F.O. Stanley, Night Message to F.E. Stanley, International Ocean Telegraph Company, January 26, 1906, SMA.

[12] Quoted in Marshall, "Interviews with the Late Fred Marriott," p. 23.

[13] Ibid.

[14] *Scientific American*, 96 (February 9, 1907): 128. See also *The Automobile*, (January 31, 1907): 247.

[15] *New York Times*, 56 (January 26, 1907): 3.

[16] Augusta Stanley's Diary, January 25, 1907.

[17] Davis, *The Stanleys*, p. 28.

[18] *The Automobile* (January 31, 1907): 250.

[19] Davis, *The Stanleys*, p. 28.

[20] See Campbell, "Models H & K." The year 1905 was one of transition for the Stanley Motor Carriage Company. It saw the Stanleys manufacture the last of their horseless-carriage, tiller-steered cars and the first of their famous coffin-nosed vehicles. It also saw the first 20-h.p. engine.

[21] 1908 Catalog, Stanley Motor Carriage Company, EPAHM.

22 Ibid.

23 F.E. Stanley, letter to Augusta Stanley, June 14, 1897, SMA.

24 Hafen, p. 12.

25 Denver Times (September 16, 1900): 17; ibid., (August 13, 1901): 1.

26 Ibid. (August 14, 1901): 1.

27 Thomas J. Noel, "Paving the Way to Colorado: The Evolution of Auto Tourism in Denver," *Journal of the West*, 26 (July 1987): 42.

28 *Denver Republican*, reprinted in *Longmont Call*, 4 (October 5, 1901): 4.

29 The Denver chapter of the Good Roads Association found an ally in the Colorado Automobile Club, formed by 42 early auto enthusiasts in 1902. The two organizations merged in 1908 to form the Rocky Mountain Highway Association. Leonard and Noel, p. 261.

30 Thanks to such lobbying efforts, the Colorado Highway Commission was formed in 1909, the year F.O. Stanley opened the Stanley Hotel in Estes Park. Its budget was $50,000. By 1920 that budget had grown to more than $6 million.

31 *Proceedings of the Good Roads Convention, Held at Denver, December 4, 5, 6, 1906* (Denver: Denver Chamber of Commerce, 1907), p. 10. By 1925, however, Denver judge Ben Lindsey was arguing that automobiles were encouraging the young to "every inducement under the moon to irresponsible conduct." Quoted in Leonard and Noel, p. 267.

32 *Lyons Recorder*, 4 (May 12, 1904): 2.

33 *Lyons Recorder*, 7 (March 7, 1907): 1.

34 Ibid., 3 (April 23, 1903): 1.

35 *Longmont Ledger*, 28 (March 22, 1907): 1.

36 *Longmont Call*, 9 (March 23, 1907): 1

37 *Longmont Ledger*, 28 (August 23, 1907). 1

38 J. B. Hall, letter to F.O. Stanley, January 17, 1905, FNSHF.

39 *Lyons Recorder*, 7 (April 18, 1907): 1.

40 Ibid.

41 *Longmont Ledger*, 28 (August 23, 1907): 1

42 Ibid., 28 (June 14, 1907): 1; *Lyons Recorder*, 7 (April 4, 1907): 1. According to a 1933 article in the *Estes Park Trail*, the right of way was secured from Welch in March of 1907. *Estes Park Trail*, 12 (April 7, 1933): 2.

43 *Longmont Ledger*, 28 (August 23, 1907): 1.

44 Ibid., 29 (March 27, 1908): 1. This section of the 1906 road, with its careful stonework, is still visible. It is located to the immediate left as one descends the hill below Pinewood Springs heading west on Highway 36.

45 *Loveland Reporter*, 8 (June 27, 1907): 2.

46 *Longmont Call*, 9 (August 24, 1907): 1.

47 *Lyons Recorder*, 8 (November 21, 1907): 1

48 *Longmont Ledger*, 28 (August 23, 1907): 1.

Chapter 7: The Estes Park Transportation Company
Pages 107–120

1 *Longmont Call,* 5 (April 25, 1903): 1. The *Call,* citing as its source the *Denver Post,* assured its readers that the Burlington Railroad "is now building a new road from Lyons into the park that will be sixteen miles long. It will be an easy grade and is constructed especially for automobiles. It is claimed that the machines will make the trip from Lyons to the Park in one hour." The story included the statement that the coming of an automobile line, with two cars running from Lyons to Estes Park, was imminent.

2 *Loveland Reporter,* 27 (February 28, 1907): 1.

3 It would later be claimed that Stanley had intended to pioneer automobile transportation from Loveland to Estes Park; that he was rebuffed by Larimer County commissioners when he offered to lend them the money necessary to put the road up the Big Thompson Canyon "in good condition" in exchange for an exclusive franchise for a fixed period to carry passengers for hire. When the county balked, the story goes, Stanley backed off, leaving the way open for others.

The single source for this story is Pieter Hondius, a resident of Estes Park since 1896. It is found in a letter dated December 7, 1928, from Roger W. Toll, superintendent of Rocky Mountain National Park, to Hondius (copy, EPAHM). Attached to his letter is a brief memorandum, dated November 28, 1928, which Toll asked Hondius to approve and sign. The memorandum lists those who had attended the meeting with County Commissioner John Y. Munson when Stanley's offer was originally made. The memorandum concludes, "Mr. Stanley's proposition was never accepted."

Though Stanley's offer seems odd on the face of it, given his later attitude with respect to transportation monopolies, there is no reason to distrust Hondius, who went so far as to vouch for its accuracy with his own signature. On F.O. Stanley's behalf, however, three things should be noted. The first is that Hondius was relying on his memory of an event that had taken place a full two decades earlier. The second has to do with Toll's own motives. For the superintendent of Rocky Mountain National Park to raise the issue in November 1928, at a time when Stanley was still fighting the Park Service's exclusive franchise with Roe Emery (see Chapter 13), hardly seems coincidental. The third is that I have not been able to corroborate the story from other sources.

4 Incorporation Records, State of Colorado (IRSC), Book 131, p. 121.

5 *Loveland Reporter,* 28 (March 14, 1907): 1.

6 *Longmont Call,* 9 (August 24, 1907): 6.

7 *Loveland Reporter,* 28 (June 13, 1907): 4; *Loveland Daily Herald,* 6 (September 2, 1915): 1.

8 Clymer, p. 14.

9 Ibid.

10 Reproduced in Derr, p. 118. The Stanley Mountain Wagon was also used successfully at a number of resorts in New England, most notably by the

Ricker Hotel Company of Maine, which operated a number of well-known resorts, including the Poland Spring House and Mansion House at South Poland, the Samoset Hotel at Rockland, and the Mount Kineo House at Moosehead Lake. The 1917 Express Wagon, built on the same chassis, cost $2,400. See Clarence F. Coons, "Stanley Steamers in Maine in the 1912–1914 Era," *SMN*, 10 (March 1991): 9–10, 19–21.

A 1917 advertisement for the Mountain Wagon put forth yet another reason for purchase: "One of the most fashionable eastern resorts does not permit internal-explosive automobiles, even pleasure cars, to come up to its principal entrance because the noise they make disturbs the guests on the piazzas; but a separate entrance is provided for them at some distance. The Stanley Mountain Wagons which this hotel owns, however, make regular stops at the carriage entrance and disturb no one." SMA.

11 Roy and Hazel Baldwin, transcript, "A Museum Interview" (June 7, 1974), p. 7, CCEPPL.

12 *Longmont Ledger*, 29 (June 19, 1908): 2.

13 Ibid., 29 (August 14, 1908): 8. F.O. Stanley's automobile line had accidents as well. "Auto No. 6, belonging to Mr. Stanley," the Longmont Ledger reported on June 26, 1908, "run [sic] off the road about 500 yards west of the P.O. Monday at 10:30 and nearly upset. They had to get a team to pull them out. Several passengers badly scared, but no one hurt." *Longmont Ledger*, 29 (June 26, 1908): 8. There is also the photograph reproduced here of the wrecked Stanley on Pingree Hill west of Fort Collins.

14 *Longmont Call*, reprinted in the *Lyons Recorder*, 8 (February 6, 1908): 1. The *Call* reiterated the message later that month: "Longmont has never had the recognition due us, from the Park. Let's keep after it." Ibid., 10 (February 22, 1908): 1.

15 IRSC, Book 132, p. 196; *Lyons Recorder*, 9 (June 25, 1908): 1. Incorporators were Oscar Peter Low, Frank P. Secor, and Gray Secor. Secor and his son, Gray, were lawyers who practiced together in Longmont.

16 Late in 1897, Milton Clauser (1867–1948), a graduate of Haverford College, filed on 80 acres in Estes Park immediately to the east of the site of the Stanley Hotel, where he built the summer home that he occupied for many years. In 1903, Clauser purchased a 1903 Model CX Stanley Steamer, one of the first three to be shipped to Colorado, for $750. On one occasion, Clauser later recalled, he was driving his tiller-steered machine from Golden toward Denver when the steering knuckle on the front axle broke. "In these early days," he wrote, reminding us of the ingenuity of early automobile drivers,

> wrecking-cars were non-existent and drivers were usually their own mechanics. I borrowed a spring wagon wheel and axle from a farmer's scrap pile, tied it under the car and came home at the rate of ten miles an hour on my own steam. While I was making the repairs the driver of a passing team gave the usual advice of "better get a horse," accompanied by the no less usual elated grin. However, as I approached Denver I overtook and passed this same team. I was sort of proud of my handiwork and took this photograph upon my return home.

The photograph and the story accompanying it were published by the Denver Chamber of Commerce on September 28, 1944. Clauser subsequently purchased a 1914 Stanley Model 607.

[17] *Longmont Call*, 10 (July 4, 1908): 1.

[18] *Lyons Recorder*, 8 (March 19, 1908): 1.

[19] *Longmont Ledger*, 29 (June 12, 1908): 1.

[20] *Longmont Call*, 10 (June 13, 1908: 1.

[21] Ibid., p. 7.

[22] *Lyons Recorder*, 8 (November 21, 1907): 1.

[23] *Longmont Ledger*, 29 (June 19, 1908): 8.

[24] LCRD, Book 245, p. 279. On October 29, 1909, Stanley then transferred the lots to the Estes Park Transportation Company (for the sum of one dollar). LCRD, Book 266, p. 389.

[25] *Loveland Reporter*, 3 (December 3, 1908): 2. The Osborns' permanent garage in Estes Park was completed in 1909.

[26] *Longmont Call*, 17 (July 23, 1915): 1.

[27] The *Estes Park Trail* reported on September 21, 1912, that "Mr. Low will go to Los Angeles and take charge of the Stanley business on the Pacific Coast." *Estes Park Trail*, 1 (September 21, 1912): 12. Low would later return to Estes Park.

[28] Ibid., 3 (September 5, 1914): 14.

[29] *Fort Collins Morning Express*, 43 (May 11, 1916): 4. Glover, it was stated, would stay on as a stockholder in Emery's company, and continue to serve the needs of the Colorado and Southern with automobiles operating from his new garage between College and Pine in Fort Collins. Stanley automobiles were also run between Greeley and its Union Pacific depot and Estes Park. As early as June 1908 it was reported that Stanley's partner, Burton Sanborn, and D. A. Canfield proposed to initiate such a venture with the blessings of the railroad. *Longmont Call*, 10 (June 27, 1908): 6.

[30] *Boulder Daily Camera*, 27 (May 28, 1917): 1.

[31] *Rocky Mountain News*, 90 (October 30, 1949): 22.

[32] Interview with Walter Emery, Denver, August 20, 1998. Walter Emery, Roe Emery's son, was named for Walter White.

[33] F.O. Stanley, letter to William E. Sweet, October 1, 1928.

[34] Quoted by Forest Crossen, *Estes Park Trail*, 18 (April 23, 1938): 20.

[35] Forest Crossen, *The Switzerland Trail of America* (Boulder: Pruett Press, 1962), p. 229.

Chapter 8: The Stanley Hotel
Pages 121–142

[1] *Rocky Mountain News*, 50 (June 13, 1909): Section 3, 2.

[2] *Longmont Ledger*, 28 (January 25, 1907): 5.

[3] Stanley clearly had developed his hotel plans well before he formally concluded his arrangement to purchase the Dunraven estate with Sanborn June 16, 1908, by which time actual construction work on the hotel had begun. Stanley may well have obtained the property, or reached agreement to obtain the property, from the Estes Park Development Company, the entity organized in February 1906 by Miller Porter of Denver and his partners following their assumption in October 1905 of Guy LaCoste's lease-purchase agreement with the Earl of Dunraven. The exact details of Stanley's purchase, however, remain unclear. The actual warranty deed on the property was not executed with the Estes Park Development Company until October 2, 1911. The company was then owned jointly by Sanborn and Stanley. LCRD, Book 242, p. 285.

[4] Gary Long, "The Stanley Hotel," unpublished typescript (March 6, 1987), p. 2. Copy, SMA.

[5] Stanley's relationship with another architect, Albert Dow, though it occurred years later, may well shed light on his working relationship with the architect he hired in Colorado. Dow, a resident of Tuftonboro, New Hampshire, near Lake Winnipesaukee, had been involved with the building of Hebron Academy's gymnasium and infirmary, and had written to the school's principal offering his services on a new project. Principal Hunt sent Dow's letter on to F.O. Stanley, who responded on May 18, 1937, with a letter rebuking Dow for overstating his contribution. "There should be no question as to who designed the Hebron gymnasium and the infirmary," Stanley told him.

> Before I had ever seen you or heard of you, I had a very complete design of the gymnasium, the various rooms, their sizes, and location, including the swimming-pool, and the two-story Doric porch. The same was true of the infirmary. We wanted an architect to take my designs and make the necessary drawings. For this purpose we hired you.

Stanley then went on to chastise Dow for having changed his design. All said, Stanley concluded: "I am now engaged in designing an important building for Hebron Academy, and I know of no architect I had rather have assist me than Albert H. Dow." F.O. Stanley, letter to Albert H. Dow, May 18, 1937, SMA.

[6] The single contemporary reference to Wieger's involvement with the construction of the Stanley Hotel is found in the December 1907 issue of the *American Architect and Building News*: "Denver, Colorado—T. Robert Wieger, 628 Fourteenth Street, is said to be preparing plans for a summer hotel, to be erected by F.O. Stanley at Estes Park, at a cost of $150,000. . . . Frank Kirchoff will have charge of the building." American Architect and Building News, 92 (December 21, 1907): 154.

Wieger (1877–1929), a native of Cincinnati, had come to Denver with his parents at the age of 12, where he attended the public schools before going into partnership with Franklin Kidder in 1900. By 1906, Wieger was self-employed, in an office on 14th Street. While nothing in Wieger's career suggests any familiarity with Georgian architecture, it is also clear that F.O. Stanley respected his work, for they collaborated again beginning in the fall of 1916, see below. Wieger committed suicide in 1929, apparently over money problems. At that time he was described as "a prominent architect," known locally for having designed Temple Emanuel, for his assistance on the new addition to the Denver Athletic Club, as well as for his service as president of the Colorado Chapter of the American Institute of Architects and as secretary to the Colorado Board of Architectural Examiners. See Rocky Mountain News, 80 (March 10, 1929): Section 2, 1; Denver Post (March 9, 1929): 1.

7 According to the newspapers of the day, the W. J. Pinney Company got the plumbing contract, the Smith & McCallin Company did the plastering work; the H. A. Koble Tinning Company did the tinning, and Homer Wright received the contract for putting on the Elaterite roofing. All were from Denver. The painting contract, however, went to the Daniels & Howlett Company of Boston, while the electrical and telephone wiring was done by a Mr. Howard and his son, Robert, of Chicago. *Longmont Ledger*, 30 (December 25, 1908): 1.

8 The original register for Elkhorn Lodge is the property of Eleanor Jane Owen, a descendant of the original owners. It covers the period June 1880 to September 1913.

9 *Longmont Ledger*, 30 (December 11, 1908): 8.

10 In July 1908, well before the Casino was started, Rogers got into a dispute with one Charley Spencer who was putting in the concrete fireplaces and sidewalks at the hotel. It ended with Spencer leaving for Denver, "taking his two helpers along with him." Ibid., 29 (July 17, 1908): 8. Such behavior evoked the following jibe from the Estes Park correspondent of the Ledger: "We will change our item about Mr. Rogers being acting superintendent for the architect. He is only the architect's critic." Ibid., 30 (October 9, 1908): 8.

11 Ibid., 29 (October 25, 1907): 4.

12 Ibid., 30 (October 30, 1908): 4.

13 Ibid., 29 (May 8, 1908): 8.

14 Ibid., 30 (December 25, 1908): 1.

15 The Longmont Ledger reported in October 1908 that "Mr. Motz and Fred Brown have a winter's job hauling 450,000 foot [sic] of lumber from Stanley's mill to Dr. James' lumber yard. Some of it will be seasoned and planed before being hauled to the various places to be used." Ibid., 30 (October 23, 1908): 8.

16 Donald L. Griffith, "Homestead Trails and Tales," unpublished typescript, CCEPPL, pp. 35–39. At Bierstadt Lake the Griffiths had a contract with the Forest Service that allowed them to harvest lumber killed by the great Bear Lake fire of 1900.

17 *Longmont Ledger*, 29 (June 12, 1908): 8.

18 Ibid., 29 (June 8, 1908): 8.

19 Ibid., 29 (June 19, 1908): 2.

20 Ibid., 29 (August 7, 1908): 8.

21 Ibid.

22 Ibid.

23 Ibid., 29 (August 14, 1908): 8.

24 Ibid., 30 (September 4, 1908): 8.

25 Ibid.

26 Ibid., 30 (October 16, 1908: 8.

27 Ibid., 30 (October 30, 1908): 8.

28 Ibid., 30 (November 13, 1908): 8.

29 *Loveland Reporter*, 29 (November 26, 1908): 2.

30 *Longmont Ledger*, 30 (December 11, 1908): 8.

31 Ibid., 30 (December 18, 1908): 8.

32 Ibid., 29 (July 31, 1908): 8.

33 Ibid., 29 (August 14, 1908): 8.

34 The *Mountaineer*, 1 (August 27, 1908): 1; *Longmont Ledger*, 29 (August 27, 1908): 8.

35 Ibid., 30 (October 23, 1908): 8.

36 Ibid., 30 (October 2, 1908): 2.

37 Ibid., 30 (October 16, 1908): 8.

38 The $150,000 figure came from the *Longmont Call* (10 [September 28, 1907], 1); the figure of $1,000,000 was from the *Loveland Herald* (3 [March 18, 1909]: 1); $500,000 was the amount reported by both the *Rocky Mountain News* (50 [June 23, 1909]: 7) and the *Longmont Ledger* (37 [June 30, 1911]: 1). By the date of the News' estimate, however, the Manor House was not yet complete. The other major newspaper to offer a guess was the *Denver Post*, which advanced the figure of $250,000 ([June 24, 1909: 6]), though both the *Greeley Tribune* and the *Loveland Reporter* had mentioned that same figure the year before in October 1908 (*Greeley Tribune*, 38 [October 7, 1908]: 3; *Loveland Reporter*, 29 [October 15, 1908]: 1). When asked about the cost of his new hotel, Stanley is said to have replied, "No one ever counts the cost, when they are getting what they want." *Denver Republican*, 31 (June 20, 1909): 23.

39 *Longmont Ledger*, 30 (November 27, 1908): 8.

40 Ibid.

41 Ibid., 29 (August 14, 1908): 8.

42 The *Mountaineer*, 1 (August 13, 1908): 6.

43 Ibid., 1 (August 27, 1908): 1.

44 *Loveland Reporter*, 29 (October 15, 1908): 1.

45 The deerskin petition—still in excellent condition—is preserved in the Estes Park Area Historical Museum.

46 *Longmont Ledger*, 30 (January 15, 1909): 1.

47 Ibid., 30 (December 25, 1908): 1. Boynton was wrong about the "hot air furnaces." During the years of F.O. Stanley's ownership, the Stanley Hotel lacked winter heating. The discrepancy in the number of bathtubs, reported earlier by Boynton's paper as 52, is difficult to account for.

48 *Rocky Mountain Druggist*, 23 (July 1909): 3.

49 *Loveland Reporter*, 30 (June 24, 1909): 6. Stanley was sufficiently impressed

(or alarmed) by these conditions that he telephoned Burton D. Sanborn on June 23 to inform him "that Lawn Lake is still frozen to a depth of four feet and that snow banks several feet deep surround the lake."

50 *Denver Post* (June 24, 1909): 6.

51 Ibid. "We were also shown the tires," the Post reporter added.

52 Loveland Herald, 3 (June 24, 1909): 6.

53 Ibid.

54 Ibid.

55 *Denver Post* (June 25, 1909): 6.

56 Ibid.

57 *Rocky Mountain Druggist*, 23 (July 1909): 14–15.

58 *Denver Republican*, 31 (June 25, 1909): 12.

59 The room that Mrs. Ford calls the rest room was the smoking room, and she seems to have confused the fireplace in the parlor with the fireplace in the smoking room, which was made of lichen-covered gneiss. Also, she has the hotel on a north-south axis rather than an east-west one for the location of rooms.

60 *Rocky Mountain Druggist*, 23 (July 1909): 10–13. Her cursory view of the kitchen would not have pleased F.O. Stanley. The kitchen was his pride. For another detailed contemporary account of the Stanley see "Hotel Stanley of Estes Park," *Hotel Monthly* (August 10, 1910): 36–42. This is cited later, starting on page 152.

61 *Loveland Herald*, 3 (July 1, 1909): 2. A more serious accident occurred two years later, in June 1911, at about 8 P.M. on a Sunday evening, when leaking gas from a line fed by the hotel's acetylene plant was ignited by Elizabeth Wilson, the chief chambermaid, as she was lighting a gas jet in one of the guest rooms directly above the dining room. The electric plant, the usual source of illumination, had been put out of commission by a storm during the day. The acetylene plant, used only in the case of emergency to produce bright white light, had then been tested for use that night. The gas line that Miss Wilson tried to light with a candle had apparently been on for some time. The room was immediately enveloped in flames. An explosion followed, causing the ceiling and several heavy steel girders to fall. Miss Wilson was hurled through the floor to the dining room below, fracturing both her ankles. There was extensive damage, estimated at $50,000–$60,000, to the southwest end of the Hotel. Four black waiters were also injured. In the dining room at the time were hotel manager Alfred Lamborn and his family. F.O. Stanley, fortunately, was in the lobby. Ironically the hotel had been opened for the season only the day before. *Loveland Herald*, 5 (June 29, 1911): 1; *Longmont Ledger*, 37 (June 30, 1911): 1; *Lyons Recorder*, 12 (June 29, 1911): 1.

62 *Rocky Mountain News*, 50 (June 23, 1909): 7.

63 *Longmont Ledger*, 30 (January 15, 1909): 5. By contrast, according to a 1910 Colorado and Southern Railroad brochure, the other hotels all charged a weekly rate, the most expensive of which were the $12–$25 charged by the Estes Park Hotel, the $12–$28 charged by the Elkhorn, the $12–$20

charged by the Rustic, and the $12–$15 charged by Wind River Lodge. CCEPPL.

Chapter 9: The Infrastructure of Estes Park
Pages 143–168

[1] Charles F. Hix claimed in an interview in September 1971 that "Mr. Sidney W. Sherman had been contacted by F.O. Stanley to organize the bank." Hix, who was originally hired as a seasonal clerk and bookkeeper in 1912, served as the bank's cashier and director from 1919 to 1937, at which time he was made president. Charles F. Hix, "Oral Interview with Charles and Elsie Hix," September 1, 1971, CCEPPL, p. 6. I have not been able to corroborate this statement from other sources.

[2] Sherman brought with him from Michigan his 44-year-old wife, Jennie, and 11-year-old son, Howard. While the work on the bank building went forward, "the new banker" made do with lodging consisting of two tents that he erected across the Big Thompson just south of E. M. A. Foot's store (at the corner of Elkhorn and Moraine). This was in late May. Within three weeks he let it be known that he planned to build "a fine residence" on Moraine Avenue. Ground was broken for the foundation and the carpenter's contract was let on June 6, the day marking the 13th wedding anniversary of Sidney and Jennie Cole Sherman. The cornerstone was laid on June 12, inside which the Sherman family carefully placed a tin box containing their signatures, a short note, a photograph of Estes Park (used as illustration here), two postcards, and an Indian head penny. When the house was torn down in the 1930s to make way for a building occupied by the telephone company, the tin box was recovered. The box and its contents are now on display at the United Valley Bank in Estes Park (the successor institution of the Estes Park Bank).
Jennie Cole Sherman died in Grand Rapids, Michigan, in May 1961 at the home of a daughter. Of Sidney Sherman there is no surviving record (he is not mentioned in her obituary), though presumably he returned with his wife to Grand Rapids. *Longmont Ledger*, 29 (May 29, 1908): 8; 29 (June 19, 1908): 8; *The Mountaineer*, 1 (June 11, 1908): 8; (June 18, 1908): 8.

[3] Stanley's purchase was recorded on May 27, 1908. On August 2, 1911, Stanley purchased an additional 20 shares from Sidney Sherman for $2,000. The original five shares were sold on March 19, 1919, at cost; the remaining 20 shares were sold by Stanley's estate on May 18, 1946, for $2,000. Estes Park Bank Stock Book. The stock book is kept in the vault of the United Valley Bank in Estes Park, the successor institution to the Estes Park Bank.

[4] *Loveland Reporter*, 28 (February 27, 1908): 1; *Longmont Ledger*, 29 (February 28, 1908): 1.

[5] Minutes of the third meeting of the board of directors, March 9, 1908, EPAHM, p. 11.

[6] Sherman's 20 shares were formally purchased on June 2, 1908. He then purchased an additional 21 shares between July 6, 1908, and May 13, 1910, at a cost of $2,100. Sherman sold all 41 of these shares between August 2

and August 5, 1911, for $4,100, recouping his entire investment. These included the 20 shares sold to F.O. Stanley on August 2, 1911. Estes Park Bank Stock Book.

7 LCRD, Book 202, p. 288.

8 *Longmont Ledger*, 29 (June 16, 1908): 8.

9 Ibid., 29 (July 3, 1908): 8. An addition to the west was completed in 1910.

10 *Loveland Daily Herald*, 11 (October 18, 1920): 1; *Longmont Ledger*, 41 (October 22, 1920): 1. In 1999 the original Estes Park Bank building survives as a camera store.

11 *Loveland Reporter*, 29 (July 16, 1908): 1.

12 Ibid., 29 (September 24, 1908): 1.

13 IRSC, Book 131, p. 108.

14 Both structures still survive, though the concrete reservoir on the hill above the Elkhorn Lodge has long since been converted to the basement of a summer cottage.

15 *Loveland Reporter*, 29 (September 24, 1908): 1.

16 F.O. Stanley, letter to William E. Sweet, October 1, 1928, SMA.

17 *Longmont Daily Call*, 24 (December 18, 1928): 1.

18 Ibid., 24 (June 12, 1928): 1; 24 (December 24, 1928): 1.

19 *Estes Park Trail*, 8 (April 5, 1929): 1; MBTEP, December 29, 1928, p. 307; February 11, 1929, pp. 308–309.

20 The land on which the power plant was sited, like the land farther west in Horseshoe Park, was never part of the Dunraven holdings. Horseshoe Park itself was homesteaded and used for cattle ranching in the 1880s, before being acquired by Pieter Hondius and others. Burton Sanborn's name does not appear on any of the tracts in this area, however, and just how he acquired the water rights on Fall River itself remains unclear.

21 IRSC, Book 131, p. 117.

22 *Longmont Call*, 11 (November 14, 1908): 1.

23 The history of the Stanley power plant and its equipment is described in the application submitted for its inclusion in the National Register of Historic Places. Copy, SMA. Most of the information in the application is taken from William B. Butler's "The Fall River Hydroelectric Plant, Town of Estes Park, Larimer County, Colorado" (1997), typescript copy, CCEPPL. Butler's study, it should be noted, is unfortunately flawed by errors of fact concerning the addition of diesel equipment. According to Butler the first diesel room (to house the Fairbanks Morse diesel generator) was "constructed somewhere between 1907 and 1919" and one of the existing rooms was expanded to house a second diesel generator sometime after 1928 or 1929 (two separate dates are supplied). However, the 1927 survey of the plant mentioned below (see Note 25), made, in part at least, to support the need for expanded equipment, makes reference only to the existence of the two hydro units. Contemporary newspapers, on the other hand, provide a specific date, January 1931, for the installation of the first diesel unit.

The origin of the third building on the power plant site, located about 150 feet southeast of the plant itself and referred to in recent years as

Operator's Cottage No. 2, has consistently troubled those who have sought to reconstruct the history of the power plant. The wooden structure appears on a September 1, 1929, site map, and has clearly been modified since that date.

Even more intriguing is the story that appeared in the *Estes Park Trail* on November 4, 1947, indicating that a house that had once been John Cleave's residence had been moved that week to the power plant site on Fall River, where it was to be "made available to Town employees as living quarters." Estes Park Trail, 27 (November 7, 1947): 16. Until 1907, the article explained, Cleave's house had stood at the corner of Elkhorn Avenue and Anderson Lane. That year it was moved to the rear of the lot by John Manford in order to make room for his new hotel. What happened to the Cleave house once it reached the power plant site is but one of a series of questions that research into the historical development of F.O. Stanley's power plant has yet to answer.

[24] *Loveland Reporter*, 29 (October 15, 1908): 1.

[25] "General Survey of The Stanley Power Company of Estes Park, Colorado," courtesy of Frank Hix. This typescript, dated March 23, 1927, was evidently prepared shortly after Stanley relinquished the power plant to the newly formed Stanley Corporation (see below). It shows that income from sales increased from $5,820.02 in 1916 to $28,236.91 in 1926, figures that reflect the growth of Estes Park.

[26] *Loveland Reporter*, 30 (June 10, 1909): 8.

[27] *Loveland Herald*, 3 (June 24, 1909): 1.

[28] Laurence Thomson, "An Interview with Laurence Thomson," April 30, 1972, CCEPPL, p. 3. Thomson and F.O. Stanley became good friends. "Mr. Stanley took an interest in me," Thomson recalled, "and I think he gave me some opportunities that probably otherwise I wouldn't have gotten. He would spend hours visiting when he came over to the power plant after I became an engineer up there . . . telling me of his own experiences."

On one occasion, Thomson also recounted, when he was out driving with F.O. Stanley in his steam car, they ran over a small squirrel near the Fish Hatchery:

> We stopped the car and he got out and examined the squirrel to see if it was killed or if it could be revived or not and he dug a grave and buried that little squirrel at the foot of a rock. He was upset about things like that. He was so considerate of people and wildlife.

Ibid., p. 14.

[29] John Willy, "A Week in Estes Park, Colorado," *Hotel Monthly*, 18 (July 1910): 37.

[30] John Willy, "Hotel Stanley of Estes Park, Colorado," *Hotel Monthly*, 18 (August 1910): 37.

[31] Ibid., 37, 39.

[32] Ibid., 39, 41.

[33] Ibid., 42.

[34] *Electrical World*, 56 (December 1910): 437.

35 Ibid.

36 Ibid., 438.

37 Ibid.

38 Ibid.

39 *Estes Park Trail*, 4 (April 18, 1924): 1.

40 Ibid.

41 *Loveland Reporter*, 42 (September 16, 1921): 2; *Longmont Daily Times*, 37 (November 22, 1921): 1.

42 Quoted in Butler, p. 7.

43 Ibid.

44 *Estes Park Trail*, 18 (April 7, 1939): 8.

45 *Estes Park Trail*, 10 (January 9, 1931): 1; *Longmont Daily Call*, 25 (January 19, 1931): 1.

46 Jack R. Melton and Lulabeth Melton, *YMCA of the Rockies: Spanning a Century* (Estes Park: YMCA of the Rockies, 1992), p. 80. The Y steam power plant, which had originally been put in use in 1919, was located east of the current Buildings and Grounds building in what is now a parking lot. It was sold during the Depression to raise money. Jack R. Melton, letter to James H. Pickering, February 10, 1999.

47 *Longmont Times Call*, 60 (February 16, 1933): 5. This was not the first time the power plant was forced to turn to the YMCA for help. In the fall and winter of 1929–1930 and again in January 1931, at a time when the new diesel was being installed, arrangements were made to use the Y steam boiler in order to be able to supply electricity on a 24-hour basis. Both times the culprit was a dry winter and the low flow of water in Fall River. *Estes Park Trail*, 12 (April 7, 1933): 35; 10 (January 16, 1931): 1.

48 A Public Service Company of Colorado drawing, dated October 4, 1933, shows the expanded diesel room with its Fairbanks Morse equipment in place. An expanded set of Public Utilities Commission drawings, dated September 7, 1937, shows how the installation was to proceed. These drawings are in the files of the Town of Estes Park's Lighting and Power Department.

49 Interview with C. Byron Hall, cited in Florence Johnson Shoemaker, "The Story of the Estes–Rocky Mountain National Park Region," M.A. thesis, Colorado State College of Education, Greeley, 1940, pp. 49–50.

50 In April 1943, following 16 months of study by the village trustees, residents voted 143 to 35 to acquire the portion of the system within town limits. After additional study, and another vote of the residents in September 1944, the entire system was purchased for $225,000, financed by $250,000 in Light and Power Revenue Bonds. *Estes Park Trail*, 25 (April 27, 1945): 1.

51 Quoted in *Hotel Monthly*, 18 (July 1910): 36.

52 Quoted in ibid.

53 *Loveland Herald*, 3 (September 23, 1909): 7.

54 Stanley's gift was accepted by the town trustees at their meeting of

October 4, 1935, followed on October 12 by a formal conveyance of the property through a warranty deed. MBTEP, II, p. 58; LCRD, Book 639, p. 207; *Estes Park Trail*, 15 (October 25, 1935): 3.

55 IRSC, Book 152, p. 198.

56 *Loveland Herald*, 5 (January 19, 1911): 1.

57 *Loveland Daily Herald*, 6 (September 22, 1914): 1; 6 (September 27, 1914): 1.

58 *Loveland Daily Herald*, 6 (September 24, 1915): 2. See also Loveland Reporter, 36 (September 22, 1915): 1; *Fort Collins Morning Express*, 42 (September 23, 1915): 1.

59 *Loveland Daily Herald*, 6 (September 23, 1915): 1.

60 *Loveland Reporter*, 36 (September 24, 1915): 1. See also *Fort Collins Morning Express*, 42 (September 25, 1915): 1.

61 MBTEP, I, 13, 27; *Loveland Daily Herald*, 9 (January 5, 1918): 1; 9 (July 12, 1918): 1.

62 Frank L. Woodward (1866–1930) was a prominent Denver lawyer; Thomas B. Stearns (1859–1946) owned T. B. Stearns Manufacturing Company in Denver. Stanley had come to know both men well during the long campaign culminating in the creation of Rocky Mountain National Park in 1915. Stanley had served with Woodward, C. H. Bond, and others as an elected director of the Estes Park Protective and Improvement Association in 1913. Stearns, as president of the Denver Chamber of Commerce, played a key role in keeping his organization actively interested and committed to the cause, and his name appeared, with F.O. Stanley's, on the park dedication program. Woodward was sent to Washington in 1914 as a "Special Representative" of the Colorado Mountain Club to lobby, during the critical period when the park bill was before the Congress. Both men were longtime Estes Park summer residents. In December 1916 the Colorado press indicated that Woodward and Stearns were part of a syndicate prepared "to construct, maintain and operate a chain of hotels and camps for tourists in the Rocky Mountain and Mesa Verde National parks." *Boulder Daily Camera*, 25 (December 5, 1916): 1.

In the spring of 1920, Woodward donated funds to erect an "ornamental" gate at the eastern Fall River entrance to Rocky Mountain National Park. *Loveland Reporter*, 40 (May 5, 1920): 1.

63 *Fort Collins Express*, 44 (September 15, 1917): 2; *Loveland Daily Herald*, 8 (September 15, 1917): 3.

64 *Larimer County Democrat*, 7 (July 1, 1927): 3.

65 *Fort Collins Express*, 44 (November 7, 1917): 6; *Loveland Daily Herald*, 8 (November 7, 1917): 1; *Denver Post* (December 2, 1917): Section 2, 1.

66 *Estes Park Trail*, 1 (June 24, 1921): 11. It is not clear just where the site was located or whether Stanley ever actually deeded title to the Town of Estes Park.

67 *Estes Park Trail* (September 14, 1912): 12.

68 F.O. Stanley, letter to Dorothy F. Schwartz, June 9, 1913, FNSHF. Dorothy Schwartz was the wife of Estes Park lumberyard owner Julius F. Schwartz.

69 Bertha Ramey, "An Oral Interview with Bertha Ramey," May 1974, CCEP-PL.

Chapter 10: The Coming of Rocky Mountain National Park
Pages 169–182

1 Quoted in Lloyd K. Musselman, Rocky Mountain National Park: Administrative History, 1915–1965 (Washington: Department of the Interior, 1971), p. 27.

2 Memoirs of Herbert N. Wheeler," typescript copy, Boulder Public Library, p. 55. Accounts of the creation of Rocky Mountain National Park may be found in Curt W. Buchholtz, *Rocky Mountain National Park: A History* (Boulder: Colorado Associated University Press, 1983), pp. 104–137; Alexander Drummond, *Enos Mills: Citizen of Nature* (Niwot: University Press of Colorado, 1995), pp. 222–247; Patricia M. Fazio, "Cragged Crusade: The Fight for Rocky Mountain National Park, 1909–1915," M.A. thesis, University of Wyoming, Laramie, 1982; and Musselman, pp. 17–27.

3 Though the date of September 1906 has been generally cited for the formation of the Estes Park Protective and Improvement Association (for example, by Enos Mills in his *Story of Estes Park* and by an article on the subject published in the August 24, 1912, issue of the *Estes Park Trail*), an organization with virtually the same name, The Estes Park Protection [sic] and Improvement Association, and the same purpose was in fact founded 11 years earlier in 1895. Its president was Abner Sprague. Ella (Mrs. William) James of Elkhorn Lodge was chosen treasurer, and James Ferguson, Horace Ferguson's son who was then operating his father's Highlands Hotel, was chosen secretary. *Longmont Ledger*, 16 (June 21, 1895): 2.

4 Ibid.

5 *Estes Park Trail*, 1 (August 24, 1912): 2.

6 *Loveland Reporter*, 29 (October 15, 1908): 1.

7 Ibid., 30 (June 17, 1909): 1; *Longmont Call*, 11 (June 19, 1909): 1.

8 Ibid., 30 (September 23, 1909): 1.

9 *Estes Park Trail*, 1 (August 24, 1912): 5.

10 Ibid., p. 8.

11 Ibid., 3 (August 1, 1914): 3.

12 Enos A. Mills, *The Rocky Mountain National Park* (New York: Doubleday, Page & Co., 1924), p. 86.

13 On Wednesday, September 9, 1914, at the age of 63, Stanley climbed Longs Peak in the company of a guide, having ridden on horseback with Flora from Longs Peak Inn to the Keyhole with a small party. *Estes Park Trail*, 3 (September 12, 1914): 19. Seven years later, on September 22, 1921, Charles Edwin Hewes recorded in his journal that Stanley had ridden past the Hewes-Kirkwood Inn up the old Longs Peak trail as far as the Keyhole. Charles Edwin Hewes, Journal of Charles Edwin Hewes, September 22, 1921, EPAHM.

[14] *Longmont Ledger*, 29 (August 14, 1908): 8.

[15] *Longmont Call*, 10 (June 20, 1908): 1; ibid., 10 (June 27, 1908): 1.

[16] *Longmont Ledger*, 29 (August 14, 1908): 1.

[17] *Loveland Reporter*, 30 (April 15, 1909): 6.

[18] F.O. Stanley, letter to Pieter Hondius, March 20, 1913, copy EPAHM.

[19] *Estes Park Trail*, 2 (June 21, 1913): 4.

[20] Charles Hewes writes about the Mills-Stanley relationship in the March 4, 1912, entry of his journal. Hewes and a small group of his neighbors in the Tahosa Valley had become suspicious of Mills's motives in promoting the new park. Fearing that their property might be appropriated by the government, they banded together to oppose the park by forming the so-called Front Range Settlers League. This set them on a collision course with their neighbor, Enos Mills. Hewes recounts how Stanley took great offense when a young man named Arthur Cole, whose parents were both Settlers League members, hauled Mills into court in Loveland, where he was convicted of assault. One of the important witnesses against Mills was the Reverend Elkanah J. Lamb, the park's first resident preacher (and the cousin of Enos Mills's own father). Hewes also tells of a dinner party, six weeks after Mills' conviction, to which the Stanleys invited the Lambs and which ended in an angry debate over the character of Enos Mills. The Stanleys nonetheless became friends with the Lambs, and on at least one occasion Flora Stanley had made a contribution to the annual benefit held in Elkanah Lamb's honor.

"Mr. Lamb responded," Hewes noted, recalling the dinner party, "in no uncertain terms as to Mills's contemptible character and also as to his own opinion of Stanley's unfairness and ungentlemanliness in endorsing such a man as against others, without carefully investigating his character and also for his inviting himself and wife to dinner and forcing upon them a subject which was so wholly disagreeable." Flora Stanley cried and the Lambs departed from dinner table and house. A few days later, in Hewes's retelling, Lamb received a letter from Stanley "of the most abject apology," closing with the statement "even if you cannot overlook the insult offered by me at our table, I shall always cherish you as one of my dearest friends." Lamb, in response, wrote a letter of forgiveness, and the breach was healed. Hewes, Journal, March 4, 1912.

[21] *Estes Park Trail*, 1 (August 24, 1912): 3.

[22] Enos A. Mills, letter to F.O. Stanley, September 6, 1910, SMA. Some years later, in discussing the park campaign, Mills indicated that "the four people who helped me the most—who from the first to the last constantly gave me their moral support and at times their intellectual assistance—were John Muir, J. Horace McFarland [president of the American Civic Association], George Horace Lorimer [editor of the *Saturday Evening Post*], and C. H. Bond." Enos A. Mills, *The Rocky Mountain National Park*, p. 91. Oddly, F.O. Stanley is not mentioned, though admittedly Mills is perhaps talking here about moral and intellectual rather than financial support. Bond's role, it should be noted, which was substantial, has been almost totally overlooked by historians.

[23] When hearings on the park bill were held before the House Committee on Public Lands on December 23, 1914, Mills was invited to speak by Colorado Senator Edward Taylor. He might also have asked F.O. Stanley, whose reputation would have carried considerable weight before an eastern audience. Taylor, however, was probably unaware of Stanley's interest and involvement, most of which occurred behind the scenes. It can be assumed, on the other hand, that Stanley was instrumental in gaining and keeping the support of the Appalachian Mountain Club (AMC), then as now headquartered in Boston. The AMC sponsored a speech in Boston by Mills during the park campaign.

[24] F.O. Stanley, letter to Enos A. Mills, January 26, 1915, SMA.

[25] F.O. Stanley, letter to Enos A. Mills, June 7, 1915, Enos Mills Cabin Collection.

[26] Fort Collins *Weekly Courier*, 37 (September 3, 1915): 5.

[27] Ibid., 37 (September 10, 1915): 5.

[28] Charlene Tresner, "Charles Tresner's Summer at Long's Peak Inn," typescript, Fort Collins Public Library. Twenty-five-year-old Tresner drove the Mountain Wagon for Enos Mills that summer, for which he received $3.50 per day plus room and board for him and his wife. On June 7, 1915, F.O. Stanley wrote Mills from Newton about his new machine, a letter that not only sheds light on their relationship but on the 1915 Stanley Mountain Wagon as well.

> We are about to ship you tomorrow the new mountain wagon. It ought to reach Lyons in about eleven days, which would bring it June 19th. We are sorry we could not get this machine off earlier, but we are very anxious to have everything about it in perfect condition. I have been running it quite a number of miles today, and it is certainly a beautiful running car. While it is geared much lower than your present car, at the same time the pumps run much slower and have a much longer stroke, as they are driven not from the engine but from the rear axle, and have a stroke of 4 inches. Running slow as they do, entirely eliminates the noise from the pumps, which was somewhat annoying in the old model. I know you will find this car very satisfactory, and after you receive it and have tried it out, I would like to have you drop me a line telling me how you like it.

F.O. Stanley, letter to Enos A. Mills, June 7, 1915.

[29] See, for example, the *Loveland Reporter*, 36 (September 3, 1915): 1.

[30] *Loveland Reporter*, 36 (September 6, 1915): 2.

[31] *Longmont Ledger*, 36 (September 10, 1915): 4.

[32] *Denver Post* (September 15, 1915): 1.

[33] *Longmont Ledger*, 36 (September 10, 1915): 4. Stanley apparently seriously miscounted, for according to the *Loveland Herald*, "At two o'clock 267 cars were parked in the natural amphitheater in Horseshoe."

[34] Ibid. *Loveland Daily Herald*, 6 (September 6, 1915): 1.

[35] *Denver Post* (September 25, 1922): 9.

[36] Ibid., pp. 1, 9.

[37] Edna Ferber, letter to Esther Mills, September 23, 1922, FNSHF.

Chapter 11: The Grand Years, 1909–1919
Pages 183–214

[1] *Estes Park Trail*, 1 (August 31, 1912): 7–8.

[2] Raymond W. Stanley, letter to Emma E. Walker, December 12, 1940, SMA. Chansonetta and Augusta had problems as well. In a two-page letter, written on July 31, 1904, Augusta addressed their relationship head on. "But I have always, & especially of late," she wrote, "felt you did not like me, or anything pertaining to me, my children included." Small wonder that Chansonetta and her daughter Dorothy preferred the company of her other sister-in-law. Augusta Stanley, letter to Chansonetta Emmons, July 31, 1904, SMA.

[3] The building of the Waverly Avenue house was one of very few events that caused the Stanleys to cut short their summers in Estes Park. They left for home in early September that year because Mr. Stanley was "very anxious to observe the progress which has been made during his summer in Estes Park." *Estes Park Trail*, 2 (September 6, 1913): 11.

[4] "Freelan O. Stanley," p. 4. Unsigned typescript dated October 25, 1940, SMA.

[5] SMA.

[6] For biographical information about Chansonetta Stanley Emmons and her photographic career see Marius B. Peladeau's introduction to *Chansonetta: The Life and Photographs of Chansonetta Stanley Emmons, 1858–1937* (Waldoboro, Maine: Maine Antique Digest, 1977), pp. 7–15; Brook Merrow, "Chansonetta," *SMN*, 8 (June 1989): 8-9; Raymond W. Stanley, "Chansonetta Stanley Emmons," *SMN*, 9 (March–June 1990), 10–12; Rebecca Bryant Lockridge, "The Photographs of Chansonetta Stanley Emmons, 1859–1937," *SMN*, 10 (March 1991): 4–6.

[7] Peladeau, pp. 10–11. While Peladeau indicates that both brothers provided Chansonetta with financial support, the specific gestures mentioned here are all attributed by Peladeau to F.O. Stanley. He cites as his source a March 4, 1976, interview with Raymond W. Stanley.

[8] The F.E. Stanleys' home amid the cliffs and dells of Squirrel Island, half an hour's ferry ride from Boothbay Harbor, invites comparison with the far more rustic life that his brother and sister-in-law preferred in Estes Park. Squirrel Island, with its turreted and gabled "cottages," some with as many as 20 rooms, like Newport, was an exclusive, social, and private summer enclave whose life revolved around the 104-room Squirrel Island Inn, with its bowling alley, spa, and 120 x 56–foot casino. The island was so exclusive, in fact, that in 1903 the Squirrel Island Association obtained a charter from the state granting the island autonomous government. By 1906 it boasted 115 cottages, a hotel, chapel, post office, telegraph office, library, and store.
  Though "Rockside" in Estes Park and the nearby Stanley Hotel certainly had their share of amenities, especially for a mountain community, the summer society in which the F.O. Stanleys moved was far more egalitar-

ian. The Stanley brothers nevertheless served their summer communities in very similar ways. On Squirrel Island, where F.E. and Augusta built a barn-red, white-trimmed cottage with wraparound porches in 1908–1909, and where their daughters for a time each had houses, Augusta took the lead in running the island association. F.E. Stanley, on his part, designed and oversaw the building of an elaborate concrete sidewalk system to protect the island's lush vegetation and the cement water tower that secured its water supply. See Susan Stiles Dowell, "Squirrel: Visitors Please Keep to the Sidewalk," *Down East Magazine* (January 1986): 60–63; Francis Byron Greene, *History of Boothbay, Southport, and Boothbay Harbor, Maine* (Portland, Maine: Loring, Short, and Harmon, 1906), pp. 412–413.

9 This gift turned out to be one of the major public embarrassments of F.O. Stanley's life. According to Raymond Stanley, at the time of the gift, Stanley gave the school $50,000 in cash, enough to begin construction. The balance was made up of the 5 percent bonds he had received from the Stanley Corporation at the time of the sale of the Stanley Hotel (see below). When the Hebron trustees later tried to cash some of these bonds, however, they were found to be worthless. Stanley had to ask the school to return the bonds so that he could foreclose on them. The gymnasium, built in 1929, was apparently eventually paid for with some of the preferred stock he received from Roe Emery at the time of his purchase of the hotel. The Hebron trustees, in turn, sold the stock to Hebron alumni and friends. This stock, too, had little or no value. Raymond W. Stanley, letter to Emma E. Walker, December 12, 1940. Harold E. Hall, *History of Hebron Academy, Hebron, Maine, 1804–1972* (Trustees of Hebron Academy, 1979), p. 159.

10 Some of the details of Stanley's long relationship with Hebron are found in Hall, pp. 158–160 ff.

11 Raymond W. Stanley, *Stanley Family Reunion*, p. 20. There are also stories of other students whose Hebron educations Stanley also financed, including a young Japanese man named Motoi Tuschia, who had come to America before World War I where he found work as a hat check boy at Boston's Adams House. There F.O. Stanley met him, and became so impressed with Tuschia's politeness and quickness that, according to the Hebron Semester, "he financed Motoi through Hebron, Tufts Dental College, and set him up in practice on Central Park West in New York City." Hebron Semester (December 1986): 25.

Not all of F.O. Stanley's efforts on behalf of Hebron Academy were as successful. In February 1927 he attempted to solicit his old friend George F. Eastman for a gift to Hebron, indicating that he was prepared, if necessary, to come to Rochester. Eastman, no doubt, seemed a promising candidate, for in 1918 he had invested heavily in education by giving a substantial sum to the University of Rochester to found the Eastman School of Music. Stanley, on the other hand, got nowhere. "Hebron belongs to a class that is entirely outside the scope of my activities," Eastman wrote him on February 11, 1927. "If I contributed to institutions of this kind it would open up a new field which is too big to warrant my tackling it. I have been over the subject many times and my mind is fully fixed; so it would be a waste of your time to come here." George Eastman, letter to F.O. Stanley, February 11, 1927, SMA.

[12] *Fort Collins Express,* 44 (February 25, 1917): 5.

[13] Roger W. Toll, *Mountaineering in the Rocky Mountain National Park* (Washington, D.C.: Government Printing Office, 1919), p. 105.

[14] Superintendent's Annual Report, 1919, LRMNP, p. 29; *Hotel Monthly,* 29 (September 1921): 47. In 1927 the Stanley Corporation sold 4.62 acres of Tuxedo Park to Charles H. Woods. Woods acquired an additional 14.42 acres in 1930. This became the site of Camp Woods, consisting of a store and a series of cottages. It operated under government franchise until 1958. LCRD, Book 495, p. 142; Book 619, p. 295.

[15] Quoted in Leonard and Noel, p. 263.

[16] *Denver Post* (June 13, 1919: 20.

[17] *Estes Park Trail,* 1 (August 31, 1912): 7-8.

[18] *Estes Park Trail,* 2 (July 12, 1913): 8. Lamborn also enjoyed the respect of his peers in the industry, who in early 1910 elected him president of the Rocky Mountain Hotel Men's Association.

[19] In small towns, small gestures matter. In the fall of 1915, for example, Lamborn announced that members of the Estes Park Golf Club, which had closed for the season, were welcome to use the Stanley Hotel course free of charge. The following March, the Rocky Mountain News pointed out that at the very time members of the Colorado Mountain Club were enjoying their annual ski outing in the snow at Fern Lake, 10 to 20 members of the Estes Park Golf Club were using the Stanley golf course each day. Rocky Mountain News, 56 (December 12, 1915): Section 2, 2; 57 (March 10, 1916): 8.

[20] *Estes Park Trail* (August 17, 1912): 6, 8.

[21] Flora Stanley's Diary, April 9, 1910, SMA. F.O. returned to Newton on April 19. The Manor House was formally opened on September 14, 1910, with guests moving over from the main hotel building.

[22] Mary B. K. Sherman, "Unique Among 1,500 Clubs," p. 5. Typescript dated June 1914, EPAHM.

[23] Ibid., p. 3.

[24] Flora Stanley's Diary, August 4, 1910, SMA.

[25] See Eleanor E. Hondius, *Memoirs of Eleanor E. Hondius of Elkhorn Lodge* (Boulder, Colo.: Pruett Press, 1964), pp. 40–41.

[26] Flora Stanley's Diary, September 10, 1910, SMA.

[27] *Lyons Recorder,* 19 (August 16, 1919): 1. See also *Denver Post* (August 8, 1919): 1; *Loveland Daily Herald,* 10 (March 31, 1919): 1; *Lyons Recorder,* 18 (April 12, 1919): 1; *Longmont Ledger,* 40 (May 19, 1919): 1.

[28] *Estes Park Trail Talk,* 1 (July 16, 1920): 5; 1 (August 20, 1920): 3; *Fort Collins Courier,* 48 (August 17, 1920): 1. While the *Courier* cited "unfavorable" weather conditions and Alberta Yore's insistence on making the flight as the probable cause, *Trail Talk* assured its readers that "the smash-up was a purely unavoidable accident. If the airplane had attained a good elevation, Mr. Swift would have had no trouble in landing safely. It was just such a combination of circumstances as causes many automobile accidents."

29 Estes Park resident Henry Dannels, who as a young man was employed at

the hotel doing renovation work about 1919, recalled the day that Stanley accosted him to point out such a deficiency. Dannels, perched on a plank protruding from a window high up on the hotel's third story, was in the act of replacing one of the dentils. F.O. Stanley, passing by, looked up to notice that the distance between two of the small projecting blocks had been thrown off by an eighth of an inch. His response was immediate: "Well, . . . Son, if it isn't too much trouble, let's take it off and wait until we get a piece the right size!" Dannels, if only later, accepted the lesson philosophically. "He had the right to look," he acknowledged, "it was his place." Henry Dannels, "An Interview with Henry D. Dannels," January 15, 1981, typescript, CCEPPL, p. 6.

It should perhaps be noted that more than 20 years earlier, on August 3, 1959, Estes Park electrician Walter Baldridge told precisely the same story. This time the man on the ladder was fellow resident David Usher. Ferrel Atkins, "Interview with Mr. Walt Baldridge," LRMNP.

30 Norman Dunham scrapbook, SMA.

31 *Longmont Call*, 19 (December 1, 1916): 1.

32 John Willy, "A Vacation in the Colorado Mountains," *Hotel Monthly*, 29 (September 1921): 46.

33 Robert B. Marshall, letter to L. C. Way, October 16, 1916, copy, SMA.

34 John E. Macdonald, Pieter Hondius, and Samuel Service, letter to Robert B. Marshall, October 26, 1916, copy, SMA.

35 Lewis C. Way, letter to Robert B. Marshall, October 30, 1916, copy, SMA.

36 *Fort Collins Morning Express*, 43 (November 11, 1916): 1; 43 (December 26, 1916): 1. See also *Lyons Recorder*, 17 (November 16, 1916): 1, and *Longmont Call*, 19 (December 1, 1916): 1; *Fort Collins Express*, 43 (February 25, 1917): 5.

37 *Fort Collins Morning Express*, 43 (December 26, 1916): 1.

38 Undated newspaper clipping from Columbia, Pennsylvania, citing as its source the *Denver Post*, SMA. The *Morning Express* also reported on December 26, that Stanley intended to buy "the greater part of the town, . . . raze the buildings and put up a picturesque, model town." *Fort Collins Morning Express*, 43 (December 26, 1916): 1; *Boulder Daily Camera*, 15 (December 28, 1916): 1.

39 *Fort Collins Express*, 43 (January 25, 1917): 1.

40 Lewis C. Way, letter to Robert B. Marshall, November 30, 1916, SMA.

41 Ibid.

42 "Administration Building and Residence in the Rocky Mountain National Park," copy, SMA.

43 T. Robert Wieger, letter to Lewis C. Way, SMA.

44 *Fort Collins Express*, 43 (February 7, 1917): 1. Rumors about Stanley and his plans were rife. Three weeks earlier, on January 20, 1917, the same paper reported that he intended to build a new hotel in Grand Lake. Ibid., 43 (January 20, 1917): 6.

45 *Loveland Daily Herald*, 8 (September 3, 1917): 1.

46 *Fort Collins Express-Courier*, 52 (September 23, 1923): 2; *Estes Park Trail*, 4 (September 18, 1925): 4. LCRD, Book 514, p. 251.

[47] The land was formally transferred to the district by a warranty deed dated July 20, 1937, SMA. LCRD, Registry of Deeds, Book 680, p. 305.

[48] Augusta Stanley's Diary, August 25, 1917, SMA.

[49] Ibid., August 26, 1917.

[50] Ibid., August 27, 1917.

[51] Ibid., August 29, 1917.

[52] Ibid., September 4, 1917.

[53] Ibid., August 31, 1917.

[54] Ibid., September 2, 1917.

[55] Augusta Stanley letter, Undated newspaper clipping, SMA.

[56] Augusta Stanley's Diary, August 15, 1922, SMA.

[57] Ibid., August 16, 1922.

[58] Ibid., August 17, 1922.

[59] Ibid.

Chapter 12: Disengagement
Pages 215–244

[1] LCRD, Book 359, p. 520.

[2] According to Blanche Stanley Hallett, her husband, Ed, had been asked by her father, F.E. Stanley, to give up his job as manager of Watson, Hallett and Company, a paint business, and join the Stanley Motor Carriage Company in 1905, during a period when workmen had been stealing parts. Some time later, Prescott Warren, who had married F.E. Stanley's younger daughter, Emily, was given a job as well. "I knew he didn't want to [take Prescott Warren in]," Blanche wrote years later, "but my mother talked him into it. It was a different situation entirely after that. Emmie and I never got on too well and there were always disagreeable things coming up. We all lived too near together. It was a great mistake." Blanche Stanley Hallett, "Memoirs, 1899–1908," pp. 184–185.

[3] The Stanleys' Unit Railway Company succeeded in producing several 50–foot-long prototype cars with 60-h.p. engines that were given trial runs between Boston and White River Junction, Vermont. The venture largely came to an end with the death of F.E. Stanley in 1918; see below.

[4] Carlton Stanley, letter to Raymond W. Stanley, February 2, 1943, SMA. Carlton told Raymond that the figures cited "were gotten up by Prescott Warren and are probably about correct." Carlton gives the net profits for the six years between 1908 and 1913 as follows: 1908, $169,355; 1909, $87,706; 1910, $32,000; 1911, $90,703; 1912, $71,500; 1913, $60,000. Gross receipts ranged from a low of $828,420 in 1911 to a high of $920,087 in 1913.

[5] Quoted in Volti, "Why Internal Combustion?" 42.

[6] *Rocky Mountain News*, 57 (January 1, 1916): Automobile Section, 20.

[7] *The Automobile*, 31 (March 1, 1917): 465.

[8] Volti, 42.

[9] Ibid., 44.

[10] Quoted in ibid., 43.

[11] Davis, *The Stanleys*, p. 31.

[12] *The Steam Car*, I, No. 16 (1919?): 1.

[13] Augusta Stanley's Diary, September 14, 1916, SMA.

[14] Ibid., November 28, 1917.

[15] F.O. Stanley, letter to Frank L. Woodward, May 25, 1923, SMA.

[16] F.O. Stanley, letter to N. W. Currier, May 24, 1923, SMA.

[17] F.O. Stanley, letter to Byron Spence, April 27, 1939, SMA.

[18] Emma E. Walker, letter to Raymond W. Stanley, February 7, 1937, SMA. This was the same kind of accounting process that the Stanleys employed with their dry plate business. Emma E. Walker, letter to Raymond W. Stanley, December 11, 1940, SMA.

[19] "When the Stanley Motor Carriage Company needed more capital to carry it over the 'hump' of an unsuccessful year . . . , it was F.E. Stanley who supplied the capital. . . . In the end when the business was sold, F.E. retrieved the money that he had furnished. Both brothers received stock in the new company that was formed but never any dividend payments and in the end when the banks took over . . . the stock was worthless." Raymond W. Stanley, undated typescript, "Notebooks," SMA. In a note dated February 6, 1958, he sets the amount loaned by his father at "about $500,000." Raymond W. Stanley, "A Few Errors Noted in Article on the Stanley Steamers by F.O. Stanley," typescript, ibid.

Raymond Stanley, it should be noted, spent most of his adult life trying to suggest that it was his father and not his uncle who deserved most of the credit for the success of the Stanley dry plate and the Stanley steam car, and in this instance he may have overstated his father's financial commitment.

[20] "I do not enjoy autoing with Frank he drives so fast," Augusta Stanley wrote in her diary on September 10, 1916, of her trip home that day from Wilton, New Hampshire. "We came awfully near having an accident just above Waltham but by Frank's turning to the left just in the nick of time to avoid it." She had reason to worry. Three years before, in November 1913, while driving in Bradford, F.E. Stanley turned out to avoid a collision and hit a telephone pole. Augusta was thrown from the car and seriously injured. Augusta Stanley's Diary, September 10, 1916, SMA.

[21] *Newton Crier* (August 2, 1918): 1; *Newton Circuit* (August 2, 1918): 1; *Newton Graphic* (August 2, 1918): 1. His death was widely reported in the Boston press.

[22] J. S. Maxcy, letter to F.O. Stanley, May 12, 1923, SMA. Josiah S. Maxcy of Gardiner, Maine, served as trustee of Hebron Academy from 1909 to 1935.

[23] Raymond W. Stanley, letter to Emma E. Walker, December 9, 1940, SMA.

[24] *Denver Post* (August 1, 1942): 4.

[25] LCRD, Book 358, p. 381.

[26] Ibid., Book 394, p. 206. The Haydens' property was located in what became the Broadview subdivision in which they owned eight rental summer cabins.

[27] Ibid., Book 395, p. 241. Storer's son and namesake, George Storer (1899–1975), then a student at Cornell, would go on to become president of the Storer Broadcasting System. The previous month, Storer had purchased the 200 adjacent acres from Milton Clauser, thus creating The Storer Ranch, a property that remained in the family for another 75 years. On November 1, 1919, Stanley sold an additional tract of 17.27 acres in the same area to the Stearns Investment Company of Denver, owned by his friend, Thomas B. Stearns. Ibid., Book 395, p. 520; Book 401, p. 151.

[28] Ibid., Book 428, p. 235. Mills purchased his original 21.01-acre tract on January 15, 1914; on June 20, 1925, he purchased an additional 15.42 acres from Stanley. Ibid., Book 311, p. 265; Book 513, p. 540.

[29] Clatworthy (1875–1953) purchased 12.55 acres for an unspecified amount on November 18, 1920, and another .66 acre, for which he paid $300, on July 1, 1922. Ibid., Book 428, p. 299; Book 439, p. 180.

[30] Birch (1882–1972) purchased 1.05 acres on August 13, 1921. The purchase price is unspecified. Ibid., Book 428, p. 4.

[31] Wolfrom (1872–1950) purchased 5.73 acres for $500 on October 4, 1921. Ibid., Book 439, p. 267.

[32] Ibid., Book 440, p. 179.

[33] See Melton and Melton, pp. 90–94.

[34] Ibid., p. 120.

[35] Jackie Hutchins, "Community Insight," *The Estes Park Trail-Gazette*, 29 (August 26, 1998): 4. LCRD, Book 358, p. 299. On September 18, 1919, and June 25, 1925, Alpha Somerville purchased two additional small parcels from Stanley, containing .78 and .86 acre. LCRD, Book 395, p. 277; Book 514, p. 142.

[36] LCRD, Book 580, p. 497. *Estes Park Trail-Gazette*, 12 (October 27, 1982): 4.

[37] LCRD, Book 506, p. 59.

[38] *Estes Park Trail*, 7 (June 10, 1927): 19; ibid., 4 (October 31, 1924): 1. On June 10, 1927, Rollins's filling station lease was assigned to the Continental Oil Company. This property was located on lower Elkhorn Avenue, in the vicinity of what is today the Valley National Bank. LCRD, Book 561, p. 186.

[39] *Longmont Ledger*, 37 (September 15, 1916): 1.

[40] *Estes Park Trail*, 2 (January 12, 1923): 1. Superintendent's Monthly Report (SMR), December 31, 1922, p. 3, LRMNP.

[41] Dannels, p. 6.

[42] SMR, March 5, 1926, p. 5.

[43] See *Estes Park Trail*, 5 (February 5, 1926): 1; *Rocky Mountain News*, 67 (February 3, 1926): 4; *Denver Post* (February 2, 1926): 1, 4; *Fort Collins Express-Courier*, 52 (February 4, 1926): 4; *Boulder Daily Camera*, 35 (February 4, 1926): 1.

[44] Shaw (1879–1947), a law graduate of the University of Wisconsin and a partner in the firm of Shaw, Muskat & Van Dyne, served for a number of years as an attorney for the Wisconsin Electric Power Company and its subsidiaries. A quiet man known for his gift of "simplicity and brevity,"

Shaw was feared by other lawyers "because of his maddening ability to cut the ground out from under an opponent with a few well chosen words." Though it was reported at the time of his death in 1947 that he enjoyed "considerable engineering and mechanical ability" and "understood the complete operation of every machine operated by the Transport and Electric companies," Shaw's obituary in the *Milwaukee Journal* says nothing about expertise in real estate transactions or other types of investment. As indicated below, less is known about the other principals, George Frederick and Erna Bond and E. T. McCarthy, beyond the fact that Bond Incorporated was located in the May Building, at 38th and North Avenue in Milwaukee. The names of Shaw and the two Bonds appear on the incorporation papers of the Stanley Corporation. The names George Frederick Bond, E. T. McCarthy, and James D. Shaw appear on the incorporation papers of both the Stanley Hotel Company and the Stanley Power Company (see below).

45 Cornelius H. Bond (1855–1931) was married twice. By his first wife, Frona Sullivan, whom he married in 1888, he had one child, a daughter, Doris. After Frona's death in 1895, Bond married Alma Sanborn (1861–1958). They had four children: the twins Frank Cornelius (1897–?) and Florence Camelia (1897-1980), George Frederick (c. 1899–?), and Mae (May) Sanborn (?–1964). Florence and Mae Bond never married, and both died in Estes Park. Frank Bond attended the South Dakota School of Mines. Returning to Estes Park, he launched a successful business career with his father and served seven years as the town's mayor, 1929–1935. In 1936, Frank Bond sold the Bond Agency and moved to New York and Connecticut, where he designed and built houses until his retirement in 1969.

Of George Frederick Bond we know even less. His Loveland High School "college prep" diploma is in the archives of the Estes Park Area Historical Museum and is dated May 25, 1916. I have been able to locate only two early newspaper references that establish and document the relationship between George Frederick Bond and Cornelius and Alma Bond, his mother and father. Both occur in their obituaries. In the case of Cornelius Bond, who died in May 1931, the reference is to Fred "of Milwaukee"; in the case of Alma Bond, who died in 1958, the reference is to Fred, without an address. *Estes Park Trail*, 11 (May 29, 1931): 1; 38 (August 15, 1958): 3.

The relationship is also mentioned in Ansel Watrous's *History of Larimer County*, published in 1911, and in a 1977 newspaper account of Frank Bond's return to Estes Park where he refers to his brother as George. *Estes Park Trail-Gazette*, 7 September 28, 1977): 7.

46 IRSC, Book 259, p. 585.

47 *Estes Park Trail*, 5 (May 21, 1926): 1.

48 "General Survey of the Stanley Power Company," p. 2; *Estes Park Trail*, 7 (July 29, 1927): 7; ibid., 7 (November 18, 1927): 3.

49 *Fort Collins Express-Courier*, 53 (August 17, 1926): 1.

50 *Estes Park Trail*, 5 (September 3, 1926): 1, 6. On June 14, 1928, the Stanley Corporation and Mountain Parks Air Lines, Inc., signed a lease agreement on 80 acres of the proposed park to create "The Stanley Air Port," to be

used for commercial and other kinds of flights. The one-year agreement called for a payment of $500. LCRD, Book 586, p. 179.

51 *Estes Park Trail*, 7 (June 10, 1927): 6.

52 Ibid., 7 (July 8, 1927): 1, 4.

53 *Longmont Daily Call*, 23 (June 8, 1927): 1; *Estes Park Trail*, 7 (May 27, 1927); 6. 288. The only major recorded transaction during this period was on June 9, 1927, when F.O. Stanley, for reasons that are not clear, repurchased, through Cornelius H. Bond, all the unplatted lands held by the Stanley Corporation within the incorporated town of Estes Park for $13,250. These lands had been held by the Corporation as the so-called Park Land Mortgage given to Stanley at the time of the original sale to Fred Bond and the others. LCRD, Book 568, p. 207.

54 *Fort Collins Express-Courier*, 53 (November 8, 1926): 3; Estes Park Trail, 6 (January 28, 1927): 9.

55 IRSC, Book 269, p. 558.

56 Ibid., Book 269, p. 266.

57 *Rocky Mountain News*, 68 (March 10, 1927): 1.

58 The Shaffers arrived at the Stanley Hotel on their "annual vacation" during Augusta Stanley's visit of 1922 and immediately renewed their relationship with the Stanleys. On the day before their return to Newton, F.O., Flora, and Augusta were invited to drive out from Denver and be the guests of the Shaffers at their Ken Caryl Ranch. Even Augusta Stanley was impressed. "The ride was twenty two miles," she noted in her diary, "—the nearest town Littleton. Seven miles before we reached the house, after we turned into their estate. There are 1000 cattle and over 40 help about the place. The house is a *palace*, with several guest houses in different parts of the ranch. It was far from my idea of a *Ranch House*, and lovely." Augusta Stanley's Diary, September 3, 1922, SMA.

59 *Longmont Daily Call*, 24 (April 7, 1928): 1.

60 LCRD, Book 586, pp. 499–501.

61 *Longmont Daily Call*, 24 (September 13, 1928): 1; Estes Park Trail, 8 (September 21, 1928): 11; Longmont Daily Times, 34 (November 17, 1928): 1. The deal was consummated after a careful study by engineers reported that they had found "the plant in much better condition than most plants they have acquired." Credit for this was given to Byron Hall who, it was announced, would stay on as manager.

62 *Longmont Daily Times*, 34 (November 17, 1928): 1. In August 1929, Warnock received a judgment in his favor of $1,676.40 plus court costs of $14.76. LCRD, Book D, p. 249.

63 *Denver Post* (December 14, 1928): 6.

64 A decade before, in December 1916, Boettcher's name had been linked to a syndicate that included two of F.O. Stanley's Estes Park friends, Frank L. Woodward and Thomas B. Stearns, and a plan to build and operate a series of "hotels and camps for tourists" in Rocky Mountain National Park and Mesa Verde National Park. *Boulder Daily Camera*, 25 (December 5, 1916): 1.

65 As in the case of E. T. McCarthy and the two Bonds, little is known about Daniel Breslauer. The 1926 Milwaukee *City Directory* lists him as a salesman for the S. E. Tate Printing Company, and the 1929 *Directory* as a salesman for the Meyer-Rotier-Tate Company. In 1929, Breslauer and his wife, Beatrice, made their home in an apartment on Summit Avenue in Milwaukee. How someone with Breslauer's credentials was able to gain the attention of a man of the stature of Charles Boettcher is, of course, far from clear.

66 *Longmont Daily Call*, 25 (May 18, 1929): 1; *Longmont Times*, 35 (May 18, 1929): 1.

67 *Estes Park Trail*, 9 (May 17, 1929): 3.

68 LCRD, Book 586, p. 458.

69 Ibid., Book 586, p. 528.

70 Ibid., Book 524, p. 72.

71 *Estes Park Trail*, 9 (June 7, 1929): 1.

72 LCRD, Book 587, pp. 95–96.

73 These figures were cited in court records dated September 24, 1929. Ibid., Book 587, p. 483.

74 Ibid., p. 485.

75 Ibid., Book 612, p. 21.

76 *Longmont Daily Call*, 25 (July 26, 1930): 1; ibid., 25 (September 8, 1930): 1. The sale was confirmed by Judge Smith in chambers on September 5, 1930. LCRD, Book 587, p. 486.

77 The eulogy published in the *Estes Park Trail* as early as June 1927 summarizes the attitude of the town. "Mr. Bond," wrote editor A. B. Harris, speaking almost as if his subject were dead, "was ever known as a helper that needed no bidding in the time of sorrow or trouble. He always seemed to know just what to do and when to do it. His lifetime has been one of unselfish devotion to the community in which he lived, and Estes Park has been blessed with his presence for more than a score of years." *Estes Park Trail*, 7 (June 17, 1927): 4.

78 Horace W. Bennett (1862–1941), one of the original founders and developers of Cripple Creek, was a Denver realtor and investment broker and had contributed a great deal to the development of the city. He was, in other words, an important man.

79 F.O. Stanley, letter to Alma Bond, April 10, 1936, FNSHF.

80 See Chapter 11, Note 9.

81 According to the *Estes Park Trail*'s issue of October 25, 1929, which cited the *Denver Post*, Stanley had just concluded a special trip from Newton to Denver to discuss a possible sale with Emery. *Estes Park Trail*, 9 (October 25, 1929): 6; 9 (November 1, 1929): 3.

As noted, there was no final agreement until a year later, when the Trail informed its readers that Emery had consolidated the Stanley and the Chalets in a new corporation, the Estes Park Hotel Company, directly controlled by the Rocky Mountain Motor Company. Roe Emery was to serve as president of both. Ibid., 10 (October 10, 1930): 3.

[82] LCRD, Book 612, p. 21. F.O. Stanley's sale was made to the Estes Park Hotel Company.

[83] The Estes Park Chalets at Marys Lake, four miles from the Estes Park post office, had its beginning as the Rockdale Hotel, built in 1912–1913 by Charles Robbins and Clarence Nevins. Its opening at the beginning of the 1913 season was celebrated by a dance held in the dining room and attended by 75. In 1919, following the suicide of his partner and a winter storm whose winds left the place in shambles, Robbins sold Rockdale to Claude Erwin Verry, a recent arrival from Nebraska. That same year the site was sold to Verry's half-brother, A. D. Lewis, who developed the property and also built the Lewiston Chalets. In 1923, Lewis, in turn, sold both the Chalets and the Grand Lake Lodge, opened in 1920, to Emery's Rocky Mountain Parks Transportation Company. Emery immediately changed the name to the Estes Park Chalet, made $50,000 worth of improvements, and increased his new hotel's capacity to 300. See *Estes Park Trail*, 4 (October 10, 1924): 1.

[84] Rowena Emery Rogers, "The Stanley Hotel: A Love Story," p. 1. Undated typescript, courtesy of Mrs. Rogers. Interview with Walter Emery and Rowena Emery Rogers, Denver, August 20, 1998. This story and its variations have become legendary. Pieter Hondius, a lifelong resident of Estes Park, cites as a source Sam Russel, Roe Emery's bookkeeper, who was asked to be present at the closing. "According to Sam the total price was $160,000—one-half cash and one-half stock. After carefully putting the check in his billfold and wadding the stock certificate in his pocket, Stanley said 'I have just sold my beautiful hotel for $80,000.00.'" Pieter Hondius, letter to James H. Pickering, December 14, 1998.

[85] E. G. Knowles, letter to Bingham, Dane & Gould, March 11, 1941, Stanley Trust File, FNSHF.

[86] Raymond W. Stanley, letter to Glenwood J. Sherrard, November 10, 1943, ibid.

[87] *Estes Park Trail* (April 10, 1938): 3.

[88] Arthur K. Underwood, letter to Frank W. Hatch, November 27, 1940; Raymond W. Stanley, letter to Glenwood J. Sherrard, November 10, 1943, Stanley Trust File, FNSHF.

[89] See, for example, *Time Magazine*, 28 (July 13, 1930): 15–16.

[90] *Longmont Times-Call*, 44 (July 8, 1936): 2.

[91] Ibid., 44 (June 25, 1936): 2. Estes Park was scheduled to host another well-known American that summer. On June 19 it was reported that Clark Gable had leased the Crocker ranch and had "definitely planned to come to Colorado . . . to spend the summer." Gable never arrived. Ibid., 44 (June 17, 1936): 1; 44 (June 19, 1936): 5.

[92] Regina Emery Rogers, "The Stanley Hotel," p. 5.

Chapter 13: The Rocky Mountain National Park
Pages 245–256

[1] *Chicago Commerce*, 11 (November 19, 1915): 32.

[2] SMR, July 1919, pp. 5–7. For accounts of the transportation controversy see Drummond, pp. 267–290, and Musselman, pp. 29–75.

[3] Arno B. Cammerer, letter to Senator Reed Smoot, May 4, 1920, LRMNP.

[4] Lewis C. Way, letter to Stephen T. Mather, December 13, 1919, Mills vs. Way Correspondence, LRMNP.

[5] Lewis C. Way, letter to Stephen T. Mather, September 9, 1919, ibid.

[6] Lewis C. Way, letter to Stephen T. Mather, December 13, 1919, ibid.

[7] Roger Toll, letter to Director, October 27, 1921, File 112, ibid.

[8] *Denver Post* (December 4, 1921): 6.

[9] *Loveland Reporter-Herald*, 43 (September 3, 1923): 1.

[10] F.O. Stanley, letter to Esther B. Mills, September 21, 1923, FNSHF.

[11] *Estes Park Trail*, 8 (September 14, 1928): 1. *Longmont Daily Call*, 24 (September 13, 1928): 1; *Longmont Daily Times*, 24 (September 13, 1928): 1. The other three officers were Carl Sanborn, Frank Bond, and Milton Clauser.

[12] F.O. Stanley, letter to William E. Sweet, October 1, 1928, SMA.

[13] F.O. Stanley, telegram to Esther B. Mills, February 2, 1929, FNSHF.

[14] See, for example, *Longmont Daily Call*, 34 (February 18, 1929): 3.

[15] F.O. Stanley, "After the Depression, What?" *Estes Park Trail*, 13 (October 13, 1933): 6. Originally written on May 2, 1933 for presentation to the Tuesday Club in Newton, it was later delivered as a talk to the Estes Park Rotary before being published in three installments by the *Trail*. See *Estes Park Trail*, 18 (September 29, 1933): 6; (October 6, 1933): 6; October 13, 1933: 6.

[16] See, for example, Stanley's essay, "The Arithmetic of the Labor Problem," 1919, originally written for the Tuesday Club in Newton, and later printed. SMA.

[17] F.O. Stanley, letter to William T. Foster, quoted in Normali, p. 58.

Chapter 14: "The Grand Old Man of Estes Park"
Pages 257–280

[1] F.O. Stanley, letter to William E. Sweet, October 1, 1928, SMA.

[2] *Longmont Times-Call*, 44 (September 16, 1936): 1.

[3] The epithet itself seems to have first been applied to Stanley in an article that appeared in the *Estes Park Trail* in April 1933, which reviewed his years in Estes Park and his contributions to the development of the town and region. See *Estes Park Trail*, 12 (April 7, 1933): 10.

[4] F.O. Stanley, letter to "My very dear friends," 1932, SMA.

[5] Raymond W. Stanley, Stanley Family Reunion, pp. 11–12.

[6] Freelan O. Stanley, *The Tobacco Habit, Its Evils*, typescript dated May 5, 1931, p. 1, SMA.

[7] For example, see Stanley's 1933 paper, "After the Depression, What?" ibid.

[8] *Longmont Times-Call*, 44 (September 16, 1936): 1.

[9] *Lyons Recorder*, 23 (July 18, 1927): 3.

[10] *Newton Graphic* (August 26, 1898): 1. Correspondence regarding this early event is to be found in the Stanley Archives at Kingfield. The seriousness of F.O. Stanley's commitment is attested to by the bond he signed for John D. Allen, the guardian of Rachel Pearl Johnson, on June 18, 1897, pledging financial support until she turned 21. Copy, SMA.

[11] "Interview with Mr. Walt Baldridge," LRMNP. "Now this is kind of a hard thing to believe," Ted Scott, a resident of Estes Park since 1916, recalled in 1990,

> but he had a board, a board that was about 8 x 8, would be 64 square inches, and he had that cut in such a way that he'd put it together and made 9 x 7 pieces, 63 square inches. And he'd ask, "Where'd that other square inch go to?" I never could figure it out, and I've tried.

Ted Scott, "An Interview with Ted Scott," September 22, 1990, CCEPPL, p. 26.

[12] Mabel Clatworthy, the wife of Estes Park photographer Fred Clatworthy, recalled the day when her two children, Fred, Jr., and Helen, ages five and three, were allowed to go to the top of Little Prospect to watch the arrival of an airplane at the airfield below. They were told to go no farther than the top of the hill. The two children, who then decided to go down to have a closer look, were brought home by Mr. Stanley in his steam car. Mabel Leonard Clatworthy, "An Interview with Mabel Leonard Clatworthy," August 20, 1981, CCEPPL.

[13] F.O. Stanley, letter to Jean and Jane McNab, May 3, 1929, FNSHF.

[14] F.O. Stanley, letter to Jean and Jane McNab, June 30, 1930, ibid..

[15] F.O. Stanley, letter to Jean and Jane McNab, June 5, 1938, ibid. The faithful Minnie Lundburg remained F.O. Stanley's housekeeper until 1940. She died, unmarried and without known relatives, in January 1952 at the age of 81.

[16] Notes from a telephone conversation between George Hopewell and James H. Pickering, July 16, 1999, SMA. Recorded remembrances of Robert Hopewell, summer 1999, SMA.

[17] Pieter Hondius, "An Oral Interview with Pieter Hondius," August 3, 1979, CCEPPL, p. 19. F.O. Stanley's crossbows were famous among the neighborhood boys in Newton as well. He built one for his next-door neighbor, a young George Hopewell (see Note 16), and the two then spent hours together in sessions of target practice. George Hopewell recalled that Mr. Stanley was "very competitive."

One of those fortunate enough to be given a Stanley violin was Frankie Haberl, the son of hotel manager Frank J. Haberl. "The violin I gave Frankie," Stanley wrote the father from Newton on January 4, 1930, "is as good as can be made and with proper care will last a life time. I am going to write him a letter telling him just how to take care of it." F.O. Stanley, letter to Frank J. Haberl, January 4, 1930, FNSHF.

18 Forrest Williamson, Transcript, "Oral Interview, The Twenties in Estes Park," June 24, 1979, CCEPPL.

19 See, for example, Sandra Dallas, *No More Than Five in a Bed: Colorado Hotels in the Old Days* (Norman: University of Oklahoma Press, 1967), p. 176; Dunning, *Over Hill and Vale: History of Larimer County* (Boulder: Johnson Publishing Company, 1971), III, 301.

20 Dunning, Ibid.

21 "Interview with Mr. Walt Baldridge, *Estes Park Trail*, 7 (February 17, 1928): 7; *Estes Park Trail-Gazette*, 4 (June 21, 1974): 5. Margaret Houston, another Baldridge daughter, recalled F.O. Stanley with great fondness: "I was the lucky one," she told the *Estes Park Trail-Gazette* in November 1998, "—I always got a [Christmas] present from Mr. (F O) Stanley. . . . I was Mr. Stanley's pet. . . . He usually sent books—I had a whole bunch of them and I gave them to my grandkids. . . . One year he sent me a doll that had a kid body and the head moved. Boy I tell you that was something." Margaret Houston, "Memories of Christmas Past," *Our Life in Estes, Estes Park Trail-Gazette* (November 20, 1998): 37–38.

22 The best single source of information on William Currence is Jack R. Melton's *The Blue Mist: An Estes Park Legend* (Estes Park: YMCA of the Rockies, 1993), pp. 4–18, which draws on original documents in the Estes Park Area Historical Museum, particularly the affidavit regarding his mining activities that Currence filed with the General Land Office on June 23, 1919.

23 *Mountaineer*, I (August 20, 1908): 1.

24 *Longmont Call*, 11 (July 10, 1909): 1.

25 Lewis C. Way, letter to M. B. Tomblin, June 26, 1919, copy, EPAHM.

26 Quoted in Melton, p. 5.

27 F.O. Stanley, letter to W. C. Currence, March 15, 1930, EPAHM.

28 F.O. Stanley, postcard to W. C. Currence, July 11, 1931, ibid.

29 F.O. Stanley, "The Violin: Its History and Construction," *SMN*, 7 (September 1988): 5; *SMN*, 8 (June 1989): 3, 7, 14-15.

30 Louis Allbright, "America's Best Violins Made in Newton Garage," *Boston Post Magazine* (April 18, 1945): 6.

31 Augusta Stanley's Diary, December 25, 1908, SMA.

32 Ibid., March 22, 1908.

33 Allbright, p. 6.

34 *Estes Park Trail*, 4 (June 20, 1924): 6. See also *Fort Collins Courier-Express*, 51 (June 1, 1924): 9. Both articles were reprinted from the *New York World*.

35 Ibid.

36 Leland H. Long, "Steam, Strings and the Stanley Twins," Monterey, California, *Peninsula Herald* (January 15, 1984): Magazine Section, 8.

37 F.O. Stanley, letter to William L. Fletcher, May 31, 1923, SMA. Carlton Stanley continued to manufacture violins until 1953, when he reached the age of 81.

38 Note, Susan S. Davis to James H. Pickering, December 1999.

[39] John H. Fairfield, *Known Violin Makers* (New York: The Bradford Press, 1942), p. 175.

[40] F.O. Stanley, letter to Mrs. Leland R. Long, October 28, 1933, FNSHF.

[41] William Trufant Foster, "Freelan O. Stanley," p. 4. Typescript eulogy delivered at the time of Stanley's death, presumably to the members of the Newton Tuesday Club. SMA.

[42] Ralph L. Hunt, tribute to F.O. Stanley, published in the *Hebronian*, 18 (November 1940): 1. Hunt served as principal at Hebron from 1922 to 1940.

[43] Foster, "Freelan O. Stanley," p. 3.

[44] *Estes Park Trail*, 17 (March 25, 1938): 1. In the "Longevity Inquiry" that Stanley filled out in 1931, he lists a single operation: for an enlarged prostate at age 62 (1911).

[45] Ibid., 18 (April 21, 1939): 20.

[46] *Longmont Daily Call*, 24 (August 13, 1928): 1; F.O. Stanley, letter to Jane and Jean McNab, July 1928, quoted in Normali, p. 56.

[47] Ferrel Atkins, Memorandum on an Interview with Howard McIlrath, August 26, 1959, LRMNP.

[48] F.O. Stanley, letter to Henry Lynch, May 14, 1935, SMA.

[49] LCRD, Book 674, p. 22.

[50] Ibid., Book 665, p. 69. See also *Estes Park Trail*, 16 (August 28, 1936): 1; *Longmont Times-Call*, 44 (August 29, 1936): 1. While the warranty deed gives the acreage as "54 acres more or less," other contemporary reports cite 57 acres.

[51] *Estes Park Trail*, 2 (July 26, 1913): 1.

[52] Ibid.

[53] *Estes Park Trail*, 7 (July 1, 1927). 3.

[54] Ibid., 17 (January 21, 1938): 2.

[55] Ibid.

[56] LCRD, Book 687, p. 186.

[57] Ibid., September 10, 1938, Book 693, p. 23. Reclamation Village encompassed what is now First to Fourth Streets in Estes Park; its administrative building now belongs to the American Legion.

[58] *Estes Park Trail* (August 29, 1941): 9.

[59] Town of Estes Park, Engineer's Office, Flat File 55, Sheet 2.

[60] Dorothy Kremser-Stoddard, letter to Raymond W. Stanley, postmarked April 10, 1944, SMA. During one of her visits to Estes Park, Dorothy Emmons met Harry Edward Kremser-Stoddard (1890–1942), a man wealthy enough to ride a motorcycle and wear Mexican silver spurs and a western hat. He was also, according to reports, a dashing figure on horseback. He was born in York, Nebraska, the son of William H. Kremser (1853–1928), and raised in nearby Fremont. For reasons not clear, sometime after his discharge from the army in January 1918, Kremser was adopted by a woman named Mary K. Stoddard, with whom he spent considerable time traveling the world. He first visited Estes Park in 1923 and, later, became a long-time summer resident.

Harry Kremser-Stoddard and Dorothy Emmons were married in Phoenix, Arizona, on February 5, 1941, following a whirlwind courtship. They were given a wedding dinner at the Westward Ho Hotel by Frank Haberl, once manager of the Stanley in Estes Park. Until Kremser-Stoddard's sudden death following a stroke two years later, the couple made their home in Pasadena, where he had an estate, and in Estes Park. Their Estes Park summer home was on the slopes of Little Prospect Mountain, built on a lot that Kremser-Stoddard had purchased from Stanley in September 1937. When the Estes Park Summer Residents Association was formed in August 1941, the popular Kremser-Stoddard was elected its first president.

61 Jackie Hutchins, *Estes Park Trail-Gazette*, 25 (April 26, 1995): 1–22, 14.

62 Father Flanagan wrote from Boys Town in Omaha on September 6, 1940, thanking F.O. and Dorothy for their hospitality. "It was the first real rest I have had all year," he noted, "and I enjoyed it immensely." Rt. Rev. F. J. Flanagan, letter to F.O. Stanley, September 6, 1940, SMA.

63 Daniel Tyler, *The Last Water Hole in the West: The Colorado-Big Thompson Project and the Northern Colorado Water Conservancy District* (Niwot: University Press of Colorado, 1992), p. 122. Stanley was photographed on that occasion with fellow-pioneer Abner Sprague. See ibid., p. 124.

64 *Longmont Times-Call*, 48 (October 3, 1940): 1.

Chapter 15: Afterword
Pages 281–284

1 *Hebronian*, 18 (November 1940): 1. From a resolution by the trustees of Hebron Academy honoring F.O. Stanley.

2 See, for example, *Boston Herald*, 189 (October 3, 1940): 15; *Boston Evening Transcript*, 111 (October 3, 1940): 8; *Boston Daily Globe*, 138 (October 3, 1940): 17; *New York Times*, 90 (October 3, 1940): 25; *Lewiston Daily Sun*, 48 (October 3, 1940): 1, 6; *Denver Post* (October 3, 1940): 5; *Longmont Times-Call*, 48 (October 2, 1940); 1; *Estes Park Trail*, 20 (October 4, 1940): 1, 7.

3 *Denver Post* (October 3, 1940): 5.

4 *Estes Park Trail*, 20 (October 4, 1940): 4.

Selected Bibliography

Athearn, Robert G., *The Coloradans*. Albuquerque: University of New Mexico Press, 1976.

Bacon, John H., *American Steam Car Pioneers, A Scrapbook*. New York: The Newcomen Society of the United States, 1984.

Bentley, John, *Oldtime Steam Cars*. New York: Arco Publishing, 1953.

Bird, Anthony, *The Stanley Steam Cars, 1987–1907, Classic Cars in Profile*. New York: Doubleday and Company, 1968.

Bird, Isabella Lucy, *A Lady's Life in the Rocky Mountains*. Norman, Oklahoma: University of Oklahoma Press, 1960.

Buchholtz, Curt, *Rocky Mountain National Park: A History*. Boulder, Colorado: Associated University Press, 1983.

Calhoun, Charles C., *A Small College in Maine: Two Hundred Years of Bowdoin*. Brunswick, Maine: Bowdoin College, 1993.

Crossen, Forest, *The Switzerland Trail of America*. Boulder, Colorado: Pruett Press, 1962.

Daggett, John, *Sketch of the History of Attleborough, From Its Settlement to the Present Time*. Dedham, Massachusetts: H. Mann, SMA, 1834.

Dallas, Sandra, *No More Than Five in a Bed: Colorado Hotels in the Old Days*. Norman, Oklahoma: University of Oklahoma Press, 1967.

Davis, Susan S., *The Stanleys: Renaissance Yankees, Innovation in Industry and the Arts*. New York: The Newcomen Society of the United States, 1997.

Derr, Thomas S., *The Modern Steam Car and Its Background*. Los Angeles, California: Floyd Clymer Publications, 1944.

Drummond, Alexander, *Enos Mills: Citizen of Nature*. Niwot, Colorado: Univeristy Press of Colorado, 1995.

Dunning, Harold, *Over Hill and Vale: History of Larimer County*. Boulder, Colorado: Johnson Publishing Company, 1956.

Ferber, Edna, *A Peculiar Treasure*. New York: Garden City Publishing Co., Inc., 1940.

Fairfield, John H., *Known Violin Makers*. New York: Bradford Press, 1942.

Galbreath, Thomas Crawford, *Chasing the Colorado Cure*. Denver: published by the author, 1908.

Greenleaf, Benjamin, *National Arithmetic*, Boston, Massachusetts: Robert S. Davis &, 1862.

Hall, Harold E., *History of the Hebron Academy, Hebron, Maine 1804–1972*. Hebron, Maine: Trustees of Hebron Academy, 1979.

Hatch, Louis C., *The History of Bowdoin College*. Portland, Maine: Loring, Short & Harmon, 1927.

Hearn, Charles, *The Practical Printer, A Complete Manual of Photographic Printing*. Philadelphia, Pennsylvania: Benerman & Wilson, 1874.

Hondius, Eleanor, *Memoirs of Eleanor E. Hondius of Elkhorn Lodge*. Boulder, Colorado: Pruett Press, 1964.

Jackson, Robert, *The Steam Cars of the Stanley Twins*. New York: Henry Z. Walck, 1969.

Jenkins, Reese V., *Images and Enterprise: Technology and the American Photography Industry*. Baltimore, Maryland: The Johns Hopkins University Press, 1975.

Leading Business Men of Lewiston, Augusta and Vicinity. Boston, Massachusetts: The Mercantile Publishing Company, 1889.

Leonard, Stephen J., and Noel, Thomas J., *Denver: Mining Camp to Metropolis*. Niwot, Colorado: University Press of Colorado, 1990.

Mallett, Richard, *University of Maine at Farmington: A Study in Educational Change (1864–1974)*. Farmington, Maine: The University of Maine at Farmington, 1974.

Melton, Jack R., *The Blue Mist: An Estes Park Legend*. Estes Park, Colorado: YMCA of the Rockies, 1993.

Melton, Jack R., *YMCA of the Rockies: Spanning a Century*. Estes Park, Colorado: YMCA of the Rockies, 1992.

Mills, Enos, *The Story of Estes Park*, SMA, 1914.

Mills, Enos, *The Rocky Mountain National Park*. New York: Doubleday, 1924.

Musselman, Lloyd, *Rocky Mountain National Park: Administrative History, 1915–1965*. Washington, D.C.: Department of the Interior, 1971.

Peladeau, Marius, "The Life and Photographs of Chansonetta Stanley Emmons, 1858–1937." Waldoboro, Maine: Maine Antique Digest, 1977.

Pickering, James H., *This Blue Hollow: Estes Park, The Early Years, 1859–1915*. Niwot, Colorado: University Press of Colorado, 1999.

Prescott, John R., *The Story of Newton, Massachusetts*. Newton, Massachusetts: Newtonville Library Association, 1936.

Proceedings of the Good Roads Convention, Held at Denver, December 4–6, 1906. Denver, Colorado: Chamber of Commerce, 1907.

Punnett, Dick, *Racing on the Rim, A History of the Annual Automobile Racing Tournaments Held on the Sands of the Ormond-Daytona Beach, Florida, 1903–1910*. Ormond Beach, Florida: Tomoka Press, 1997.

Stackpole, Everett S., *History of Winthrop, Maine*. SMA, 1925.

Stanley, Raymond Walker, (1894–1985), "Some Descendants of Matthew Stanley of Topsfield, Massachusetts," Volume 1, SMA.

Stanley Family Reunion: A Transcription of Conversations During the Stanley Family Gathering, June 7, 1981, at Kingfield, Maine. Kingfield, Maine: The Stanley Museum, 1981.

Sweet, Channing, *A Princeton Cowboy*. Colorado Springs, Colorado: Dentan-Berkeland, 1967.

Toll, Roger W., *Mountaineering in Rocky Mountain National Park*. Washington, D.C.: U.S. Government Printing Office, 1919.

Tyler, Daniel, *The Last Water Hole in the West: The Colorado–Big Thompson Project and the Northern Colorado Water Conservancy District*. Niwot, Colorado: University Press of Colorado, 1992.

Magazines

Name	Years Cited
American Architect and Building News	1907
Antique Automobile	
Automobile Quarterly	1985
Automotive Weekly	1903
Boston Post Magazine	1945
Chicago Commerce	1915
Down East magazine	1986
Electrical World	1910
Empire Magazine, Denver Post	1978
Estes Park Magazine, E.P. Trail Gazette	1983
Hebron Semester	1986
Hebronian	1940
Horseless age	1898
Hotel Monthly	1910, 1921
Invention & Technology	1990
Journal of the West	1987
Rocky Mountain Druggist	1909
Scientific American	1907
The Automobile	1917
The Colorado Magazine	1931
The Texaco Star	1948
Time Magazine	1930

Newspapers

Name	Year Cited
Boston Daily Globe	
Boston Evening Transcript	1940
Boston Globe	1911
Boston Herald	1898, 1940
Boulder Daily Camera	1916, 1917
Denver Post	1903, 1930
Denver Republican	1901–1909
Denver Times	1900, 1903
Estes Park Trail	1933, 1938
Estes Park Trail Gazette	1998
Fort Collins Courier	1920
Fort Collins Courier Express	1924
Fort Collins Express	1916, 1917
Fort Collins Express Courier	1923, 1926
Fort Collins Morning Express	1915, 1916
Fort Collins Standard	1874
Fort Collins Weekly Courier	1904, 1907, 1915
Greeley Tribune	1907, 1908
Larimer County Democrat	1916, 1927
Larimer County Independent	1926
Lewiston Daily Sun, Maine	
Lewiston Journal, Maine	1904
Longmont Call	1907, 1908
Longmont Daily Call	1928, 1929
Longmont Daily Times	1921
Longmont Ledger	1907, 1908
Longmont Times	1929
Longmont Times Call	1938
Loveland Daily Herald	1915, 1917, 1918
Loveland Herald	1909
Loveland Reporter	1903, 1908
Loveland Reporter-Herald	1923
Lyons Recorder	1903, 1904
New York Times	1907
Newton Circuit	1918
Newton Crier	1918
Newton Graphic	1898
Peninsula Herald, Monterey, CA	1984

Name	Year Cited
Rocky Mountain News	1864, 1874, 1909
The Country Gentleman's Newspaper, UK	1873
The Mountaineer	1908

Index

C

MR. STANLEY OF ESTES PARK

M

N

O

P

CPSIA information can be obtained at www.ICGtesting.com
Printed in the USA
BVOW03s1122230813

329289BV00009B/18/P